Developing Trauma-Informed Teachers

Creating Classrooms That Foster Equity, Resiliency, and Asset-Based Approaches

Research Findings From the Field

A Volume in Contemporary Perspectives
on Developing Trauma-Informed Teachers

Series Editors

Ofelia Castro Schepers
Purdue University

Megan Brennan
Resilient Futures

Philip E. Bernhardt
Metropolitan State University of Denver

Contemporary Perspectives on Developing Trauma-Informed Teachers

Ofelia Castro Schepers, Megan Brennan, and
Philip E. Bernhardt, Series Editors

Developing Trauma-Informed Teachers:
Creating Classrooms That Foster Equity, Resiliency, and Asset-Based Approaches:
Research Findings From the Field (2023)
edited by Ofelia Castro Schepers, Megan Brennan,
and Philip E. Bernhardt

Developing Trauma-Informed Teachers: Creating Classrooms That Foster Equity,
Resiliency, and Asset-Based Approaches (2022)
edited by Ofelia Schepers, Megan Brennan, and Philip Bernhardt

Developing Trauma-Informed Teachers

Creating Classrooms That Foster Equity, Resiliency, and Asset-Based Approaches

Research Findings From the Field

Edited by

Ofelia Castro Schepers
Purdue University

Megan Brennan
Resilient Futures

Philip E. Bernhardt
Metropolitan State University of Denver

INFORMATION AGE PUBLISHING, INC.
Charlotte, NC • www.infoagepub.com

Library of Congress Cataloging-in-Publication Data

CIP record for this book is available from the Library of Congress
http://www.loc.gov

ISBNs: 979-8-88730-107-5 (Paperback)

979-8-88730-108-2 (Hardcover)

979-8-88730-109-9 (ebook)

Cover art by Jin Baek

Copyright © 2023 Information Age Publishing Inc.

Printed in the United States of America

CONTENTS

FOREWORD

Elizabeth Dutro
University of Colorado Boulder

"The material body is center, and central. The body is the ground of thought."

—Gloria Anzaldúa (2015)

As Anzaldua (2015) writes, bodies hold deep knowledge. It is a statement, not a question. Bodies are the ground of thought. Those words resonate powerfully with Schepers, Brennan, and Bernhardt's volume and its importance for teacher education. As this collection of writing underscores, all forms of knowledge held by bodies matter, including the thought, understanding, and perspective connected to the hard experiences of life. As the idea of trauma-informed education has moved to the center of many conversations and initiatives in K–12 education, those efforts and the definitions and actions brought to "trauma" are complex and consequential for both students and teachers. As this book emphasizes, teacher preparation must engage with those complex considerations of trauma. Failing to do so is a disservice to children, youth, and teachers. As a collection, these authors ask us to consider the role and responsibility of teacher education programs in supporting new teachers to grapple with the presence and impact of trauma for students and for themselves. In its array of insights, it offers pathways for educators to consider how experiences of trauma not only count as knowledge but are central to seeing the world for what it is and what it could potentially be. In other words, readers will find equity-focused

Developing Trauma-Informed Teachers: Creating Classrooms That Foster Equity, Resiliency, and Asset-Based Approaches: Research Findings From the Field, pp. vii–ix
Copyright © 2023 by Information Age Publishing
www.infoagepub.com

and humanizing approaches to trauma here, which can never be taken for granted in how trauma is approached in education.

I began with Anzaldua's (2015) quote about knowledge grounded in experience, including trauma, because, as this book emphasizes, deficit perspectives are pervasive in schooling and attention to trauma can feed false narratives of damage and brokenness about students. Incorporating trauma responsiveness into teacher education demands that teachers and teacher educators contend with the risk that well-meaning attention to trauma will lead to an implicit or explicit message that some learners are impaired. Of course, realizing and acting on a commitment to viewing students through an asset-based lens in no way dilutes the pain of grappling with the injustice of trauma's impacts on bodies and spirits. No child or young person should have to face trauma and navigate its affects; but, of course they do, as do teachers and teacher educators. What I remind myself in my work that centers on equitable, humanizing approaches to difficult life experiences in classrooms is that trauma is both a source of knowledge and connection that matters to life and learning *and* trauma is, by definition, harmful to human beings. For these reasons and others explored in this volume, the landscape of trauma-informed schools is tricky. How can educators absorb and act on the crucial idea that traumatic knowledge *and* the toll of trauma must be honored in classrooms, at one and the same time? This volume contributes to that importantly complex project.

Readers can come to this volume anticipating that each chapter will shimmer with the depth of human experience that creates the imperative for this area of focus in teacher education. This volume is full of human stories, some explicitly told, in narrative and poetry, and others present as the animating force underlying research questions and the processes of inquiry. Recently, there has been a heartening increase in resources for equity-centered, asset-based K–12 trauma-responsive education (e.g., Dutro, 2019; Goodman, 2018; Jones, 2020; Simmons, 2020; Venet, 2021). The stories and strategies that fuel the critical work in trauma focused on K–12 contexts certainly provide support for teacher educators to weave trauma-responsive content into preservice experiences. What Schepers, Brennan, and Bernhardt's collection provides, however, is support for *how* to lace those approaches and mindsets into teacher education courses and programs in humanizing ways. Moving toward the how in teacher education is crucial if we are to realize the goal of honoring the lived experiences of children and youth, and their teachers, in schools and classrooms.

Another gift of this book is that it turns the lens toward the novice teachers who are learning to be the guides and advocates children and youth deserve while teaching within their own traumatic knowledge. It may seem obvious to say that educators also carry hard knowledge from life that necessarily impacts how they feel in classrooms, respond to students, and experience a school day. However, as Dunn (2021) emphasizes, teachers' experiences of grief and loss and pain and how those aspects of life impact teaching life is not often the focus of inquiry. As many of the chapters in this book show, teachers' life experiences and their awareness of their own vulnerability and humanity matters to pedagogy. As empathetic listeners and witnesses to students, teachers also carry students' stories in ways that have implications for their own well-being. What this volume raised for me, is that, like "trauma" the term "boundaries" cannot have a simple definition in the context of schools and classrooms. Simultaneously centering the needs of self and others is a necessary goal in teaching—and is also an ambitious aim that is often challenging to enact. Authors in this book offer tangible support for that process and draw readers into a conversation that will be ongoing for our field as teacher educators and mentors support novice teachers to engage the day-to-day navigations of the social and emotional life of classrooms.

As trauma and trauma-informed education has moved to the center of discussion in education, I have held feelings of hope and possibility alongside concern and trepidation. If we are to heed Anzaldua's (2015) words to honor the body as the ground of thought, trauma, and the ways it is ascribed to human lives and inscribed on particular people must be approached critically, intricately, and humanely in teacher education. This book helps light that crucial path for teacher educators.

REFERENCES

Anzaldúa, G. (2015). *Luz en la obscura [Light in the dark]: Rewriting identity, spirituality, reality.* Duke University Press.

Dunn, M. B. (2021). Teaching literature following loss: teachers' adherence to emotional rules. *English Teaching: Practice & Critique*, *20*(3), 354–367. https://doi.org/10.1108/ETPC-11-2020-0147

Dutro, E. (2019). *The vulnerable heart of literacy: Centering trauma as powerful pedagogy.* Teachers College Press.

Goodman, S. (2018). *It's not about grit: Trauma, inequity, and the power of transformative teaching.* Teachers College Press.

Jones, S. P. (2020). Ending curriculum violence. *Teaching Tolerance*, *64*, 47–50.

Simmons, D. (2020). The trauma we don't see. *Educational Leadership*, *77*(8), 88–89.

Venet, A. S. (2021). *Equity-centered trauma-informed education.* W.W.W. Norton & Company.

INTRODUCTION

Trauma is a public health crisis. In the United States, approximately 60% of individuals ages 17 or younger report experiencing trauma (Felitti et al., 1998). These traumatic events do not live outside of the scope of schools and teaching. As children and teachers develop communities within their classrooms and schools, trauma comes with those who have experienced it, whether invited or not (Dutro Bien, 2014). High rates of trauma exposure among youth in the United States and the detrimental effects of trauma on students' psychosocial and academic outcomes are well-established. There is a great deal of research documenting the impact of childhood trauma and stress on brain development and school performance, and cognitive, social, emotional, and physical development (Perfect et al., 2016 Porche et al., 2011).

The concepts of *trauma-informed care* (TIC) began to spread after a SAMHSA study in 1998 of the Women, Co-Occurring Disorders and Violence Study provided recommendations for "trauma-integrated services." Over the last two decades, distinctions have been made to focus TIC specifically to trauma-informed practices, and these practices have expanded to schools in the past decade. Trauma-informed practices are intended to be holistic and require a paradigm shift framing potential concerns about students with *what has happened* rather than *what is wrong with you?* Rather than seeing trauma reactions through a deficit lens of defiance, TIC reframes these reactions as adaptive, realizing they are the individual's best attempt to cope with the experiences of trauma (Substance Abuse and Mental Health Services Administration [SAMSHA], 2014).

In response to increased awareness of the impact of trauma on student behavioral, emotional, and academic outcomes, schools across the United States have begun to adopt trauma-informed approaches to

Developing Trauma-Informed Teachers: Creating Classrooms That Foster Equity, Resiliency, and Asset-Based Approaches: Research Findings From the Field, pp. xi–xiv
Copyright © 2023 by Information Age Publishing
www.infoagepub.com

better understand and meet the needs of these youth (Dorado et al., 2016; Overstreet & Chafouleas, 2016). Changing practices within schools so that children who have experienced trauma are better understood and more compassionately served is a goal shared by many schools and mental health professionals (Chafouleas et al., 2016; Wolpow et al., 2009). The use of trauma-informed practices in schools aims to create a safe, supportive climate in which school personnel are encouraged to view and respond to students' behaviors with an understanding of the potential impact of trauma and the strength of resilience. Several core assumptions include realizing the pervasive impact of trauma, identifying and understanding trauma symptoms, using knowledge of trauma to inform practice, and avoiding re-traumatization (SAMSHA, 2018). Schools that recognize and respond to child trauma have seen gains in student achievement and reduced incidence of delinquency (Brown et al., 2020; McKinney de Royston & Nasir, 2017).

Teacher education programs are primed to support the intentional weaving of trauma-informed practices into their own curriculum. This humanizing approach can be used to support preservice educators through modeling of inviting trauma into classrooms with intention and truly allowing students to bring all parts of their lives to classrooms. Though TIP have not been largely present in preservice education, in recent years there have been impactful preservice education resources that explore trauma in K–12 classrooms with intentionality and as a way to honor the lived experiences of students (e.g., Dutro, 2019; Goodman, 2018; Jones, 2020; Simmons, 2020; Venet, 2021).

The vision and development of this edited text are driven by a deep desire to ensure that teacher candidates are thoughtfully prepared to more fully address students' needs and create classroom environments that are safe and sustainable for students and teachers. Specifically, this text will provide a more informed understanding of how educator preparation programs are providing teacher candidates with the knowledge and practical skills to effectively utilize trauma-informed practices that are rooted in an asset-based approach to foster resiliency skills that support P–12 students who have or are experiencing trauma. When educators and future educators understand the impact of trauma on a child's behavior, development, social-emotional skills, and readiness for learning, they can actively work to address these needs and more effectively promote student success. The text will also consider how programs are developing equity-focused content, curriculum, and pedagogies to ensure teacher candidates understand how to develop their own resiliency skills. This resource will highlight important and relevant tools, strategies, and approaches for preparing future teachers to implement trauma-informed practices within their classrooms.

The following question situates and frames the edited text: In what ways are teacher preparation programs developing and implementing equity-focused, asset-based content, curriculum, and pedagogies to ensure teacher candidates can successfully integrate trauma-informed practices as well as develop their own resiliency skills?

The primary purpose of the chapters included in this edited text are to provide the readers with a varied set of examples from teacher preparation programs that share models and personal experiences of integrating TIP into their practices, programs, or curricula. The chapters discuss the varied ways TIP can be conceptualized and implemented into individual courses, program-wide initiatives, and cross-discipline collaboration. This text will be of primary interest to all those working in institutes of higher education, alternative licensure programs, and schools and districts involved with the preparation of teacher candidates.

REFERENCES

Dutro, E., & Bien, A. (2014). Listening to the speaking wound: A trauma studies perspective on student positioning in schools. *American Educational Research Journal, 51*, 7–35. https://doi.org/10.3102/0002831213503181

Brown, E. C., Freedle, A., Hurless, N. L., Miller, R. D., Martin, C., & Paul, Z. A. (2020). *Preparing teacher candidates for trauma-informed practices.* Urban Education. https://doi.org/10.1177/0042085920974084

Dorado, J., Martinez, M., McArthur, L., & Leibovitz, T. (2016). Healthy environments and response to trauma in schools (HEARTS): A whole-school, multi-level, prevention and intervention program for creating trauma-informed, safe and supportive schools. *School Mental Health, 8,* 163–176.

Chafouleas, S. M., Johnson, A. H., Overstreet, S., & Santos, N. M. (2016). Toward a blueprint for trauma-informed service delivery in schools. *School Mental Health, 8,* 144–162.

Dutro, E. (2019). *The vulnerable heart of literacy: Centering trauma as powerful pedagogy.* Teachers College Press.

Felitti, V. J., Anda, R. F., Nordenberg, D., Williamson, D. F., Spitz, A. M., Edwards, V., & Marks, J. S. (1998). Relationship of childhood abuse and household dysfunction to many of the leading causes of death in adults: The Adverse Childhood Experiences (ACE) Study. *American Journal of Preventive Medicine, 14*(4), 245–258.

Goodman, S. (2018). *It's not about grit: Trauma, inequity, and the power of transformative teaching.* Teachers College Press.

Jones, S. P. (2020). Ending curriculum violence. *Teaching Tolerance, 64,* 47–50.

McKinney de Royston, M., & Nasir, N. S. (2017). Racialized learning ecologies: Understanding race as a key feature of learning and developmental processes in schools. *New Perspectives on Human Development,* 258–286. https://doi.org/10.1017/CBO9781316282755.015

Overstreet S., & Chafouleas S. (2016). Trauma-informed schools: Introduction to the special issue. *A Multidisciplinary Research and Practice Journal, 8*(1), 1–6. http://dx.doi.org/10.1007/s12310-016-9184-1

Perfect, M., Turley, M., Carlson, J. S., Yohannan, J., & Gilles, M. S. (2016). School-related outcomes of traumatic event exposure and traumatic stress symptoms in students: A systematic review of research from 1990 to 2015. *School Mental Health, 8*, 7–43. https://doi.org/10.1007/s12310-016-9175-2

Porche, M. V., Fortuna, L. R., Lin, J., & Alegria, M. (2011). Childhood trauma and psychiatric disorders as correlates of school dropout in a national sample of young adults. *Child Development, 82*(3), 982–998.

Simmons, D. (2020). The trauma we don't see. *Educational Leadership, 77*(8), 88–89.

Substance Abuse and Mental Health Services Administration. (2014). *Trauma-informed care in behavioral health services.* Treatment Improvement Protocol (TIP) Series 57. HHS Publication No. (SMA) 13–4801

Substance Abuse and Mental Health Services Administration. (2018). *National Mental Health Information Center Child, Adolescent, and Family Branch.* Center for Mental Health Services. http://www.mentalhealth.samhsa.gov/child

Venet, A. S. (2021). Equity-Centered Trauma-Informed Education. W.W.W. Norton & Company.

Wolpow, R., Johnson, M. M., Hertel, R., & Kincaid, S. O. (2009). *The heart of learning and teaching: Compassion, resiliency, and academic success.* Office of Superintendent of Public Instruction (OSPI) Compassionate Schools.

CHAPTER 1

OUR STORIES BELONG HERE

Ellie Haberl Foster
The University of Colorado Boulder

I began to recognize that when I experienced testimony and witness in classrooms in productive, even transformative ways, it was not a linear, unidimensional process, but rather was circular and cyclical. I find the circular image appealing because it has no definitive end; it implies that there is not a point of leveling off and being "done." Rather, the smooth endlessness of the circle suggests that the compulsion and responsibility to witness and to testify are always present. In this view, the circle of testimony-witness begins when someone's difficult experience enters the classroom (in whatever way that occurs) and demands that others bear witness. Faced with such testimony and in acting as witness, the listener may respond with personal testimony that, in turn, must be witnessed and, again, may prompt testimony from her witnesses. (Dutro, 2011, p. 198)

The entrance to the children's hospital is a central atrium in the round with a glass elevator that goes up. But I don't walk this circle while I'm living there with my newborn son, I walk the hallways. My hallway walk is my attempt to transcend time. I am hopeful it will be a portal, that it will carry me back in time so I can relive my son's birth, and this time, warn the nurses that there will be a low oxygen event during the birth and it will cause a severe brain injury. If I could find a portal, I could go back and beg them to intervene. In my imagination I scream down the hallway with desperation. And this time, help arrives in time. And this time, I live an alternative reality, one where we snuggle our baby, cozy and safe, healthy—all of us.

Developing Trauma-Informed Teachers: Creating Classrooms That Foster Equity, Resiliency, and Asset-Based Approaches: Research Findings From the Field, pp. 1–4
Copyright © 2023 by Information Age Publishing
www.infoagepub.com

Of course, hallways are not timelines. And so I cannot walk backwards through time. But after a few weeks I discover that the elevator is a magic portal. I can take it to the atrium and walk outside of the hospital. And this is magic, too, because I can walk out into a world that doesn't know what happened, and that is almost like being in a world where it has not happened.

One day, I go to the Target, and I cannot believe it. No one knows. They are not worried about me. They do not hand me paperwork to sign or huddle around me to update me on Will's oxygen percentage. They put popsicles in their carts and buy gym shoes for their healthy children. All I see is healthy children. *How did you do it?* I want to run up to their parents and ask. I marvel and gape at their healthy children. But anonymity is relief. They don't know. It's just popsicles and gym shoes. It's just Wednesday.

In the middle of August, I flip the pages on my paper calendar, counting the weeks. Will was born on July 30th. The class I am teaching begins on August 27. My eyes, blurry, count the days left. I sit cross-legged on our plastic foldout couchbed in his room. I decide that teaching might help.

I send an email to my students—27 undergraduates who want to be elementary teachers. It is the email I always send before the writing methods class begins. I am cheery and pleasant. Hello! Welcome to a new semester! I will be your instructor! This is my favorite class to teach! I overuse exclamation points. I type the email with one hand. I balance Will in my lap, all curled up and sleeping. We are tethered to the machines, oxygen and heart rate. My email and this scene are in sharp contrast. My tone is dishonest, but I cannot imagine it another way. I cannot picture a welcome email that describes the fresh shock I am still navigating. So, instead, I ask them to prepare for our first class by reading an article by my mentor, Elizabeth Dutro (2011), *Writing Wounded: Trauma Testimony, and Critical Witness in Literacy Classrooms.*

It is the way she always began the class too. It is the framework, the foundation, the lens we hope they will bring to their work with children. She shares her pedagogy of critical witnessing and reciprocal vulnerability, the invitation to be witnesses to our students' difficult experiences. Many of those experiences get the capitol "T" trauma labels, but we will complicate the label in class. We will resist easy classification. We will be critical of those deficit perspectives that often accompany the hardest stories. And we will invite children to be our witnesses too.

A circular notion of testimony and witness in classrooms requires teachers to participate as both witnesses to student experience and testifiers to their own. I think it is tempting to view teaching as involving witness, but not testimony. It is not unusual to hear teachers referred to as witnesses to students' lives and learning. But, as witnesses, are teachers merely vessels for the testimonies of Others? (Dutro, 2011, p. 198).

It is the first article we read together because we want to begin right away. Right away Professor Dutro shared. And me, too. I always used to share right away, on the very first day. I used to talk about addiction- my family's recovery from alcoholism, my own struggle with anxiety. I used to read my writing to the class, start to chisel away at the school rules that said that teachers shouldn't cry in school.

But this first day of school will be different, and I am weighing what to share. My husband watches me get ready for my first day of teaching. I stand in our tiny NICU hospital room bathroom, no bigger than an airport bathroom, and curl my hair, cover my red face with make-up. "You could decide to wait to tell them. You don't have to tell them today?" He asks. I'm quiet, protesting. Later, he tells me he knew what I would do.

I take the elevator portal outside. I'm wearing the only dressy shirt I have that will cover my just recently pregnant belly. I wonder if I look like I live in a hospital. I wonder if my face still looks frozen with terror and if my students will mirror it to me, with their mirror neurons because we just can't help ourselves. It is empathy. It is instinct.

I reconsider the Target. The anonymity. They wouldn't need to know. We could just talk about the syllabus. But, I don't really consider it. I've done this enough to know that letting them witness my story will be better than the anonymity I felt in the Target. It is a lot harder. But also, better.

When I get to the classroom, I decide. Yes. I project a picture of Will on my first power point slide. The plastic oxygen tubes sticking out of his nose. A grey onesie with white stars on it. I will not tell them the brain injury is one of the most severe the neonatologist has ever seen. I will not tell them the prognosis. But I will tell them his name. And I will let myself cry some of my heartbroken terrified shocked feelings.

This time, the room fills with sadness, at first, and then with complicated celebration and congratulations, it is a baby after all. And then, at the end, with sadness again. They get the context. They take it in.

It is not uniform, their response. But the feelings they transmit blend together to create a sense of comfort. And I cry when I feel it. All at once, it takes me under.

I was going to teach them how to do this, how to be in the hardest place with someone but without the awful pity or positioning. It is amazing to me that they know how to do this already.

And so I focus, it is the heart of the class after all—

I will show them that my story belongs in the classroom.

I will promise them that their story does too.

And someday, I hope, when they are teachers with students of their own, they will repeat the cycle.

REFERENCE

Dutro, E. (2011, January). Writing wounded: Trauma, testimony, and critical witness in literacy classrooms. *English Education, 43*(2), 193–211.

CHAPTER 2

GUIDING LEARNERS THROUGH TRAUMA WITH RESPONSIVE MINDFULNESS THEORY

Erik Jon Byker and Merri Hemphill Davis
UNC Charlotte

Merri Hemphill Davis
Center for Well-Being and Resilience

ABSTRACT

The overall purpose of this text, *Developing Trauma-Informed Teachers: Creating Classrooms that Foster Equity, Resiliency, and Asset-Based Approaches,* is to highlight relevant tools, strategies, and approaches for preparing educators to implement trauma-informed practices within their instruction. Such a book is critical in this time of the global COVID-19 pandemic and social unrest. The year 2020 will be remembered as a whirlwind of trauma, including for educators and for children in schools. Educators—including those who are preparing to become teachers—need to be equipped to recognize and be responsive to trauma (Alvarez, 2020). The purpose of this chapter is to support educators' development of strategies and classroom practices that are responsive to trauma. This chapter has two objectives. First, the chapter intends to highlight the literature on trauma using a literature review research methodology (Creswell & Creswell, 2017). Second, the chapter analyzes the findings in literature to ground a theoretical framework, called responsive mindfulness theory (RMT) (Byker & Davis, 2021). The responsive

Developing Trauma-Informed Teachers: Creating Classrooms That Foster Equity, Resiliency, and Asset-Based Approaches: Research Findings From the Field, pp. 5–23
Copyright © 2023 by Information Age Publishing
www.infoagepub.com
All rights of reproduction in any form reserved.

mindfulness theoretical (RMT) framework is based on research-informed practices that support educators in being responsive to the trauma of their learners through mindfulness practices. Additionally, RMT incorporates a four-part heuristic for helping support and guide learners through trauma. The chapter uses the acronym ARMS to explain the heuristic approach, which includes: (1) acknowledging trauma, (2) responding to a learner's social-emotional needs in equitable ways, (3) mitigating the trauma with resources and social-emotional support, and (4) sustaining the response to the trauma.

INTRODUCTION

In March 2020, the World Health Organization (WHO) classified a new strain of coronavirus—called COVID-19—as a global pandemic, defined as an outbreak of a disease that spreads quickly and impacts populations around the world (WHO, 2020). In response to the global pandemic, schools were quickly closed with an immediate shift to online education. As health and safety concerns mandated many changes to the face-to-face format of schooling, the mental health of students and teachers has been negatively affected by the COVID-19 crisis (Bartlett et al., 2020). Currently, there is a great deal of uncertainty woven into the sociocultural context of the United States. This uncertainty often leads to trauma (Kamenetz, 2020). According to the UCLA-DUKE University National Center for Child Trauma (NCTSN), trauma is a "frightening, dangerous, or violent event that poses a threat to a child's life or bodily integrity" (NCTSN, 2011, p. 2). In many ways, the year 2020, was filled with much uncertainty that could trigger trauma for children, young people, and educators. For example, in response to the COVID-19 pandemic, schools and school districts switched to remote and online learning that was a completely new pedagogy for many teachers and learners. Families and caregivers were burdened with the demands of helping to facilitate this online instruction as well as navigate uncertainties related to their employment. These demands take a toll on the health and well-being of all stakeholders involved with the education of children and young people. Current and preservice educators need to be equipped to recognize and respond to trauma. The purpose of this chapter is to describe the contours of trauma, to report on the effects of trauma, and to investigate ways that teachers can be responsive to their students who are dealing with trauma. A secondary purpose is to develop a theoretical framework, based on research-informed practices called responsive mindfulness theory (Byker & Davis, 2021), which supports educators in being responsive to trauma. The rest of the chapter is organized into three sections. First, the chapter explains the literature review methodology for the review of the literature. Then, the literature is examined in order to define and report on the effects of trauma as well as describe programs to support children through trauma. Finally, the chapter employs a grounded theory (Glaser & Strauss, 1967) approach to develop and discuss a theoretical framework, called responsive mindfulness theory (Byker & Davis, 2021), designed to support teachers in being responsive to the trauma of their learners through cultural responsiveness, equitable practices, mindfulness, and social-emotional learning.

METHOD

Creswell and Creswell (2017) explain how a literature review is a systematic way for conducting an initial summation of knowledge about a problem or phenomenon under study. They recommend the following steps for conducting a literature review: (1) developing a set of research questions to guide the study; (2) identify the selection criteria for the literature review including key terms or words to begin the search for the literature; (3) locating the literature in reliable databases, international reports, and peer-reviewed journals; (4) checking the relevance of the literature; (5) reading the literature and coding into categories; and (6) re-reading the literature, organizing the categories into themes, and then reporting out the findings. Creswell and Creswell's step-by-step approach was used for the literature review methodology that centers the investigation in this chapter.

Research Questions

Three research questions guided the literature review inquiry for this study:

1. What are the indicators of trauma in children and in adults?
2. What is the impact and effects of trauma in schools and for young learners?
3. What are programs that help to prepare teachers to be responsive to trauma?

Selection Criteria

To conduct this literature review, a list of selection criteria was developed to help guide the systematic methodology. For example, candidate studies were located using research databases like Academic Search Complete, ERIC, Education Research Complete, Google Scholar, and ProQuest. The search criteria was narrowed to studies published by reputable organizations such as the Center for Disease Control (CDC) as well as international organizations like the United Nations (UN), United Nations Educational, Scientific, and Cultural Organization (UNESCO), and the World Health Organization (WHO). Studies that were in peer reviewed journals and published within the past 10 years were also reviewed. This ensured that the studies chosen for the literature review were an accurate representation of the most up-to-date research on trauma. Using combinations of the following keywords and terms: "programs to mitigate trauma," "school settings," "trauma-informed practices," and "trauma" were searched in databases. Once possible research studies were identified, the References section of each study was investigated to examine the cited research for other potential studies to include in the literature review.

FINDINGS—LITERATURE REVIEW

The literature review findings were organized by answering the three research questions. First, reports on the indicators of trauma in children and in adults are reviewed. Second, the impact and effects of trauma in schools and for young learners are described and summarized. Third, reports on programs to prepare educators to be responsive to trauma are reviewed.

Theme 1: Indicators of Trauma

Trauma, as defined by the literature, is when an individual is overwhelmed by an event or events that it impedes the person's ability to adapt and leads to negative emotions about life or about the person's self (Blaustein, 2013; Phelps & Sperry, 2020). There are many indicators of trauma in children and adults. Research shows that children can exhibit a range of emotions in response to trauma including separation anxiety, depression, attachment disorders, and difficulty in emotion regulation (NCTSN, 2011; Phelps & Sperry, 2020). Additionally, a child's personality, temperament, and prior exposure to trauma will likely increase the child's vulnerability to additional trauma, such as recent events in the current COVID-19 pandemic and the perpetual social unrest caused by the killings of Ahmaud Arbery, Breonna Taylor, and George Floyd (Blume Oeur, 2020; CDC, 2020a; Kamenetz, 2020). The NCTSN, a joint project between UCLA and Duke University, developed a core curriculum to help child-serving professionals improve outcomes for children and families experiencing trauma. According to

The 12 Core Concepts for Understanding Traumatic Stress Responses, a part of the NCTSN (2011) core curriculum, the following are indicators related to trauma in children:

- Children can exhibit a wide range of reactions to loss and trauma including separation anxiety, depression, attachment disorders and emotion regulation
- Children experiencing multiple or recurrent trauma exposure or where a primary caregiver is a perpetrator often experience increased complexity in their reactions
- Both child-intrinsic and child-extrinsic factors influence a child's reaction to a traumatic event
- A child's personality, temperament, prior exposure to trauma or dangerous and exposure to unsafe situations may increase vulnerability to new traumas (e.g., the COVID-19 pandemic)
- Reminders of loss of parents, grandparents, friends or neighbors to traumatic events (e.g., like the COVID-19 pandemic) add layers of stress and may produce fluctuation in children's post-traumatic emotional and behavioral functioning
- Trauma can disrupt major functioning at school, home, and in the community

Adults are also susceptible to trauma. The indicators of trauma in adults relate to the force and the duration of one or more stressors (Krupnik, 2019). The COVID-19 pandemic is an example of such duration as there are a multitude of stressors—such as employment, food insecurity, and concerns about maintaining good health—that have lasted several months and have had an impact on adults (Phelps & Sperry, 2020; Wang et al., 2020). Teachers are an important population that were deemed essential workers during the COVID-19 pandemic (CDC, 2020b; Kamenetz, 2020). The demands on teachers during the COVID-19 pandemic were overwhelming as they had to quickly implement synchronous online learning options for instruction as well as learn new socially distanced, face-to-face models of instructions and at the same time they managed the ever-changing expectations from their districts (CDC, 2020a; Quezada et al., 2020). Zhou (2020) found that teachers are prone to the following indicators of trauma: burnout, depression, emotional numbing, fatigue, guilt, hopelessness, lack of trust in the institutions and government officials, a sense of hypervigilance, and shame.

Theme 2: Effects of Trauma

The impact and effects of trauma can be long-lasting for both children and adults (WHO, 2020; Zhou, 2020). For example, trauma impacts mental health by perpetuating uncertainties that disrupt a child's academic and social performance in school (Wang et al., 2020). During the COVID-19 pandemic, the CDC (2020a) data suggested that more than half of all U.S. children experienced some form of an adverse experience due to the pandemic. In 2009, the CDC and the World Health Organization formed a partnership to strengthen their work on understanding and documenting adverse childhood experiences, which is known by the acronym ACEs (Atchison et al., 2020). The partnership has created a global focus on the effects of trauma and adverse experiences to children (CDC, 2019). Along with exposure to neglect and physical and sexual violence; the experiences of many children and adolescents during the COVID-19 pandemic were classified as an ACE (CDC, 2020b; Wang et al., 2020). The impact of these adverse childhood experiences could mark an entire generation in terms of deleterious mental, physical, and educational outcomes.

While there is limited research regarding the adverse traumatic effects of the COVID-19 among students, the literature does show an increase in post-traumatic stress scores in children who have been quarantined as a result of the virus (Wang, et al., 2020). According to UNESCO (2020a) the effects of the COVID-19 pandemic resulted in a plethora of adverse educational and health consequences for children and families, such as: (1) interrupted learning; (2) inequitable distribution of resources, especially technological resources, (3) poor nutrition; (4) parents or guardians feeling unprepared or confused by distance learning; (5) gaps in childcare or afterschool care; (6) a rise in school dropout rates; and (7) an increase in exposure to violence, neglect, and exploitation.

The effects of trauma has increased teacher vulnerability to stress and burnout, which are already documented in the literature (Borntrager et al., 2012; Caringi et al., 2015; Mojsa-Kaja et al., 2015; Motta, 2012; Skaalvik & Skaalvik, 2017). International and comparative studies have found more than 60% of educators identified teaching as a stressful occupation and confirmed experiencing high rates of work-related fatigue, depression, anxiety, cynicism and low self-esteem (Mojsa-Kaja et al., 2015). UNESCO (2020b) has documented COVID-19 related environmental changes creating additional stress for teachers, counselors, school administrators and operational staff including: (1) Challenges creating and improving on distance learning; (2) assessment challenges; (3) stress related to the confusion of unknown expectations and managing constant changes; (4) increased pressure on schools and school systems that remain open; and (5) maintaining good health and positive mental attitude. The literature shows how trauma and stress are some of the factors related to dwindling numbers in the teaching cadre population as approximately 40% of teachers leave the profession within the first five years of qualifying (Skaalvik & Skaalvik, 2017). Cipriano and Brackett (2020) found that teachers who experience stress are less likely to stay in the profession and are also more likely to exhibit symptoms of burnout and chronic illness. According to Frydman and Mayor (2017), the stress of can be exacerbated by challenging student behavioral and emotional difficulties that sometimes stem from a student's adverse childhood experiences.

Theme 3: Programs to Support Students and Teachers in Trauma

The literature confirms the need for programs to support students and teachers in trauma, especially during the COVID-19 pandemic (CDC, 2020a, UNESCO, 2020b). These programs are critical for discussing and including in teacher preparation programs in order to foster and tend to the social and emotional competence of teacher candidates in helping to reduce the effects of trauma among learners (Cipriano & Brackett, 2020). Jennings and Greenberg's (2009) model of the prosocial classroom. The prosocial classroom is one in which teacher and student relationships thrive through the development of social skills, emotional competencies, and effective classroom management (Jennings & Greenberg, 2009) The prosocial classroom promotes social skills for students while providing a framework for establishing teacher social and emotional competence. The prosocial classroom is one in which teacher and student relationships thrive through the development of social skills, emotional competencies, and effective classroom management (Jennings & Greenberg, 2009). How teachers, counselors, and administrators model prosocial behavior with learners mediates their resiliency and ability to experience post-traumatic growth. Research shows that prosocial classroom programs can help mitigate behavior and emotional difficulties in the classroom (Elreda et al. 2019; Mackenzie et al., 2020). Additionally, Cipriano and Brackett (2020) found that the prosocial classroom helps to nurture social-emotional learning (SEL) for both teachers and students.

Another program in the literature is the neurosequential model of therapeutics, which developed the sequenced intervention model using the following descriptors: calm, attuned, present, predictable, do not escalate; this model is shortened to the acronym CAPPD (Perry, 2006). The CAPPD program centers on developing mindfulness as a way to navigate trauma. Mindfulness is the two-step process of "orienting attention toward what is presently happening and responding to what is happening in a purposeful and positive way" (Renshaw & Cook, 2011, p. 6). The mindfulness model in the CAPPD program includes the following features: (1) stay calm and take deep breaths; (2) be attuned to the verbal and nonverbal cues; (3) stay present and focused on the person you are with in that moment; (4) be predictable with routines and provide structure for repeated positive experiences; and (5) remain in control of emotions in order not to escalate the situation and trigger further trauma. While these features are strategies for teachers and caregivers to employ as part of trauma-informed practices, the CAPPD features can also be taught to students to support their self-regulation and social-emotional learning (Renshaw & Cook, 2011; Perry, 2006). Studies have shown how mindfulness practices help support students in reducing stress (West et al., 2017) and in being ready to learn (Napoli & Holley, 2005; Parker et al., 2014). Additionally, the use of calming strategies and mindfulness have also been found to be helpful ways to empower students to select an activity to help with self-regulating (West et al., 2017). In summary, prosocial classroom, the CAPPD model, and mindfulness programs are ways to help students and teachers navigate trauma in schools.

DISCUSSION

The findings in this literature review were used to help ground a theoretical framework, called responsive mindfulness theory (Byker & Davis, 2021). Responsive mindfulness theory, or RMT, is based in research-informed practices that support educators in being responsive to the trauma of their learners. In the rest of this section, the RMT theory is discussed, explained, and concluded with recommendations for a future research agenda.

Responsive Mindfulness Theory

RMT guides educators—including preservice teachers and in-service teachers—toward a purposeful, empowering approach to be responsive to learners experiencing adverse and traumatic events. The theory incorporates a four-part heuristic to support and guide learners through trauma. The acronym ARMS is used to explain this heuristic: (1) acknowledging trauma, (2) responding to a learner's social-emotional needs in equitable ways, (3) mitigating the trauma with resources and social-emotional support, and (4) sustaining the response to the trauma. RMT incorporates responsive mindfulness toward learners and the acquisition of mindful self-care skills for teachers. Teachers' capacity to support learners is strengthened by their recognition of and efficacious response to their own stress, trauma, or burnout. By retaining an empathic, positive attitude toward themselves, teachers are able to mindfully attend to the needs of learners and adequately model social emotional skills. An important focus of RMT is a purposeful, culturally responsive, and equitable response to the needs of learners. Research related to social emotional learning and equitable practices is a gap in the literature addressed in the RMT model. Thus, RMT considers the diverse student populations at higher risk for adverse childhood experiences or traumatic exposures. For example, prior to traumatic exposure, Black and Latinx learners are subject to much higher rates of suspension and punitive discipline compared to White learners (Byker & Davis, 2021; Wade & Ortiz, 2017). Using the principles of RMT, the environmental and economic disparities of learners' lives, including cultural, gendered, and special needs considerations, are incorporated into strategies—like cultural responsiveness, equitable practices, mindfulness, and self-care—for supporting and guiding learners toward resiliency. Figure 2.1 shows a graphic representation of the ARMS model of RMT.

Figure 2.1

Graphic Representation of the Responsive Mindfulness Theory's ARMS

As Figure 2.1 illustrates, RMT is grounded in the notions of culturally responsiveness (Gay, 2010), equitable practices (Byker et al., 2021), mindfulness, self-care, and social-emotional learning (Byker, 2019; Jennings & Greenberg, 2009). These features are foundational to the theory and help to inform the ARMS heuristic. At the same time, the ARMS heuristic also shapes how the foundational components of RMT are implemented in the classroom. Building capacity within educational systems and among preservice and in-service teachers to recognize and address indicators of trauma in learners is essential to the ARMS approach.

Acknowledge the Trauma

The first part of RMT is to acknowledge the trauma. As Phelps and Sperry (2020) explain, acknowledging trauma is a first step in being responsive by not ignoring or denying that the trauma exists and is real. This can be especially important in this post-COVID-19 pandemic where historical systems of inequalities often impact children of color living in impoverished communities in profound ways (Pinderhughes et al., 2015). The effects of traumatization vary with the severity of the trauma, the nature of the violence and preexisting vulnerability based on socioeconomic and psychological factors as well as levels of social support offered in schools (Pinderhughes et al., 2015). According to the CDC (2020a), health and social inequities experienced by people of color have resulted in disproportionate sickness and death from COVID-19. It is imperative that school systems, preservice teachers, and in-service teachers are prepared and acknowledge the potential impact of traumatization due to the pandemic.

Awareness is a key part of acknowledging trauma. Awareness training and education in causes and behavioral signals of traumatic exposure are critical in teacher preparation programs and part of the professional development of in-service teachers. Likewise, professional development related to supporting well-being is another key component to acknowledging and addressing traumatic exposure among learners (Renshaw & Cook, 2011). The Substance Abuse and Mental Health Services Administration (SAMHSA), an agency of the U.S. government, has a listing of age-appropriate, evidenced-based educational resources for school district and classroom teachers to build awareness in identifying and acknowledging trauma.

Responding to Learners' Social-Emotional Needs in Equitable Ways

Responding is the next part of the ARMS approach in the RMT framework. Responding necessitates a comprehensive, equitable, trauma-informed pedagogy. As classroom teachers view their students through a trauma-informed lens, academic instruction, behavioral, and social-emotional support can be incorporated to achieve the best possible learning outcomes. Equitable social-emotional support for special needs, immigrant, and racial and ethnic minority learners is critical. Education-based and family support interventions appropriate to types of traumatic exposure are an important component of meeting learners' needs. Student interventions like those listed from the National Child Traumatic Stress Network (NCTSN) Learning Center (see Appendix) are strategies for connecting evidence-based practices to reduce trauma.

Responding also requires the competency of cultural responsiveness (Gay, 2010). Culturally responsiveness means "using cultural knowledge, prior experiences, frames of reference, and performance styles of ethnically diverse students to make learning encounters more relevant to and effective for them" (Gay, 2010, p. 31). Related to trauma, there is a critical need for educators to be conscious of the impact of implicit biases and systemic racism on students of color. For example, Wade and Ortiz (2017) assert that because of "the racialization of school discipline, youth of color may inadvertently be punished for behaviors stemming from trauma exposure or mental health conditions" (p. 82). The inequitable application of school discipline to learners of color in America's public schools continues to persist. Alarming disparities exist for Black children—particularly boys—in public schools, who are subject to disproportionate rates of suspensions and expulsions, mediating the school-to-prison pipeline in the United States (Losen & Martinez, 2020; Wade & Ortiz, 2017). At the secondary level, Losen and Martinez (2020) document lost instructional days due to out-of-school suspensions nationally for Black boys at 103 days per 100 students, which translates to 82 days more than their White peers. Thus, to be responsive to all their learners' social-emotional needs related to trauma; educators need to be equipped with culturally responsive practices that promote equity and a culture of support for students rather than relying on punitive measures.

Mitigating Trauma With Resources and Social-Emotional Support

The third feature of ARMS is to mitigate trauma with resources and social-emotional support. While the COVID-19 pandemic has created specific challenges for responding to learners, there are many existing resources which support the ARMS approach. In the chapter's appendix, there is a list of resources for socioemotional education support. For example, social and emotional support can include facial and emotive connection activities, narrative writing or journaling, classroom persona dolls, restorative and healing circles, and peer ambassadors or buddies (Cipriano & Brackett, 2020; Reyes et al., 2012). Other positive social-emotional learning resources include the inclusion of arts-based education—especially dance, music, and theatre. Kinesthetic learning activities—like movement activities and play—can also be instrumental to encourage social-emotional learning.

Traumatic exposure impairs the ability of learners to regulate emotions resulting in diminished social relationships. Learning to identify and articulate emotions is a key facet of emotional regulation. Classroom resources for supporting learners in sharing feelings and emotional states are available through a number of NGOs and are included in the chapter's appendix. Mindfulness practices are also fruitful ways to mitigate trauma (West et al., 2017). Meditation, yoga, and other mindfulness practices can help children experiencing traumatic exposure regain control of their emotions and body space, generating acceptance toward themselves and others. Mindfulness and mindfulness training for preservice teachers and in-service teachers alike are critically important to retention, quality of life, and well-being of educators. West et al. (2017) explains how mindfulness can also help mediate the growth of resilience in learners needing social emotional support following adverse or traumatic exposures.

Sustaining the Response to Trauma

The fourth feature of RMT and the ARMS model is sustaining. The RMT framework needs to be sustained. Part of that sustaining includes the integration of the RMT framework in teacher preparation course in order to help prepare preservice teachers for trauma-informed practices. Acknowledging, being responsive to, and helping to mitigate trauma is not a solitary act. Instead, sustainability is a key component of the RMT framework as it takes commitment and a long-term version. A primary concern for learners who have experienced trauma is physical and psychological safety. Classrooms should be free from physical and verbal abuse. Safety is prioritized. Preservice teachers, in-service teachers, and administrators can become better trained and work together to support rather than penalize children experiencing behavior challenges resulting from traumatic exposure. Learners' sense of safety can be increased by teaching conflict-resolution skills and emotional regulation as well as the development of a school climate where teachers and school staff model respectful communication and conflict resolution within classroom spaces.

Sustaining the responses to trauma also includes identifying traumatic triggers. This is important to increasing perceptions of safety for learners and reducing trauma-related behavioral disruptions. With the support of behavioral specialists, teachers can structure the classroom day to identify and reduce triggers for learners with histories of traumatic exposure. These triggers may include an overly stimulating classroom environment that has too much bright, environmental print or is too noisy (Alexander, 2019). Likewise, Cole et al. (2006) recommends breaking tasks into parts and providing encouragement and reinforcement throughout the day to enhance learners' perceptions of safety. Xu et al. (2017) found that increased opportunities for outdoor play and physical activity can also help mitigate triggers. Various governmental agencies and NGOs are focused on sustained efforts to respond to trauma by addressing the causes of adverse childhood experiences (ACEs). For example, the CDC (2020b) explains how the measures to address trauma can be sustained through: (1) strengthening economic supports for families; (2) reinforces social norms—including culturally responsive norms—that protects against bullying and adversity; (3) ensure a strong start of the year for children; (4) teach mindfulness and social-emotional strategies to handle stress, manage emotions, and tackle everyday challenges; (5) and connecting youth to caring adults and activities. While school systems may be unable to impact every factor identified by the CDC, by creating trauma-informed school systems with social emotional learning and mindfulness; much can be done to help mitigate the harmful effects of traumatic exposure (von der Embse et al. 2018). Sustainable responses to trauma include multi-tiered, school and school system wide programs—see appendix for examples—aimed at introducing trauma-informed approaches in the classroom.

Implications and Future Directions

The RMT framework provides a lens for responding to trauma. The ARMS approach provides a strategy for targeting trauma through mindfulness and social emotional support by: (1) acknowledging trauma, (2) responding to a learner's social-emotional needs in equitable ways, (3) mitigating the trauma with resources and social-emotional support, and (4) sustaining the response to the trauma. In addition, self-care for preservice teachers and in-service teachers is an important component part of RMT. Self-care promotes a positive attitude about the importance of teaching. Teacher preparation programs can include a culture where self-care for preservice and in-service teachers is encouraged and prioritized. Both preservice and in-service teachers should be encouraged to take care of their health and well-being so that they can thrive in the classroom. Self-care contributes to the preservice teachers' and in-service teachers' understanding of self and tending to their emotions as educators. Self-care can include gratitude practices as a way to increase happiness and reduce stress and anxiety (Byker et al., 2021). Self-care can help to foster a healthy sense of identity, connections to others, and result in a more positive school climate (Mackenzie et al., 2020; Miller & Flint-Stipp, 2019). An implication of RMT is that it is a strategy for culturally responsive and equitable ways to address trauma in schools.

Yet, future research is needed related to further implications of RMT. A future research legend would include the examination of RMT related to mitigating trauma in students of color to reduce the school-to-prison pipeline. Another future research question would examine comparative and international ways that RMT is implemented by educators in different contexts. More research is needed related to the implementation of RMT in order to reduce the punitive disciplinary measures on students—especially students of color—in various school locations (i.e., urban schools, suburban schools and rural schools). Future research documenting the availability, use, and outcomes of such research-based training would be a beneficial next step in validating the efficacy of RMT. Finally, and more particular to the context of the current COVID pandemic would be a follow-on investigation of how or whether the virtual classroom is effectively providing social emotional support for learners with histories of adverse experiences or trauma. In conclusion, RMT prioritizes mindfulness and social-emotional learning as a way to target trauma in culturally responsive and equitable ways for the good of educators, teacher candidates, and the students—including the future leaners—under their care.

APPENDIX

ARMS Related Resources to Address Social-Emotional Learning and Trauma

ACES in Education,
https://www.acesconnection.com/g/aces-in-education/collection/resources-books

Attachment and Trauma Network. (2020).
https://creatingtraumasensitiveschools.org/resources/

American Institutes for Research. (2017). *Center on great teachers and learners: Social and emotional learning in the daily life of classrooms.*
http://www.gtlcenter.org/technical-assistance/professional-learning-modules/social-and-emotional-learning-daily-life-classrooms

CASEL. (2017). *SEL in the home.*
http://www.casel.org/in-the-home/

Edutopia. (2017). *Social and emotional learning.*
https://www.edutopia.org/social-emotional-learning

Feelings & Needs Share Out Tool
https://www.morningsidecenter.org/teachable-moment/lessons/feelings-needs-share-out-tool

The Charles A. Dana Center, University of Texas at Austin (2017). *Inside mathematics: Social and emotional learning through mathematics.*
http://www.insidemathematics.org/common-core-resources/mathematical-practice-standards/social-and-emotional-mathematics-learning

Robert Wood Johnson Foundation (2017). *Social and emotional learning: A series of resources on the importance of supporting children's social and emotional learning and development so that they can lead healthier, more successful lives.*
http://www.rwjf.org/en/library/collections/social-and-emotional-learning.html

National Child Traumatic Stress Network (NCTSN) Learning Center https://www.nctsn.org/trauma-informed-care NCTSN fact sheet *Coping in Hard Times* include:

- Including fun, free or inexpensive activities in lesson plans
- Encourage students to talk about their safety concerns
- Model calm behavior in the classroom
- Teach, model and review effective problem-solving
- Download and teach guided visualizations/meditations and mindfulness exercise
- Have students keep a journal

Cultivating Awareness and Resilience in Education (CARE for Teachers) http://www.garrisoninstitute.org/care
This is a 4-day, 36-h program held over the course of 5–6 weeks with intersession coaching provided to participants by phone to support the application of CARE skills. It is also offered as a week-long retreat at the Garrison Institute. CARE utilizes three primary instructional components: (a) emotion skills instruction, (b) mindfulness and stress reduction practices, and (c) listening and compassion exercises. Program components are linked to specific strategies for improving classroom management, teacher-student relationships, and instructional strategies.

Mindfulness, Courage, and Reflection for Educators.
http://umassmed.edu/cfm
A blend of mindfulness-based stress reduction (MBSR) programing and the Courage to Teach Program Mindful Schools http://www.mindfulschools.

org/ Online and live training for educators and administrators in the form of courses, curriculum trainings, and customized mindfulness workshops.

Passageworks Soul of Education Course for Teachers.
http://passageworks.org/
This 2.5-day program focuses on building heart, spirit, and community in the classroom. The program covers the theory of social and emotional learning, the integration of play, ritual, stillness, expressive arts and community building, developing reflection, and "teaching presence"

Stress Management and Relaxation Techniques (SMART-inEducation).
http://www.smart-in-education.org/ http://margaretcullen.com/
Promotes skills sets (e.g., regulation of attention and emotion) and mindsets (e.g., dispassionate curiosity, compassion and forgiveness for self and others) associated with mindfulness that are conducive to occupational health and well-being and teachers' capacities to become more effective teachers. This training includes group discussions, dyadic exercises, didactic presentations and practices such as breath awareness meditation, mindfulness meditation, loving-kindness and forgiveness meditations, a progressive "body scan," and mindful movement Inner Resilience http://www.innerresiliencetidescenter.org/ Promotes the skills of self-regulation and caring for others through residential retreats for school staff, professional development workshops, individual stress reduction sessions, and parent workshops at school sites

REFERENCES

Alexander, J. (2019). *Building trauma-sensitive schools: Your guide to creating safe, supportive learning environments for all students*. Paul H. Brookes.

Alvarez, A. (2020). Seeing race in the research on youth trauma and education: A critical review. *Review of Educational Research*, *90*(5), 583–626.

Atchison, C. G., Butler, J., & Damiano, P. (2020). Adverse childhood experiences: A model for effective 21st-century clinical-community partnerships. *American Journal of Public Health, 110*(4), 450–451.

Bartlett, J. D., Griffin, J., & Thomson, D. (2020, March 8). Resources for supporting children's emotional well-being during the COVID-19 pandemic. *Child Trends Blog*. https://www.childtrends.org/publications/resources-for-supporting-childrens-emotional-well-being-during-the-covid-19-pandemic

Blaustein, M. (2013). Introduction to childhood trauma and a framework for intervention. In E. Rossen & R. Hull (Eds.), *Supporting and educating traumatized children: A guide for educators and professionals*. Oxford University Press.

Blume Oeur, F. (2020). Fever dreams: WEB Du Bois and the racial trauma of COVID-19 and lynching. *Ethnic and Racial Studies Journal*, *16*(4), 1–11.

Borntrager, C., Caringi, J. C., van den Pol, R., Crosby, L., O'Connell, K., Trautman, A., & McDonald, M. (2012). Secondary traumatic stress in school personnel. *Advances in School Mental Health Promotion, 5*(1), 38–50.

Byker, E. J. (2019). Study abroad as social and emotional learning: framing international teaching with critical cosmopolitan theory. *Journal of Research in Innovative Teaching & Learning, 12*(2), 183–194. https://doi.org/10.1108/JRIT-02-2019-0023.

Byker, E. J., & Davis, M. H. (2021). *Introduction to responsive mindfulness theory: A model for trauma-informed practices.* https://www.cwbr.center/

Byker, E. J., Crawford, E., & Lee, H. D. (2021). Giving equity a voice: supporting school administrators with global equitable practices. In R. Shankar-Brown's (Ed.), *Bending the arc towards justice: Equity-focused practices for educational leaders.* Information Age Publishing.

Caringi, J. C., Stanick, C., Trautman, A., Crosby, L., Devlin, M., & Adams, S. (2015). Secondary traumatic stress in public school teachers: Contributing and mitigating factors. *Advances in School Mental Health Promotion, 8*(4), 244–256.

Centers for Disease Control and Prevention [CDC]. (2019). *Preventing adverse childhood experiences: leveraging the best available evidence.* https://www.cdc.gov/violenceprevention/pdf/preventingACES.pdf

Centers for Disease Control and Prevention [CDC]. (2020a). *Health equity considerations and racial and ethnic minority groups report.* Updated July 24, 2020. https://www.cdc.gov/coronavirus/2019-ncov/community/health-equity/race-ethnicity.htm

Centers for Disease Control and Prevention [CDC]. (2020b). *COVID-19 critical infrastructure sector response planning report.* Updated December 9, 2020. https://www.cdc.gov/coronavirus/2019-ncov/community/critical-infrastructure-sectors.html

Cipriano, C., & Brackett, M. (2020). Teacher, interrupted: Leaning into social-emotional learning amid the COVID-19 crisis. *EdSurge.* https://www.edsurge.com/news/2020-03-18-teacher- interrupted-leaning-into-social-emotional-learning-amid-the-covid-19-crisis

Cole, D. C., Van Eerd, D., Bigelow, P., & Rivilis, I. (2006). Integrative interventions for MSDs: Nature, evidence, challenges & directions. *Journal of Occupational Rehabilitation, 16*(3), 351–366.

Creswell, J. W., & Creswell, J. D. (2017). *Research design: Qualitative, quantitative, and mixed methods approaches.* SAGE.

Elreda, L. M., Jennings, P. A., DeMauro, A. A., Mischenko, P. P., & Brown, J. L. (2019). Protective effects of interpersonal mindfulness for teachers' emotional supportiveness in the classroom. *Mindfulness Journal, 10*(3), 537–546.

Frydman, J. S., & Mayor, C. (2017). Trauma and early adolescent development: Case examples from a trauma-informed public health middle school program. *Children & Schools Journal, 39*(4), 238–247.

Gay, G. (2010). *Culturally responsive teaching: Theory, research, and practice* (2nd ed.). Teachers College Press.

Glaser, B. G., & Strauss, A. L. (1967). *The discovery of grounded theory: Strategies for qualitative research.* Aldine.

Jennings, P. A., & Greenberg, M. T. (2009). The prosocial classroom: Teacher social and emotional competence in relation to student and classroom outcomes. *Review of Educational Research, 79*(1), 491–525.

Kamenetz, A. (2020, April 24). *9 ways schools will look different when (and if) they reopen.* National Public Radio: All Things Considered. https://www.realcleareducation.com/ 2020/04/29/9_ways_ schools_will_look _different_when_if_they_reopen_48499.html

Krupnik, V. (2019). Trauma or adversity? *The Journal of Traumatology, 25*(4), 256–261. https://doi.org/10.1037/trm0000169

Losen, D., & Martinez, P. (2020). *Lost opportunities: How disparate school discipline continues to drive differences in the opportunity to learn.* University of Southern California Civil Rights Project.

Mackenzie, E. R., Fegley, S., Stutesman, M., & Mills, J. (2020). Present-moment awareness and the prosocial classroom: educators' lived experience of mindfulness. *Mindfulness Journal, 11*(12), 2755–2764.

Miller, K., & Flint-Stipp, K. (2019). Preservice teacher burnout: Secondary trauma and self-care issues in teacher education. *Issues in Teacher Education, 28*(2), 28–45.

Mojsa-Kaja, J., Golonka, K., & Marek, T. (2015). Job burnout and engagement among teachers: Worklife areas and personality traits as predictors of relationships with work. *International Journal of Occupational Medicine and Environmental Health, 28*(1), 102–119.

Motta, R. W. (2012). Secondary trauma in children and school personnel. *Journal of Applied School Psychology, 28*(3), 256–269.

National Center for Child Trauma [NCTSN]. (2011). *The 12 core concepts for understanding traumatic stress response.* Duke University Press.

Napoli, M., & Holley, L. (2005). Mindfulness training for elementary school students: The attention academy. *Journal of Applied School Psychology, 21*(1), 99–125.

Parker, A., Kupersmidt, J., Mathis, E., Scull, T., & Sims, C. (2014). The impact of mindfulness education on elementary school students: Evaluation of the mastermind program. *Advances in School Mental Health Promotion, 7*(3), 184–204.

Perry, B. D. (2006). Applying principles of neurodevelopment to clinical work with maltreated and traumatized children: The neurosequential model of therapeutics. In N. B. Webb (Ed.), *Working with traumatized youth in child welfare* (pp. 27–52). Guilford Press.

Phelps, C., & Sperry, L. L. (2020). Children and the COVID-19 pandemic. *Psychological Trauma: Theory, Research, Practice, and Policy, 12*(1), 73–75.

Pinderhughes, H., Davis, R., & Williams, M. (2015). *Adverse community experiences and resilience.* Prevention Institute.

Quezada, R. L., Talbot, C., & Quezada-Parker, K. B. (2020). From bricks and mortar to remote teaching: A teacher education program's response to COVID-19. *Journal of Education for Teaching, 46*(4), 472–483.

Reyes, M. R., Brackett, M. A., Rivers, S. E., Elbertson, N. A., & Salovey, P. (2012). The interaction effects of program training, dosage, and implementation quality on targeted student outcomes for the RULER approach to social and emotional learning. *School Psychology Review*, *41*(1), 82–99.

Renshaw, T. L., & Cook, C. R. (2017). Introduction to the special issue: Mindfulness in the schools—Historical roots, current status, and future directions. *Psychology in the Schools*, *54*(1), 5–12.

Skaalvik, E. M., & Skaalvik, S. (2017). Dimensions of teacher burnout: Relations with potential stressors at school. *Social Psychology of Education*, *20*(4), 775–790.

United Nations Educational Scientific and Cultural Organization [UNESCO]. (2020a). *Report on the adverse consequences of school closures*.

United Nations Educational Scientific and Cultural Organization [UNESCO]. (2020b). *Report on distance learning strategies*.

von der Embse, N., Rutherford, L., Mankin, A., & Jenkins, A. (2019). Demonstration of a trauma-informed assessment to intervention model in a large urban school district. *School Mental Health Journal*, *11*(2), 276–289.

Wade, D. T., & Ortiz, K. S. (2017). Punishing trauma: How schools contribute to the carceral continuum through its response to traumatic experiences. In K. J. Fasching-Varner, L. L. Martin, R. W. Mitchell, K. P. Bennett-Haron, A. Daneshzadeh (Eds.), *Understanding, dismantling, and disrupting the prison-to-school pipeline*. (pp. 181–191). Lexington Books.

Wang, G., Zhang, Y., Zhao, J., Zhang, J., & Jiang, F. (2020). Mitigate the effects of home confinement on children during the COVID-19 outbreak. *The Lancet*, *395*(2), 945–947.

West, M., Melvin, G., McNamara, F., & Gordon, M. (2017). An evaluation of the use and efficacy of a sensory room within an adolescent psychiatric inpatient unit. *Australian Occupational Therapy Journal*, *64*(3), 253–263.

World Health Organization [WHO]. (2020). *Key messages and actions for COVID-19 prevention and control in schools: Report*.

Xu, T., Byker, E. J., & Gonzales, M. (2017). Ready to learn: The impact of the morning blast physical activity intervention on elementary school students. *Journal of Movement, Health, and Exercise*, *6*(1), 1–12.

Zhou, X. (2020). Managing psychological distress in children and adolescents following the COVID-19 epidemic: A cooperative approach. *Psychological Trauma: Theory, Research, Practice, and Policy*, *12*(1), 76–78.

CHAPTER 3

"CHECKING IN" WITHIN CLASSROOM AND DIGITAL SPACES TO BUILD COMMUNITIES OF SUPPORT

Cassandra Lo
St. Thomas Aquinas College

ABSTRACT

This chapter discusses the benefits of check-ins in both in-person and digital spaces for preservice teachers who are completing their fieldwork semester. The chapter is informed by trauma studies, the relational teaching framework, informal writing practices and modeling strategies. The chapter centers on a study by the author in which a group was formed outside of class time for secondary preservice teachers to meet with the author, engage in check-ins, and form a community through reciprocal witnessing as they traversed the many difficulties of student teaching. The study found that the unique role of the student teacher presented many challenges, including navigating relationships and carving out an identity in the classroom; journaling and group meetings provided a space to build a community that was beneficial for the students; and additional modes of communication, such as group text messages, must also be incorporated into these practices to best serve the students in our modern classrooms. The author also discusses how to use these strategies, especially checking in, inside and outside of the classroom space to best develop candidates into effective and empathetic teachers.

Developing Trauma-Informed Teachers: Creating Classrooms That Foster Equity, Resiliency, and Asset-Based Approaches: Research Findings From the Field, pp. 25–47
Copyright © 2023 by Information Age Publishing
www.infoagepub.com
All rights of reproduction in any form reserved.

I was first given the opportunity to work with secondary preservice teachers in an adjunct position while finishing my doctoral degree. I worked with the same cohort over the course of a year as they completed their pre-practicum and practicum semesters. During the fourth week of the Fall semester, the preservice teachers in my seminar were silent. I always asked them to share updates about their fieldwork and noticings from their site. Usually, this portion of class elicited a cacophony of responses, with shared joys and frustrations. This week was different, however. The candidates looked at each other, but they were silent. Then, finally, one candidate said, "A student at our school died of a drug overdose this week and we don't know what to do." There was a heaviness surrounding them that I had not noticed before this moment. I thought back to the first time I experienced this type of incident as a high school English teacher. Moments of student trauma can stun us to silence, as our minds race thinking of the perfect response. But is there a perfect response? Is there a perfect action? The preservice teachers began to talk through the instance and shared stories about how their students were reacting to the loss. While there were no "perfect" answers at the end of class, knowing that they were experiencing the same difficulty with this incident and sharing their concerns and ideas allowed these teachers to have more supportive conversations with their students.

As candidates in subsequent semesters have embarked on their student teaching experiences, they have approached me with concerns about students who are experiencing trauma. This is an unfortunately common occurrence—the 2018 National Survey of Children's Health showed that one in three children under the age of 18 had experienced at least one type of traumatic incident (Health Resources & Services Administration, 2019). The stories candidates share with me about their students are heartbreaking. One student died by suicide. Another student's brother was shot. As we have faced the COVID-19 pandemic, candidates have shared that their students have lost family members and families have lost their homes. Remote learning has brought on a whole new set of challenges, with students lacking proper technology resources or being required to watch their younger siblings while attending class. Every candidate is faced with unique and sometimes difficult circumstances, but the desire to support their students is consistently demonstrated. As situations arise, the question they always ask is, "What do I do?"

A common conversation amongst faculty about the student teaching seminar is that there isn't enough time to do anything other than navigate the challenges of graduation and certification requirements, especially the edTPA, a performance-based portfolio assessment that is used for certification in several areas within the United States. As soon as the semester begins, candidates must create in-depth lesson plans, make filming decisions, and create and analyze assessments in addition to the usual day-to-day activities of student teaching. Simultaneously, students share that there is no space to decompress during those fast-paced months. Unlike my first class, candidates at other universities where I have worked have not been able to work in one school system. They are scattered in a one-hour radius from campus, and many commute to school, so the only time they have with other preservice teachers is the weekly seminar class. Of course, edTPA and other aspects of certification are critical, but preservice teachers are severely missing a space where they can build a community with their peers and discuss both triumphs and challenges.

As faculty members working with preservice teachers, we must support our candidates during difficult moments in their field experiences so that they can, in turn, better support their own students. We can start this work by engaging preservice teachers in check-ins during class because it is necessary to create classroom spaces that support the sharing and witnessing of testimonials of trauma (Dutro, 2019). Despite time constraints during seminar, it is necessary to allow space for check-ins at the beginning of each class. This finding was discovered by conducting a study over the course of two semesters where secondary preservice teachers met biweekly outside of class time and was confirmed through my work in seminar during the 2020–2021 school year. In the study, students were asked to informally write about their experiences between meetings and then share with peers.

The study set out to answer the following questions:

Which writing and sharing practices can preservice teachers engage in when witnessing their students' traumas?

As a preservice teacher educator, how can I provide the space necessary for teacher candidates to write and share about the traumas that they experience and witness in their classrooms?

THEORETICAL FRAMEWORK

This study used trauma studies, the relational teaching framework, informal writing practices and modeling strategies to highlight the importance of implementing written and spoken trauma-informed strategies with preservice teachers. As they begin interacting with students in their fieldwork experiences, many preservice teachers witness traumatic incidents or are called upon to support students who are experiencing trauma. They can help improve their comfort level when confronted with difficult situations by encouraging writing and speaking practices that are rooted in trauma support. These practices can help candidates improve the relationships with their students.

Nontraditional, informal writing practices in classrooms can encourage students to write their truths. It is important when utilizing these trauma-informed practices that teachers emphasize the process over the product. Informal writing practices such as journaling, "free writes," or "do nows" allow for students to write freely without traditional constraints. Writing allows for immediate processing to occur after witnessing a difficult incident. In addition to independent informal writing, digital communication, and other nontraditional outlets such as text messaging or messaging applications allows for connectivity, community building, and "writing back to power" (Bouhnik et al., 2014; Janks, 2010, p. 155). In this study, processing through informal and nontraditional writing occurred independently through journal entries and jottings or collectively through group messages. The immediacy of informal writing was implemented in many forms by different candidates and the flexibility of the genre led to candidates sharing in the ways they felt most comfortable.

The sharing of testimonials of trauma through both written and oral storytelling allows for a connection that would not surface otherwise, because it is a connection of wounds (Dutro, 2008, 2009). Trauma studies researchers discuss the importance of testimonies, or testimonials, to recognize the impact of an experience; testimonies are not necessarily complete accounts of traumatic events, but rather are pieces of stories in process without a clear conclusion (Caruth, 1995; Felman & Laub, 1992). Testimonials can be written or spoken, and can arise when others are experiencing an incident, recalling a difficult moment, or listening to someone else share about their traumas. In this study, candidates engaged in unconventional storytelling by completing "jottings" (Marshall & Rossman, 2011), quick, shorthand notes that occur in the moment to capture true experiences and emotions, as well as through group text messages. The candidates shared their testimonials of trauma through storytelling during group meetings, often by retelling stories from their jottings, text messages, or journal entries. Another aspect of trauma studies relevant to this study is the notion of witnessing, where an audience is present for a person's testimony of trauma. Witnessing and sharing testimonies becomes a circular process through reciprocal witnessing (Dutro, 2019; Felman & Laub, 1992). Through witnessing, a person's trauma is affirmed, but without witnessing, trauma testimonials are often suppressed in unhealthy ways. Candidates witnessed both their peers' testimonials in the group chat and our meetings and their students' stories in their fieldwork experiences.

Reciprocal witnessing (Christie et al., 2016; Dutro, 2017) utilizes storytelling and cross-storytelling as both students and teachers share about their grief and trauma collectively. Reciprocal witnessing involves a deeper understanding between students and teachers, and students and other students, especially about testimonials of trauma. This type of interaction also affirms a student's experience in ways that traditional listening does not because it involves connecting and relationships. Having students and teachers share in the same way provides a level playing field for interaction in the classroom. One of the main reasons teachers do not want to present moments of vulnerability is because they do not want to get too close to their students, making their classroom an emotional space, but Kinloch (2010) argues that both teachers and students must take risks in order to get to know each other through written and spoken encounters.

Throughout this study, relational teaching practices were utilized within the research group and candidates were encouraged to use these practices with their own students. Relational teaching is a framework that encourages teachers to consider a student's lived experiences when forging connections in the classroom (Gross & Lo, 2018). Rogers (2009) defines a successful student-teacher relationship as an "alliance" that collaborates with a common goal in mind. Relational gestures, such as responding to personal interests, maintaining high standards, sharing common traits, or revealing a vulnerability, can create a strong community between teachers and students (Reichert & Hawley, 2013). While relational teaching is beneficial for all students, it is especially critical for boys who are often required to participate in schooling without sharing emotion in order to conform to gender roles (Raider-Roth, 2008; Reichert & Hawley, 2013). Additionally, students who have experienced trauma are better able to succeed in school when they feel that they have the support of their teachers, so implementing relational teaching strategies is necessary for community building (Gross & Lo, 2018).

Modeling relational teaching strategies, witnessing, and sharing testimonials of trauma, and journaling can help preserve teachers utilize these activities with their students. In modeling, a teacher shows their students what a strategy or way of learning looks like so that they can apply those skills. Explicit teacher instruction has especially been effective when modeling strategies and organization skills for students with learning disabilities (Troia & Graham, 2002). Explicit strategy instruction has been used with K–12 students in all subjects, but Watson and Bradley (2009) discuss how this instruction can also be effective in teacher education classes because preservice teachers can see strategies modeled and participate in them to see how they can be adapted for their own content areas. Similarly, as members of our group, candidates participated in check-ins and relational teaching strategies and were able to consider how they could be applied to their classrooms.

METHODOLOGY

This study utilized practitioner inquiry, group meetings and analysis of two forms of informal writing, journaling, and group text messages, as research methods. Practitioner inquiry is a valuable research method because it centers both teachers' and students' experiences (Ballenger, 2009). I took an "inquiry stance" (Cochran-Smith & Lytle, 2009) as I conducted my research, and constantly reflected on my own work in order to improve the group and classroom experience for my students. The practitioner inquiry used in this study was two-fold: I examined at how I could incorporate support strategies into my teacher education courses, and the participants reflected on their practice and thought about ways that they could better support their own students.

The research group met biweekly throughout the spring 2019 and fall 2019 semesters. A group setting was ideal for this study as groups are socially oriented and allow for more natural conversations than traditional one-on-one interviews (Marshall & Rossman, 2011). In between meetings, the preservice teachers journaled about moments of student trauma that they witnessed either formally or informally. At our first meeting, we devised a journaling protocol that was used throughout the year. The candidates opted to journal about the incident, their reactions, and any quotes from others that they overheard during the incidents.

The primary sources of data for this study were group meeting transcripts, preservice teachers' journal entries, and their group text messages. The transcripts, journal entries and text messages were first reviewed and then coded them into several different categories and subcategories. Data was coded twice, utilizing Saldaña's "First Cycle and Second Cycle" coding (Miles et al., 2013). The two main approaches to coding this data were In Vivo Coding and Emotion Coding. During the first cycle, I used In Vivo coding to pull out important quotes and phrases from each interview. During the second cycle of coding, I used Emotion Coding, which "labels the emotions recalled and/or experienced by the participant or inferred by the researcher about the participant" (Miles et al., 2013, p. 75). These two types of coding helped to draw connections between the coding categories and formalized my analysis of the transcripts. I used both emic and etic codes when categorizing my data. Emic codes are "taken from participants' own words and concepts" while etic codes are derived from "researcher's concepts" (Maxwell, 2013, p. 108). The majority of my codes were emic in nature, as the emic perspective is the one that is privileged in practitioner inquiry (Lytle, 2000).

In addition to the candidates' contributions, researcher data that was collected was reflective in nature through memos and shorthand notes. These reflective writings aided in understanding the research at a deeper level and contributed to creating findings categories (Maxwell, 2013; Ravitch & Riggan, 2012). The themes that emerged after two cycles of coding and analysis of researcher data produced four distinct findings, which will be shared in a subsequent section.

PARTICIPANTS AND DESCRIPTION OF GROUP ACTIVITIES

Participants in this study were part of a small teacher education program at a private university on the East Coast. During the student teaching semester, candidates were enrolled in a reflective practice seminar once a week which primarily served as a certification and graduation requirement preparation course. Our research group met outside of seminar class time in order to provide an outlet for student support and sharing. Six preservice teachers working in middle and high schools in four different districts participated in this study over the course of two semesters. All secondary education candidates in the school's program were invited to join, and participation was not mandatory. Pseudonyms were used to protect the candidates' identities. Ben, a social studies teacher and Jackie, a biology teacher, joined Athena and Madeline, two English teachers, during the first semester. Julia, a math teacher, and Natalie, an English teacher, were a part of the research group during the second semester. Ben identified as a White male, and the other participants identified as White females. They ranged in age from 21–35. Collectively, the group identified as a combination of lower and middle class.

The two main components of our group meetings were check-ins and discussing relational teaching strategies. For the check-ins, candidates would take turns updating the group on the happenings from school. Some participants would come to our group meetings with a written list of talking points or a journal entry, but others would speak extemporaneously during this portion of the meeting. After each candidate shared, their peers would respond and sometimes share their own check-ins that were connected, allowing for reciprocal witnessing and cross-storytelling. Some sessions that covered particularly difficult topics, such as a shooting that occurred outside of school or a student dying by suicide, solely focused on check-ins. The candidates would discuss what they would do in that circumstance, or how they could approach it differently next time. It is important to note that check-ins were always *optional* in both group meetings and my classes. Candidates were invited to share, but not required, as being forced to share traumatic stories could re-traumatize the storyteller. Those who did not feel comfortable sharing their own stories were invited to share just with me via email or focus on witnessing and affirming their peers during the group. Due to the community established in our group, all candidates shared stories and participated in reciprocal witnessing throughout our time together. The check-ins were modeled so that the preservice teachers could participate in the activity and consider how to use them within their own spaces (Watson & Bradley, 2009).

When time permitted, a discussion on relational teaching methods ensued. Relational gestures (Reichert & Hawley, 2013) that could be used with future classes were reviewed. While all of the gestures shared by Reichert and Hawley (2013) are valuable, the three focus gestures were "reach out, often improvising measures to meet a student's need, respond to a student's personal interest or talent, and reveal a vulnerability" (p. 51). These relational gestures often applied directly to the difficult situations that candidates shared during check-ins. We discussed relational teaching methods that would help to build community in classes and that would show support, which was especially important after students experienced trauma. I would issue a challenge or goal for candidates to try before our next meeting. For example, I encouraged candidates to share a vulnerability with students if they felt comfortable. One preservice teacher wrote a personal narrative and shared it when she assigned a personal essay to her students. Another candidate surveyed his class about their favorite movies and offered to show the (appropriate) winning film at the end of the week as a reward for productive class time. He found much less resistance from his class when he spent a few moments discussing their favorite movies. Follow-up regarding their relational teaching efforts was then folded into the next meeting's check-ins.

FINDINGS

Findings show that check-ins during class can be beneficial. The preservice teachers reported that sharing, journaling, and digital communication gave them time to process incidents from their teaching experience in new ways. They used the sharing of their journal entries and digital messages during the check-ins as moments to figure out how to approach classroom situations in the future. Participants were able to create a community through immediate group texting, which also allowed them to reciprocally witness as incidents occurred.

Four main findings of this study were discovered after coding all group meeting transcripts and written student contributions via journals and group messages. The first two findings are emotion-based while the second two findings are more practical in nature. First, preservice teachers noted their unique role as both student and teacher in the classroom and how they struggled to carve out their own identity with their students. They also noted the difficulty in navigating relationships with school staff members when faced with student traumas. Next, candidates reported that journaling and group meetings created a community that gave them time to process incidents from their teaching experience in ways that they were unable to do before. Finally, additional literacies have to be considered as valuable practices within the relationship building of preservice teachers as they develop these communities of support.

The Unique and Difficult Position of "Student Teachers"

The title of "student teacher" left the participants in this study with confusion over their role within the classroom. Several students demonstrated a lack of self-confidence in their actions at school. The first time Madeline had to pull a student into the hallway, she said "that was my first time having to bring her outside, or bring anyone outside, so it was kind of scary. I don't even know if I was necessarily supposed to be doing this, like if I'm allowed to" (Semester 1 Group Session 2). Jackie was concerned about bringing up upsetting topics during her genetics and disease units in biology class: "I know that there's a chance of that, and I don't wanna accidentally say anything that might make someone upset, like, whether I see it escalate or if I, like what if I don't know?" (Semester 1 Group Session 3). Madeline's lack of clarity about her role in the classroom caused her to doubt her judgment, while Jackie feared making a mistake in class and if her position even allowed her to have these difficult discussions.

During Natalie's student teaching semester, she experienced a shooting in the town in which she taught. She taught English in a middle school and one of her students' brothers went to the high school. Her students' brother was crossing a street by the high school when he was shot by someone in a car driving by. He was grazed by the bullet and ran back into the high school to seek medical assistance. This automatically put the high school and middle school into a lockdown. When Natalie was explaining how she handled the situation to us, she said "The scariest thing was being in the dark and not knowing anything and having all of your kids look at you like what's happening? Are we okay? Are we in danger? … I can't even tell them no I'm only a student teacher and I don't know what to do" (Semester 2 Group Session 3). Natalie's cooperating teacher had children in the high school, so while she attempted to contact her children, Natalie assumed the lead teacher role and tried to assuage the fears of her students. Midway through the lockdown, they discovered that the student who was shot was the brother of her student, and Natalie had to figure out how to notify her student of the issue.

Natalie mentioned several times throughout the semester that she wanted to "be a mom" and keep her students safe. In addition to the lockdown, during the first week of Natalie's fieldwork, one of her students was very upset after losing her uncle. This moment made Natalie particularly emotional, as she lost her mother to cancer while she was in high school. Natalie wanted to be a teacher because of the wonderful support she received from her teachers during that difficult time in her life. During our first meeting, Natalie talked about how she wanted to help her student in the same way others had helped her:

> So my mom was diagnosed with cancer when I was a junior in high school ... in April, and she passed away that June. So two months later. Yeah, right before my senior year of high school. But honestly I think it almost like makes it harder for me, because I want to just like take her and be like, "I'm here for you, like whatever you need. If you just need a smile—if you just need like a high five, or whatever. Like if you need an extra day to fin- ish this..." whatever they do on the computer, "Like you just need to ask, because I don't want to hover." Like I don't know how to handle that-as like a professional, and especially because they know I'm a student teacher, I don't want them to think (laughs), "Oh, who is she?" You know? But I think it almost makes it harder, because my heart. Just like I have such a big heart already, and then going through that. (Semester 2 Group Session 1)

Natalie mentioned her "heart" as both a factor in her desire to care for her students and a possible challenge to her role as a student teacher. Natalie's difficulty in supporting students who were grieving was a common discussion amongst the candidates throughout both semesters, but her unique viewpoint on familial grief made it even more difficult for her.

In a later meeting that semester, Julia shared about a difficult moment during a classroom observation. As she went around and checked home- work at the beginning of class, one of her students looked visibly upset. Julia asked her if she was okay, and the student shared:

> She was up the whole night crying ... her parents found out she was gay (and) went through her phone ... (their) religion is very against it (and) they have a counselor trying to fix her ... I didn't really know what advice to give her, I was very limited because I was being observed. (Semester 2 Group Session 3)

In that moment, Julia shared, she told the student she would speak with her after class. While being watched by her cooperating teacher, who Julia shared did not nurture relationships within the classroom, and her univer- sity supervisor, Julia did not feel that she could fully support the student. Her position in the classroom prevented her from handling a difficult situ- ation, but we were able to discuss how she would handle that situation in her future classroom during our group meeting.

For some preservice teachers, the most difficult experiences they faced happened outside of the classroom. Both Ben and Jackie were involved in an event called "Challenge Day" at their school. Challenge Day was a time when students got together to do ice breakers and teachers facilitated. There was no professional development or training before this event, but rather a 15-minute briefing before students arrived. Students began sharing extremely personal stories and some were even brought to tears. Reflecting on these moments, Ben said:

> I was surprised at, I think, how well I handled it on the spot. Once, you know, a student starts crying in front of you, the alarm bells go off. What do I do? I said to the students, "Just remember that you were brave enough to show yourself to other people. That's something a lot of people don't do, and they go through their whole life not doing it." (Semester 1 Group Session 2)

By sharing these mutual moments, the candidates began to feel less uncomfortable. Madeline heard about how Athena pulls students aside during class, which reassured her about her choices. Ben and Jackie shared about their experiences about Challenge Day. Julia and Natalie were able to discuss difficult moments together. In this sharing, participants drew connections between their experiences and saw that they were not alone in their struggles during their fieldwork experiences.

Navigating Relationships and Supporting Peers Through Difficult Incidents

One common thread in candidates' stories was tension with other staff members. In many circumstances that involved staff tensions, the preservice teachers noted that other teachers in the school were not as empathetic or kind in their responses to students who shared traumas, but they felt silenced due to their identity as a preservice teacher. For example, Athena wrote a journal entry about a moment when a student reacted strongly to an activity relating to Huxley's (1932) novel *Brave New World*. She ran out of the classroom crying after a discussion of a deceased child began. When Athena followed the student to check on her, she discovered that the student had recently lost a brother. Athena's cooperating teacher told her that the student has to learn how to "handle" these discussions, regardless of her own grief.

Similarly, Jackie noted two incidents with a veteran teacher during our group sessions. The first referred to a student in her class that was having seizures and was behind in her work. Jackie overheard a teacher in the lounge talking about this student:

I'm not gonna try to like throw anyone under the bus, but somebody was like, "Oh she needs to pull herself up by her bootstraps." And I'm like, "Please don't say that about someone who's in foster care and is on medication for seizures at like 16. It's not very nice." (Semester 1 Group meeting 2)

The second incident elicited strong reactions from other group members. Jackie shared dissatisfaction with how a teacher handled a racist, homophobic incident in her classroom. A student in her class who identifies as gay and Black did not stand for the Pledge of Allegiance, and several White classmates hurled insults at him as a result. The teacher did not reprimand the students:

Jackie: The other cooperating teacher in that classroom was like, "He only does this because he's gay and Black," and I'm like, "Oh my God."

Athena: The teacher?

Jackie: Yeah, she's like, "Oh I get it, I get that you're gay and you're Black, but you should stand up for the flag. If I was tenured I would tell him to stop being disrespectful and stand."

Athena: Oof. The teacher said that?

Madeline: That is rude.

Jackie: Yes! Ten more days. Ten more days! Yeah, I told him, I was like, "I'm sorry they're giving you a hard time."

Ben: Just think of the position that kid's in now. So now he's got the kids, and the teacher.

Athena: That's crazy. (Semester 1 Group Session 5)

During this difficult time when teachers should be supporting underrepresented students, it is baffling that the teacher responded in this way. While she felt helpless witnessing this incident, Jackie reported that she appreciated having the ability to share with peers and think through how to handle this situation differently in the future. We discussed the importance of allyship and how to better build communities that affirm instead of isolate underrepresented students. As a woman of color myself, the candidates often came to our meetings with questions that came up from their school interactions or experiences that they wanted to debrief with me. In our time together, participants shared that providing space and a platform for witnessing and sharing of testimonials during our group meetings was beneficial as they navigated relationships and experiences at school.

As evidenced by the example above, the community that was built by these preservice teachers was cited as a valuable support system as students reflected upon their experience. During the second semester, Natalie and Julia demonstrated many moments of support as they checked in with each other. When Natalie shared about the shooting in her district, Julia said, "I think you played it right … you handled it very well" (Semester 2 Group Meeting 3). Similarly, when Julia shared about a difficult conversation she had with a student, Natalie responded, "That's kind of amazing that she opened up to you about that then … you know, you are a very trusting person" (Semester 2 Group Meeting 4). Encouragement and camaraderie were observed during group meetings as candidates shared difficult stories with one another. Ben said, "If it's not this group or class, you know, I'm not going to bring it up to other people because they don't understand it" (Semester 1 Group Session 6). Participants shared that they did not have many educators in their social networks outside of their classmates, so it was hard for their friends and family to truly empathize with the difficulty of the student teaching semester while completing other certification and graduation requirements, including tests and portfolio assessments.

The Value of Written and Spoken Activities

When candidates were faced with challenging scenarios during their fieldwork, they either wrote about them through journaling or the group text message or they shared about them aloud during our group meetings. Writing and sharing about these instances supported candidates in two ways: 1. Candidates were able to process the incidents with peers who were in similar roles and 2. Candidates were able to think through the incidents and discuss how to approach similar moments in the future. The processing and thinking-through directly addressed the questions I receive from so many preservice teachers who face moments of trauma with their students. As candidates asked, "What do I do," I turned the question back towards the group and encouraged them to think together. In this space, candidates would walk through the incident with peers in similar situations and hear about alternative solutions.

The participants used the journaling and the sharing of their experiences as moments to think about the happenings in their classroom and start to figure out how to approach situations in the future. While I intended to spend a considerable amount of time on the preservice teachers' journal entries, they actually became a less prominent data source than our group conversations and the candidates' group chats via text message, which will be discussed further in the next section. Three of the six candidates shared occasional journal entries with me via Google Docs. Julia hand wrote some jottings and shared them during her turns, but overall, the students valued the speaking and listening more than the writing component.

While the preservice teachers did not utilize much journal writing, they did mention a few instances where their students shared traumas with them through writing. Both Madeline and Athena, the two English teachers, talked about assignments where their students shared testimonials of trauma through writing. Madeline had students submit weekly blog posts that were personal in nature. One of her students shared about his father who had stage four cancer: "In that autobiography entry, he wrote two paragraphs on that and how that was his best experience, because it changed his view on life and how, like, um, he's closer with his family now, like, they bought a dog for his dad. He actually was asking on Monday, he was like, 'Did you guys read my entry?'" (Semester 1 Group Session 3). One of Madeline's students shared about a time he was arrested: "He said it was his best experience, because if he kept going that way, he would've had, like, an awful life, because he wouldn't have been in colleges or anything" (Semester 1 Group Session 3). Madeline did not know how to respond to these two students' blog posts, so she asked for support from her teacher, who told her to thank the students for sharing. Athena assigned her students a personal essay, and then wrote one herself. She shared her essay as an example and told the class about her life as a single mother and going to college later in life. After she shared, "every essay I got back was some sort of tragedy, almost. Like going through divorce ... this person passed away in my life. I wrote them all notes, like ... it took me a long time to grade because I wrote them all paragraph notes" (Group Session 2). Although journaling did not have as much of an impact on our group as I had originally intended, the students did see value in informal, non-traditional writing and sharing practices in their own classrooms.

These written and spoken activities would not be possible within the confines of a traditional student teaching seminar, which requires the dedication of a significant amount of time to certification and graduation requirements, such as the edTPA. For candidates who need to discuss the emotional weight of student teaching, the student teaching seminar in its current format is not sufficient.

Group Text Messaging as an Additional Mode of Support and Communication

Finally, the preservice teachers utilized an external mode of communication during their student teaching semester outside of our group meetings that provided them with instant support. In a seminar where time is limited, having an additional mode of support for candidates can be extremely beneficial. Early in each semester, the students created a group chat text message system. I did not ask to join the conversations, as they valued the independence from the university within their conversations so they could speak freely. The two groups discussed in this chapter both used text messages, but other groups have used group chat applications such as GroupMe.

When asked about why they created this group text, Madeline said, "So it started on the first day of class so we kind of understood more what edTPA is all about. And so we called it edTPA Survival" (Semester 1 Group Session 6). Participants shared the following about the purpose of the group chat (Semester 1 Group Session 3):

Madeline: "I'm just always stressing. If no one else is stressing, I'm like okay, I'll just stop. We were all struggling together, so it's kind of nice."

Jackie: "When other people are stressed out, I try and, like, cheer them on, because I need it. That would be nice."

Athena: "We always have ideas for each other."

In addition to providing support and ideas, the group chats provided a space for levity during a difficult semester. The candidates shared humorous pictures and fun stories when they arose. Julia shared that the second semester group would send each other memes to provide small moments of laughter during their busy days. They also used this space to share pep talks and words of encouragement, especially when the candidates were being observed or as they worked on their certification exams and portfolios. The following two images show examples of conversations held in the group chats during each semester. While I was not a part of these conversations, the candidates shared screenshots with me for the purpose of this study.

Figure 3.1, from the second semester of this study, shows preservice teachers using their group chat to share about their nervousness pertaining to submitting their edTPA portfolios. They use memes from popular television shows to further elaborate on their emotions surrounding the event. Figure 3.2, from the first semester of this study, shows a conversation with a much different tone. While the first part of the image shows the candidates greeting each other and celebrating the impending weekend, the conversation quickly took a turn. One of the towns where two of the candidates were located was in a lockdown because there was an armed

Figure 3.1

Preservice Teachers Use Memes From Popular Television Shows to Demonstrate Their Feelings About Submitting the edTPA Portfolios

Figure 3.2

Preservice Teachers Use a Group Text Message to Support a Peer Who Is Experiencing a Lockdown at Their School

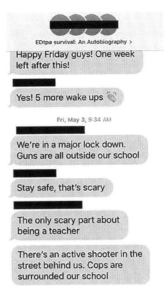

individual on the street outside of several district schools. In this moment, one candidate reached out to the group to seek support and let them know what was happening. The conversation continued to ask about the other preservice teacher in the district, Madeline, who was unresponsive in the chat at the time. They continued to check in until they located her.

The group chats were used as instant connections to the other preservice teachers, which was especially helpful since the candidates were working in several different schools and districts. Many of the moments mentioned in the previous findings mentioned in this chapter were also linked to the group messages. Natalie shared about the shooting with her peers, and Ben and Jackie wrote to their group about Challenge Day. They provided support to each other during difficult instances, but also checked in during their lunch breaks and prep periods. The immediacy of the group chat allowed for witnessing to occur as soon as an incident occurred. The candidates shared support, encouragement, and advice on a daily basis, and these daily check-ins supplemented our group meetings and the students' weekly seminar as a third way to converse about their experiences. The group messages were a critical addition to the candidates' modes of communication as the student teaching seminar was not a place where they had much time to have these necessary discussions.

CONCLUSION

This study used trauma studies, the relational teaching framework, non-traditional writing practices and modeling strategies to highlight the importance of implementing written and in-person trauma-informed methodology with preservice teachers. Ultimately, preservice teachers shared that the spaces for processing through writing and sharing were critical to their well-being and growth as educators. I focused on three strategies to develop resiliency skills with preservice teachers: self-reflections, check-ins, and discussions about the impact of students' traumas on the candidates themselves. While candidates checked in and witnessed each other's testimonials, the practice of checking in was something that I encouraged them to do with themselves as well. After incidents occurred in their teaching, I asked the preservice teachers to conduct a check-in with themselves, where they reflected on what they witnessed and how they reacted. Then, I asked candidates to determine what external resources should be consulted after witnessing an incident. Should they journal? Should they text their cohort mates? Should they consult a school administrator or their cooperating teacher? Teachers often sacrifice self-care strategies and moments in order to be there for their students, but they cannot support others if they are not mentally well. It is important to discuss how preservice teachers can receive support and guidance in difficult situations.

The witnessing of traumas also led to candidates' connecting their students' stories to their own personal traumas. Athena connected stories shared by her students to her own past experiences with loved ones who struggled with substance abuse. She asked her students to write personal essays, and she wrote her own about her past and shared it with her students. Natalie lost her mother when she was in high school. She witnessed two significant incidences of trauma during her fieldwork semester, and she discussed how she was impacted by her own grief when interacting with students in their respective situations. Candidates in this group developed an awareness of their own reactions as they witnessed students' traumas and traumatic stories. As they shared in our group, they discussed how they were impacted by their students' testimonials

Check-ins can allow for reciprocal witnessing and support to happen within school spaces, which leads to stronger student-teacher and peer relationships. These strategies can both increase resiliency and confidence in preservice teachers and can encourage community building in their own classrooms. Incorporating trauma-informed instruction and relational teaching practices into teacher education coursework can greatly benefit both preservice teachers and their future students.

Implications

Some common themes throughout both semesters included a lack of confidence when faced with difficult situations and concern about safety protocols in schools. As seen in the findings, candidates believed the title of "student teacher" did not allow them to take charge in a classroom that was not technically theirs. That title paired with a lack of experience dealing with different school circumstances led to candidates not having much confidence in their ability to confront serious issues. Work must be done with preservice teachers in semesters before fieldwork occurs in order for them to understand that while the role of student teacher does prohibit them from some independent decisions, they are an adult in the classroom who can assume responsibilities. School safety was also an issue that was noted by both groups of participants. In addition to the routine lockdown, fire, and evacuation drills that take place at schools, candidates from each semester experienced lockdowns during their student teaching experiences. While we all hope that lockdowns will not need to occur and schools will remain safe, the reality of today's world includes lockdowns and lockdown drills. The fieldwork experiences of these preservice teachers further demonstrate the need for more support for about lockdowns and threats of violence in their schools and classrooms. Both of these themes can be addressed by including more case studies and scenarios in the semesters prior to being preservice teachers. Guest speakers from local districts are also valuable, as candidates can interact with those who are currently in the field.

As preservice teachers supported students who are sharing traumas, we must consider their emotional well-being as well during these difficult situations. For those who did not have supportive cooperating teachers, our group meetings and their group chats provided a necessary community. As Ben said, "alarm bells" went off when students cried in front of him at Challenge Day. Over time, the preservice teachers will get more comfortable in their role as teacher, but they shared that having a space to discuss their triumphs and challenges helped them grow as they began their career as educators. In many circumstances, the preservice teachers noted that other teachers in the school were not as empathetic or kind in their responses to students. Candidates also struggled to support their students if testimonials triggered emotions of their own. However, participants shared that providing space for witnessing and sharing of testimonials during our meetings was beneficial as they navigated school relationships and experiences.

The benefits of a space for testimony and witness were modeled in group meetings. Candidates noted the advantages of using check-ins both on a daily basis and for processing difficult moments. Many of them mentioned that they plan to implement similar conversations within their classrooms in order to better support their students. Candidates learned questioning techniques to use during check-ins and considered how to thoughtfully introduce this type of activity rather than just launching into it. They also discussed specific ways to implement relational teaching practices. Too often, new initiatives are brought into classrooms without practice or planning. Group participants were able to see these check-ins work in our meetings and were able to practice how to facilitate this type of activity with their future students.

Researcher reflective memos discussed how as candidates checked in each week about difficult situations that were faced in their student teaching experiences, they realized that they were not alone. They had a cohort of peers to rely on when faced with tough moments, and they had colleagues at their schools to work with as well. Candidates shared that they felt that their friends and family who were not in education did not understand or want to talk to them about their experiences, so these outlets were unique places for some to share. They also discussed the fact that some of their cooperating teachers shared their uncertainty in incidents of trauma as well. As Natalie worked with her students in lockdown, her cooperating teacher told her that she still didn't know exactly what to say after over two decades in the profession. This fact also comforted the preservice teachers, who were often afraid to do the "wrong" thing in a situation. Sharing stories of how they handled situations as well as observing others in the field helped to build confidence in the preservice teachers as they graduated and became teachers of their own classrooms.

Plans for Continued Development

Moving forward, data will continue to be collected on check-ins during the seminar class. I plan to continue utilizing check-ins and time for candidates to reciprocally witness and share their testimonials in future semesters. I also plan to suggest informal journaling and digital communication between cohort members to allow for peer check-ins to occur outside of class meetings. With even more difficult times on the horizon, it is imperative to foster community within the student teaching seminar so that candidates have the space they need to build resiliency skills and learn how to implement trauma-informed strategies in their own classrooms. While it may seem like a small initiative, this model allows for candidates to see the benefits of allowing for time and space for witnessing in their own classrooms, and it will provide them with a forum to share their concerns and support for each other.

In the following school year, I integrated the work we did in our group sessions into class time. I implemented a check-in system in the student teaching seminar. Our class was remote due to the COVID-19 pandemic, and we met via Zoom once a week. This course primarily provides certification portfolio and exam support and also includes several certification workshops and training required by our state. I carved out the first segment of each week in order to introduce check-ins to candidates. Over the course of 14 weeks, each candidate shared a check-in at least three times. Candidates were assigned two check-in weeks and the whole class checked-in during our final meeting. After the scheduled check-ins, I opened the room up for any other comments. This open forum is an important part of the check-in process because incidents can occur at any time, and candidates sometimes need to debrief or ask for advice outside of their assigned weeks. Just as in the group meetings, while candidates had assigned check-in weeks, this participation was optional. We used the "rose and thorn" format for check-ins, but candidates were encouraged to share either a rose, a thorn, or both a rose and a thorn. This open format for sharing check-ins led all students to share at least one type of moment from their fieldwork, even those who were quieter during the open forum portion of class. In addition to our class check-ins, the cohort had a group chat where they shared celebrations and difficulties. They mentioned the group chat many times over the course of the semester and discussed how our check-ins and the group chat were both very helpful as they navigated the difficult work of teaching during the COVID-19 pandemic.

The weekly check-ins brought about many stories that highlighted the difficulties of the world we are currently in while also allowing candidates a space to celebrate their accomplishments. One candidate rejoiced when she finally remembered all of her students' names. Another encouraged his students to proofread textbooks and shared about how his class communicated with a publisher about correcting errors they discovered within their books. One candidate lost her grandmother during our time together. Another lost her sister. Yet another spent the first month of the semester in Mexico taking care of her ailing father. We grieved together, cried together, and laughed together as check-ins tended to run the gamut of emotions. Above all else, as they built off of each other's stories, it was clear that the candidates appreciated the community we had built in the virtual space of our class over the course of the semester.

The role of educators is expanding to better support students who have experienced trauma, more professional development and training is needed at the in-service and preservice levels (Alvarez, 2017; Thomas et al., 2019). Trauma-informed pedagogy must be implemented in a meaningful way in order to help, and not harm, our students. As the world begins to emerge from the depths of the pandemic, widespread trauma will be evident among preservice teachers and the students they work with. The stories of losses, illnesses, and caretaking will fill classrooms for years to come. This community trauma is unique from individual traumas that more frequently showed up in the past, as it will be much more pervasive. Now, more than ever, it is imperative that preservice teachers engage in activities and discussions about how best to support students, who have experienced grief and trauma, before entering their own classrooms. Incorporating check-ins into the student teaching seminar can provide candidates a space to discuss the emotionality of their fieldwork experience while modeling how to implement a similar activity with their future students.

REFERENCES

Alvarez, A. (2017). "Seeing their eyes in the rearview mirror": Identifying and responding to students' challenging experiences. *Equity & Excellence in Education, 50*(1), 53–67.

Ballenger, C. (2009). *Puzzling moments, teachable moments: Practicing teacher research in urban classrooms* (Practitioners Inquiry Series). Teachers College Press.

Bouhnik, D., Deshen, M., & Gan, R. (2014). WhatsApp goes to school: Mobile instant messaging between teachers and students. *Journal of Information Technology Education: Research, 13*(1), 217–231.

Caruth, C. (1995). *Trauma: Explorations in memory*. JHU Press.

Christie, D., McFarlane, F., Casdagli, L., & Fredman, G. (2016). Witnessing outsider witnessing: A reciprocal witnessing workshop with young people reclaiming their lives back from pain and Fatigue. *Physical Medicine and Rehabilitation Research, 1*(4).

Cochran-Smith, M., & Lytle, S.L. (2009). *Inquiry as stance: Practitioner research for the next generation*. Teachers College Press.

Dutro, E. (2008). 'That's why I was crying on this book': Trauma as testimony in responses to literature. *Changing English, 15*(4), 423–434.

Dutro, E. (2009). Children's testimony and the necessity of critical witness in urban classrooms. *Theory Into Practice, 48*(3), 231–238.

Dutro, E. (2017). Let's start with heartbreak: The perilous potential of trauma in Literacy. *Language Arts, 94*(5), 326.

Dutro, E. (2019). *The vulnerable heart of literacy: Centering trauma as powerful pedagogy*. Teachers College Press.

Felman, S., & Laub, D. (1992). *Testimony: Crises of witnessing in literature, psychoanalysis, and history*. Taylor & Francis.

Gross, N., & Lo, C. (2018). Relational teaching and learning after loss: Evidence from Black adolescent male students and their teachers. *School Psychology Quarterly, 33*(3), 381.

Health Resources & Services Administration. (2019, October). *New HRSA Data Shows One in Three US Children Have Suffered an Adverse Childhood Experience* [Press Release]. https://www.hrsa.gov/about/news/press-releases/hrsa-data-national-survey-childrenhealth

Huxley, A. (1932). *Brave new world*. Chatto & Windus

Janks, H. (2010). *Literacy and power*. Routledge.

Kinloch, V. (2010). *Harlem on our minds: Place, race, and the literacies of urban youth*. Teachers College Press.

Lytle, S. L. (2000). Teacher research in the contact zone. In M. Kamil, P. Mosenthal, D. Pearson, & R. Barr (Eds.), *Handbook of reading research* (Vol. III, pp. 691–718). Lawrence Erlbaum.

Marshall, C., & Rossman, G. B. (2011). *Designing qualitative research*. SAGE.

Maxwell, J. A. (2013). *Qualitative research design: An interactive approach* (Vol. 41). SAGE.

Miles, M. B., Huberman, A. M., & Saldaña, J. (2013). *Qualitative data analysis: A methods sourcebook* (3rd ed.). SAGE.

Raider-Roth, M. (2008). Teaching boys: A relational puzzle. *Teachers College Record, 110*(2), 443–481.

Ravitch, S. M., & Riggan, M. (2012). *Reason & rigor: How conceptual frameworks guide research*. SAGE.

Reichert, M., & Hawley, R. (2013). Relationships play primary role in boys' learning. *Phi Delta Kappan, 94*, 49–53.

Rogers, D. (2009). The working alliance in teaching and learning: Theoretical clarity and research implications. *International Journal for the Scholarship of Teaching & Learning, 3*(2).

Thomas, M. S., Crosby, S., & Vanderhaar, J. (2019). Trauma-informed practices in schools across two decades: An interdisciplinary review of research. *Review of Research in Education*, *43*(1), 422–452.

Troia, G. A., & Graham, S. (2002). The effectiveness of a highly explicit, teacher-directed strategy instruction routine: Changing the writing performance of students with learning disabilities. *Journal of Learning Disabilities*, *35*(4), 290–305.

Watson, S. W., & Bradley, J. F. (2009). Modeling secondary instructional strategies in a teacher education class. *Education*, *130*(1).

CHAPTER 4

SELF-COMPASSION PRACTICE TO MITIGATE TEACHERS' EMPATHY FATIGUE AND BURNOUT

David P. Barry
West Chester University of Pennsylvania

ABSTRACT

Though there has been an increase in research aimed at supporting trauma-tized students in recent years, less attention has been given empirically to the impact supporting traumatized students has on teachers. This chapter presents findings from a mixed-methods case study in which the researcher investigated the impact of self-compassion practices on preservice early childhood teachers enrolled in a large, urban university's teacher education program over their three-semesters of coursework and field placements in urban elementary schools. As self- compassion practice has been found to be effective in mitigating the effects of burnout and empathy fatigue among pro-fessional caregivers who support traumatized patients, the researcher utilized a self-compassionate letter-writing intervention for use with preservice early childhood teachers in order that they might enter their classrooms with the self-compassion skills to soothe and perhaps prevent potential experiences with burnout and empathy fatigue as a result of supporting their students, some of whom had experienced trauma. Findings from this study indicate

Developing Trauma-Informed Teachers: Creating Classrooms That Foster Equity, Resiliency, and Asset-Based Approaches: Research Findings From the Field, pp. 49–70
Copyright © 2023 by Information Age Publishing
www.infoagepub.com

that these self-compassion practices hold promise for teachers who support traumatized children in two important ways. First, quantitatively, participants experienced a significant increase in their self-compassion scores in ways similar to professional caregivers who practice self-compassion who also experience fewer instances of job-related burnout and empathy fatigue and greater instances of job satisfaction. Second, qualitatively, participants felt these practices could help protect them from burnout as teachers and encouraged them to be more mindful and less punitive when interacting with their students. After graduating from this teacher education program and beginning their first year as teachers, all interviewed participants continued to believe that these practices were important to their own mental health and their capacity to support their students.

The toxic impact of trauma on children and how teachers can support traumatized children is a burgeoning area of research; less studied is the deleterious effects experienced by teachers who support traumatized children that can include post-traumatic stress disorder (DSM-V), empathy fatigue and burnout (Jennings, 2019; Stebnicki, 2015), and in some instances, leaving teaching all together (Barry, 2020, 2021a, 2021b; Ingersoll, 2001; Ryan et al., 2017). The purpose of this chapter is to illuminate (1) the parallels that exist between professional caregivers (e.g., doctors, nurses, mental health clinicians, etc.) who experience these effects as a result of supporting traumatized patients and teachers, (2) how interventions aimed at reducing these effects among professional caregivers may also work for teachers, and (3) present findings from a mixed-methods case study (Creswell & Plano Clark, 2018) in which I, the researcher, examined how one such intervention appeared to work for a group of preservice teachers.

Young children's "thin agency" (Klocker, 2007) coupled with their heavy dependence on adults (i.e., teachers and parents) puts them in particularly vulnerable positions. When this vulnerability is met with the potentially damaging effects of community violence, parental abuse, and poverty, the impact on children can be traumatic (Gaikhorst et al., 2017). Often, a young child's teacher is the best known and most trusted adult outside of the family and in instances that the potential for danger exists within the homes and communities of very young children, it can often become the responsibility of their teacher to take an elevated caregiving role in his or her students' lives. A teacher's heightened responsibility and the intimate knowledge of their students' suffering can lead to burnout in ways similar to professional caregivers (Barry, 2020, 2021a, 2021b; Ryan et al., 2017). Though some might recommend these teachers practice self-care more regularly, the current standards-based accountability reforms that hold teachers, students, and schools accountable for student achievement on standardized tests leave very little room to attend to their students' social-emotional needs, let alone their own (Dunn, 2018).

Research shows that higher levels of self-compassion are often correlated with fewer instances of empathy fatigue and burnout among professional caregivers (Amrani, 2010; Barnard & Curry, 2012; Benzo et al., 2017; Duarte et al., 2016; Germer & Neff, 2019; Montero-Martin et al., 2016; Sinclair et al., 2017; Stebnicki, 2015), but little has been done to address this same need among elementary and early childhood teachers (Jennings, 2019).

The first part of this chapter will define self-compassion and address the challenges professional caregivers face when supporting traumatized patients and draw parallels to the similarities experienced by early childhood teachers—particularly those in urban contexts. Then, the second part of this chapter will present findings from a mixed methods case study (Creswell & Plano Clark, 2018) in which preservice teachers in an urban, undergraduate, university-based teacher education program engaged in a self-compassion intervention (Neff, 2011) over the course of their three semesters of coursework and fieldwork in public, urban, elementary school classrooms (Barry, 2020, 2021a, 2021b). Quantitative findings indicate a statistically significant increase in participants' self-reports of self-compassion from semester one to semester three with a large Cohen's d effect size of .77 ($n = 16$) (see Table 4.1) which is highly correlated with increased job satisfaction and reduced levels of empathy fatigue and burnout among professional caregivers (Finlay-Jones et al., 2015). Qualitative findings indicate that all interviewed participants ($n = 10$) found the practice to be beneficial to their development as teachers and believed that practicing self-compassion would help mitigate the effects of empathy fatigue and burnout in the future. Furthermore, as these preservice teachers began their first year as classroom teachers, they began to see how these practices impacted their interactions with their students—particularly those who were experiencing or had experienced trauma—to be more mindful and less punitive.

The chapter will conclude with recommendations for teacher educators to prepare preservice teachers for the emotional toll that caring for traumatized children can incur upon teachers. By encouraging teacher educators to frontload skills like self-compassion within and across their teacher education programs, they may graduate teachers who are able to withstand the extensive stressors of teaching—including supporting traumatized children—without succumbing to burnout (Jennings, 2019) and attrition (Ryan et al., 2017) in the future.

WHAT IS SELF-COMPASSION?

Neff and Germer (2013) define self-compassion as "three interacting components: self- kindness versus self-judgment, a sense of common humanity

Table 4.1

Statistical Tests

Paired Samples Test of Preservice Teachers' Mean Self-Compassion Scores (Semester 1, 2, & 3)

	Paired Differences							
				95% Confidence				
Compared Semesters (1, 2, & 3)	Mean	Std. Deviation	Std. Error Mean	Lower	Upper	t	df	Sig. (2-tailed)
Pair 1 Semester 1 - Semester 2	-0.29083	0.56659	0.16356	-0.65083	0.06916	-1.778	11	0.103
Pair 2 Semester 2 - Semester 3	-0.27077	0.35615	0.09878	-0.48599	-0.05555	-2.741	12	0.018
Pair 3 Semester 1 - Semester 3	-0.57214	0.74427	0.19892	-1.00187	-0.14241	-2.876	13	0.013

Paired Samples Effect Sizes of Preservice Teachers' Mean Self-Compassion Scores (Semester 1, 2, & 3)

		Point Estimate (Cohen's d effect size)	95% Confidence	
Compared Semesters (1, 2, & 3)	Standardizer[a]		Lower	Upper
Pair 1 Semester 1 - Semester 2	Cohen's d	0.56659	-0.513	-1.107	0.101
Pair 2 Semester 2 - Semester 3	Cohen's d	0.35615	-0.760	-1.370	-0.127
Pair 3 Semester 1 - Semester 3	Cohen's d	0.74427	-0.769	-1.358	-0.158

a. The denominator used in estimating the effect sizes.

Cohen's d uses the sample standard deviation of the mean difference.

versus isolation, and mindfulness versus over-identification when confronting painful self-relevant thoughts and emotions" (p. 28). While mindfulness teaches us to pay "attention in a particular way: on purpose, in the present moment, and nonjudgmentally" (Kabat-Zinn, 1994, p. 4), self-compassion goes deeper, showing us how to turn our awareness to our suffering as it arises. In this way, self-compassion shifts the focus from the objective "experience" (mindfulness) to the "experiencer" (Neff & Germer, 2013). Self-compassion then teaches us to attend to our suffering with the same kindness we would show a close friend (Neff, 2011, p. 42), whom we would reassure of their worthiness without judgment, and remind that suffering is part of our shared human experience (Neff & Germer, 2013). By activating the elements of self-compassion (mindfulness, self-kindness, and recognition of the shared experience of our common humanity) in unison, we can begin to attend to our suffering and heal. To better understand the three interconnected elements of self-compassion, they will be defined separately, however, it should be noted that to authentically practice self-compassion is to incorporate each element collectively.

Self-Kindness Versus Self-Judgment. Practicing self-kindness requires "that we be gentle and understanding with ourselves rather than harshly critical and judgmental" (Neff, 2011, p. 41) and that we "actively [comfort] ourselves, responding just as we would to a dear friend in need" (p. 42). As Neff (2011) noted, a barrier to practicing self-kindness is that most of us have come to see self-judgment and "disparaging internal commentary … as normal" (p. 42). However, when we expand our capacity to offer the same loving support and kindness, we would offer a dear friend or loved one, we can begin to develop our capacity for "clearly seeing the extent to which we harm ourselves through relentless self-criticism" and "understand our … failures instead of condemning them" (p. 42). Further, as the capacity for self-kindness expands and the harsh self-judgment we have been conditioned to internalize diminishes, so too expands the capacity for "actively soothing and comforting oneself" in moments of suffering (Germer & Neff, 2017, p. 5).

Common Humanity Versus Isolation. Integral to self-compassion practice—and a key element that distinguishes self-compassion from self-pity—is the understanding that other people also experience suffering; that to suffer and to feel pain is part of the experience of being human that connects human beings (Germer & Neff, 2017; Neff, 2011). By "feeling connected with others in the experience of life … rather than feeling isolated and alienated by our suffering," a developed sense of common humanity allows people to feel comforted by the fact that everyone suffers, and it offers comfort because everyone is human. The pain I feel in difficult times is the same pain you feel in difficult times. The triggers are different, the circumstances are different, the degree of pain is different, but the process is the same (p. 62). To understand that feelings of pain, suffering, and failure are experienced by all people, our sense of common humanity reminds us that we are not alone in our suffering and that our suffering is not what isolates us, rather, it is what connects us to others.

Mindfulness Versus Over-Identification. The following excerpt from Siegel (2010), concisely captures what mindfulness is and what it can do for those who practice it:

> When we are operating on automatic—daydreaming about one thing while our body is involved in another, or restlessly craving the next little treat—we don't really notice what we're doing. And if we're not aware of our experience from moment to moment, it's very difficult to gain insight into and interpret the mental habits that create suffering—which is ultimately the point of practicing mindfulness. (Siegel, 2010, p. 52)

"Operating on automatic" and "restlessly craving the next little treat" (p. 52) steals from us the satisfaction that resides in the omnipresent "present moment" and the opportunity to realize that "there is just this moment" (Kabat-Zinn, 1994, p. 22).

As stated earlier, Kabat-Zinn (1994) defined mindfulness as "paying attention in a particular way: on purpose, in the present moment, and nonjudgmentally" (p. 4) which is in direct dissonance with the way people are trained to live their lives—always striving for the promise of happiness on the other side of the hurdle, but already anxious about the next hurdle before finishing jumping the first (Siegel, 2010). Instead of ruminating on or over-identifying future obstacles to success and happiness, mindfulness gives us an appreciation for the here and now—this moment. With mindfulness, we are gentler to—and more patient with—ourselves because we come to accept that our intrusive thoughts are just thoughts, not reality. When we can see our judgements of ourselves as just thoughts that can come, fade, and be let go, they are no longer able to hold us hostage.

Kabat-Zinn (1994) acknowledged that practicing mindfulness is "simple but not easy" because "we tend to be particularly unaware that we are thinking virtually all the time" (pp. 8–9). Bishop et al. (2004) reiterated the challenge of being mindful because of our preoccupation with outcomes rather than processes (p. 235). With practice, however, mindfulness allows us to acknowledge these intrusions without judgement. By taking away our emotional attachment (i.e., our judgement and our over-identification) from these inevitable intrusions, we can "gently return to the present moment" (Neff, personal communication, 2017) and continue our mindfulness practice.

HOW IS SELF-COMPASSION DIFFERENT FROM SELF-CARE?

Corey et al. (2018) defined self-care as:

> the collection of positive actions that promote wellness and effective cop-
> ing. Stated broadly, "self-care includes routine positive practices and mind-
> ful attention to one's physical, emotional, relational, and spiritual selves in
> the context of one's personal and professional lives" ([in] Wise & Barnett,
> 2016, p. 210). (Corey et al., 2018, p. 3)

Though this definition indicates there are similarities between self-care and
self-compassion (e.g., the inclusion of mindfulness), the differences that
exist between these two constructs make them more different than alike.
For example, in Corey et al.'s book, (2018), there are several vignettes of
graduate students in a counselor training program who reflected on their
self-care practices. One such student described her experience when she
reflected,

> Although finding sufficient time is difficult, I have worked self-care into my
> life. My absolute favorite form of self-care is taking vacations. I generally
> take two vacations each year, and occasionally I add a third vacation when I
> find myself particularly in need. (p. 4)

This graduate student, Amanda, expressed how she practiced self-care in
terms of something that she needs to set aside time and money for, and
ultimately, something that she needs to get away in order to do. Self-compassion, as opposed to self-care, is not something that needs to be delayed
or paid for (as self-care practices often are). Self-compassion is a way of
relating to and responding to one's challenges and suffering with self-
kindness, mindfulness, and the understanding that all humans experience
suffering and challenging moments. Self-compassion does not require that
one wait to give themselves the love and kindness they deserve, instead,
self-compassion allows people to identify these moments of challenge as
they arise and respond to them with the same love and care they would to a
dear friend (Neff, 2011). Though Corey et al. (2018) wrote that self-care is
"an ethical mandate" (p. 3), it is not always accessible in the moments one
needs it the most—particularly professional caregivers. Self-compassion,
however, when cultivated and practiced, is accessible wherever you are,
whenever it is needed.

EMPATHY FATIGUE: A MAJOR CAUSE OF BURNOUT FOR PROFESSIONAL CAREGIVERS

Empathy fatigue is a psychological phenomenon typically attributed to a specific form of burnout experienced by professional caregivers such as healthcare workers, mental health clinicians, and religious leaders (Amrani, 2010; Barnard & Curry, 2012; Benzo et al., 2017; Duarte et al., 2016; Germer & Neff, 2019; Montero-Martin et al., 2016; Sinclair et al., 2017; Stebnicki, 2015). Stebnicki (2015) defined empathy fatigue as:

> [an] impairment that affects the whole self: mind, body, and spirit…. This type of professional work-related stress has psychological, physical, and behavioral costs that may result in the symptoms of depression, anxiety, and emotional exhaustion. From an empathy fatigue perspective, there is a cost to one's mind, body, and spiritual growth. (p. 533)

Neff (2011) extended this definition to include the causes of empathy fatigue professional caregivers experience "as a result of continually dealing with traumatized patients. When listening to tales of abuse and horror, or when tending to bodies that have been ravaged by sickness or violence, caregivers often feel their patients' trauma" (p. 192). Though the effects of empathy fatigue have the potential to be extremely damaging to professional caregivers, research shows that one way to ease the impact is by learning to be more self-compassionate (Benzo et al., 2017; Duarte et al., 2016; Montero-Martin et al., 2016).

What follows is a description of some of the research on professional caregivers who utilized self-compassion to mitigate the deleterious effects of empathy fatigue.

SELF-COMPASSION CAN MITIGATE THE EFFECTS OF EMPATHY FATIGUE EXPERIENCED BY CAREGIVING PROFESSIONALS

Research shows that practicing self-compassion can be quite successful at mitigating the effects of empathy fatigue experienced by professional caregivers (e.g., Germer & Neff, 2019). Studies of healthcare workers showed that self-compassion "facilitate[d] … psychological well-being and resilience" (Sinclair et al., 2017, p. 179) and also "predicted positive changes in perceived stress" (Shapiro et al., 2005, p. 170). Neff (2011) noted "that caregivers who have been trained in self-compassion are less likely to develop … [empathy] fatigue because they have the skills needed to avoid getting overly stressed or burned out when interacting with their patients

(p. 192). In fact, healthcare workers who are more self-compassionate are more likely to experience " 'compassion satisfaction'—the positive feelings experienced from one's work such as feeling energized, happy, and grateful for being able to make a difference in the world" (Germer & Neff, 2019, p. 25). In the case of healthcare workers who lack self-compassion, the research shows a greater degree of empathy fatigue and burnout (Benzo et al., 2017; Montero-Marin et al., 2016). In the case of nurses experiencing empathy fatigue, Duarte et al. (2016) wrote:

> Although empathy is a key component in nurse-patient relationships, re-sults from this study suggest that being overly sensitive to others' pain and suffering may have deleterious effects on caregivers' mental health, which can limit their ability to provide effective care. This is particularly so when nurses lack self-compassionate abilities. (p. 8)

Similarly, mental health professionals experience empathy fatigue as a result of repeatedly listening to "[c]lient stories that have themes such as addictions, physical or sexual abuse, and psychological trauma [which] can adversely affect the mind, body, and spirit of the counselor" (Stebnicki, 2015, p. 536). Additionally, several studies point to self-compassion being linked to stress reduction in mental health clinicians (Amrani, 2010; Finlay-Jones et al., 2015; Germer & Neff, 2019; Stebnicki, 2015). In a study of 301 psychotherapists that "examined the relationship between self-compassion, empathy and burnout, and whether self-compassion had a 'buffering effect' for a psychotherapist and could protect against the effects of high empathy, i.e., burnout" (Amrani, 2010, p. ix), it was found that "high self-reported overall empathy was associated with greater isolation, self-judgment, and over-identification (i.e., low self- compassion)" (p. 80). Results were similar in a study of "[r]eligious leaders'… experience[s of] burnout…. Clergy with high emotional exhaustion feel drained and discouraged … [however], [h]igher self-compassion was … related to increased satisfaction in ministry. Increasing self- compassion may prevent clergy burnout" (Barnard & Curry, 2012, p. 149). These positive results with professional caregivers who were high in self-compassion and experienced fewer instances of burnout and empathy fatigue have implications for other professionals who experience stress and burnout as a result of caregiving and empathy fatigue. The next section of this chapter will make the case for teachers to practice self-compassion to mitigate the harmful effects of stress, empathy fatigue, and burnout related to supporting traumatized students in order that they may experience similar benefits to professional caregivers.

TEACHERS' EXPERIENCES OF STRESS, EMPATHY FATIGUE, AND BURNOUT

To say that teachers are stressed is an understatement (Ryan et al., 2017). In fact, teachers' unique stress is a global issue (Adams, 2013; Simos, 2013; Yong & Yue, 2007). In the United Kingdom, "Teaching and education are recognised as among the most stressful occupations ... with rates of suicide running at a third above that of the national population.... [B]etween 35 and 63 teachers have killed themselves each year" (Adams, 2013). In China, overwhelming numbers of students, eight-hour days, and critical parents with high demands and expectations of teachers were cited as major sources of teachers' stress (Yong & Yue, 2007, p. 81), resulting in teachers experiencing "less self-control, self-respect, and work efficiency and a higher level of irritability ... [leading to] ... depression, probability of ulcer and hypertension, alcoholism, and overreaction to moderate amounts of stress" (p. 80). In the United States, teachers are leaving the classroom at an alarming rate, double that of "high performing countries like Finland and Singapore" with teachers' unique stress being cited as a likely cause (Westervelt, 2016).

Teachers are mandated reporters, meaning that when child abuse is suspected, they are legally obligated to report their suspicions to whatever state program governs child protection (Kulgren, 2012; Sciamanna, 2020). According to the Children's Bureau's "annual child abuse and neglect report: Child Maltreatment 2018" (Sciamanna, 2020):

> As far as who reports cases of abuse and neglect, professionals submitted 67.3 percent of reports. Professionals included teachers, police officers, lawyers, and social services staff. As in past years, education personnel (20.5%) accounted for the single biggest percentage of reporters.

This puts elementary and early childhood teachers in a particularly difficult position as they are the most likely reporters of suspected child abuse and neglect (Sciamanna, 2020). An additional challenge associated with being a mandated reporter that teachers face is the detrimental effect it can have on a teacher's relationship with the family. Unlike other professionals who are mandated reporters of suspected abuse (e.g., police officers, lawyers, social services, etc.), teachers interact frequently with the families of the children in their classrooms whereas other professionals would most likely not have sustained relationships or daily interactions. For example, if a teacher's suspicions are found to be untrue, it is unlikely that families would continue to trust that teacher which could present serious challenges to the quality of the relationships that teachers will be able to have with families thereafter.

The Impact of Urban Contexts and Child Poverty. In addition to the uniqueness of the family dynamics and age of the students in early childhood classrooms, the environmental contexts in which they live can also be quite complex. This is particularly evident in the case of young children living in high-poverty urban areas where teachers feel that "violence and poverty are important challenges for urban education" (Gaikhorst et al., 2017, p. 49). Though violent crime in cities has been on the decline since the 1990s, the rates of community violence in urban areas are still much higher than in suburbs (Kneebone & Raphael, 2011). In a study by Gaikhorst et al. (2017), the authors found

> the majority of the teachers … recognised the challenge of violence and an unsafe atmosphere [and] believed that the problem was related to teaching in urban schools … [and that] children in large cities are often hanging around in the streets at night and some of them live in unsafe neighborhoods. (p. 56)

This same study found that teachers working in high-poverty urban schools felt "that some students experience particular circumstances such as hunger, fear, illness and aggression on a daily basis at home" (p. 56). According to one of the teachers interviewed

> I find this very difficult at times, because a child has a right to affection, but also a right to have breakfast in the morning. Especially in the beginning [of my career], I found this very hard to cope with. (p. 56)

As a result of these unique challenges, "90% of high poverty schools are struggling to find enough qualified special education teachers" and "1 in 5 teachers in high-minority schools and high poverty schools is unprepared for teaching" (Westervelt, 2016). These statistics could very well be due to qualified teachers leaving the profession as result of the burnout they are experiencing (Ryan et al., 2017), and in fact, seems likely given the emotional toll that working with very young children living in poverty and witnessing or experiencing violence may take on teachers (Gaikhorst et al., 2017; Kelly & Bethelsen, 1995). The unique challenges of urban early childhood educators, therefore, present a nuanced complexity when compared to the population of teachers in general who experience burnout. Given the heavy teacher-dependence (Kelly & Bethelsen, 1995) and "thin agency" (Klocker, 2007) young children have and the additional contextual complexities experienced by children living in poverty in urban contexts (Gaikhorst et al., 2017; Kneebone & Raphael, 2011), there can be a heightened degree of caregiving required by teachers in these contexts that flavors their experience with burnout differently than in other teachers who experience burnout.

SELF-COMPASSION COULD MITIGATE THE EFFECTS OF EMPATHY FATIGUE WITH TEACHERS

Due to the striking similarities between these studies of teachers' stress and burnout and the experiences of empathy fatigue experienced by professional caregivers, particularly regarding the effects on one's mental health (e.g., Adams, 2013; Amrani, 2010; Wrobel, 2013), teachers may very well be experiencing burnout by way of empathy fatigue in ways similar to professional caregivers (Ryan et al, 2017). As Adams (2013) discovered in the United Kingdom, teachers are experiencing stress at a level higher than all other professionals besides nurses—who are included among professional caregivers who may experience empathy fatigue that benefit from practicing self-compassion (Benzo et al., 2017; Duarte et al., 2016; Montero-Marin et al., 2016). As higher levels of self-compassion are correlated to reductions in stress (Shapiro et al., 2005), increased job satisfaction (Barnard & Curry, 2012), and reductions in the negative effects of empathy fatigue with other professional caregivers (Germer & Neff, 2019), practicing self-compassion may be one way that teachers could manage their stress and stay in their classrooms healthfully and sustainably with the skills needed not only to be the teacher their students deserve, but the skills needed to care for themselves in ways that deserve.

A Self-Compassion Practice for Early Childhood Teachers in Urban Contexts.

In Neff's (2011) book, she shared a variety of strategies and practices to help her readers develop self-compassion, one of which is entitled *Exploring Self-Compassion Through Letter Writing* (pp. 16–17) and is described next.

Exploring Self-Compassion Through Letter Writing

Neff (2011) invited the person doing this exercise to first consider "an issue that tends to make [them] feel inadequate or bad about [them]self" and to "feel [their] emotions [connected to this issue] exactly as they are— no more, no less" (p. 16). The second part of the exercise asks the person doing the exercise to:

> think about an imaginary friend who is unconditionally loving, accepting, kind, and compassionate. Imagine that this friend can see all your strengths and all your weaknesses, including the aspect of yourself you have just been thinking about.... This friend recognizes the limits of human nature and is kind and forgiving towards you. (p. 16)

With this "imaginary friend" and the particular issue in mind, the person doing this exercise will then "[w]rite a letter to [them]self from the perspective of this imaginary friend" (p. 17). Neff posed the following questions to be considered while writing the letter:

> What would this friend say to you about your "flaw" from the perspective of unlimited compassion? How would this friend convey the deep compassion he/she feels for you, especially for the discomfort you feel when you judge yourself so harshly? What would this friend write in order to remind you that you are only human, that all people have both strengths and weaknesses? And if you think this friend would suggest possible changes you should make, how would these suggestions embody feelings of unconditional understanding and compassion? As you write to yourself from the perspective of this imaginary friend, try to infuse your letter with a strong sense of the person's acceptance, kindness, caring, and desire for your health and happiness. (p. 17)

The final part of the practice is to "put [the letter] ... down for a little while. Then come back and read it again, really letting the words sink in. Feel the compassion as it pours into you, soothing and comforting you like a cool breeze on a hot day" (p. 17). For a teacher experiencing empathy fatigue as a result of supporting traumatized students, it may be very challenging to give compassion directly to oneself because of the "depression, anxiety, and emotional exhaustion" (Stebnicki, 2015, p. 533) they are experiencing. Taking—and then writing from—the perspective of an unconditionally loving and accepting friend may serve as an entry point to the teacher beginning to practice self-compassion. To evaluate whether frontloading this exercise within teacher education programs would be beneficial, I, the researcher, explored the impact of practicing this self-compassion exercise among preservice elementary and early childhood teachers as they progressed through an urban teacher education program which included coursework and field placements in urban, elementary school classrooms.

METHODS

This mixed-methods case study (Merriam & Tisdell, 2016) involved a cohort of preservice teachers ($n = 16$) in an urban undergraduate teacher education program who engaged in Neff's "Exploring Self-Compassion Through Letter Writing" (2011) to address their stress over three semesters of coursework and field placements in urban public elementary classrooms. Much of research on teachers' stress and attrition is highly quantitative, relying on surveys and scales for the majority of data (Fantilli & McDougall, 2009; Ingersoll, 2001). Though this work has illuminated several aspects of pre- and in-service teachers' experiences of stress, burnout, and attrition, the conclusions that come from these studies can miss the myriad factors that influence a teacher to check "personal" or "dissatisfaction" (Ingersoll, 2001) in a survey on attrition. Therefore, it is important that research about teachers' stress, burnout, and attrition include more qualitative data sources (e.g., interviews) to provide "rich, thick description" (Merriam & Tisdell, 2016, p. 257) of their unique experiences. Using case study as a research methodology allows researchers to generate findings with "an in-depth description of a bounded system" (p. 37) through the rich description and triangulation (p. 259) of multiple data sources; both quantitative and qualitative. This work is guided by the research question, how might practicing self-compassion impact preservice teachers' experiences of burnout and empathy fatigue related to their field placements and supporting children who may be experiencing trauma in public elementary school classrooms?

Data Collection

Self-Compassionate Letters. The preservice teachers in this study wrote 11 self- compassionate letters to themselves over the course of their three-semester teacher education program about challenging experiences in their field placements from the perspective of an unconditionally loving friend using "Neff's "Exploring Self-Compassion Through Letter Writing" (2011 as a prompt during seminars. With the support of their field placement coordinator, I attended the first 15 minutes of their seminars to disseminate paper and electronic copies of the prompt to the preservice teachers. After 15 minutes, I collected and deidentified the letters and uploaded them to NVivo 12 for analysis.

Neff's Self-Compassion Scale—Short Form. Participants filled out Neff's Self- Compassion Scale—short form (Raes et al., 2011) once each semester for three semesters. Mean scores for each preservice teacher were calculated at each time period and then a group mean was calculated for each time period. The means were analyzed using paired sample t-tests to determine significance in SPSS.

Semi-Structured Interviews. Preservice teachers who wished to be interviewed ($n = 10$) participated in two semi-structured interviews (Merriam & Tisdell, 2016, p. 110)—one in the middle of their teacher education program and one after completing the program. Each interview lasted approximately 30 minutes and questions focused generally on their experiences with the self-compassion exercise in relation to their experiences in their field placements. Interviews were audio-recorded, transcribed, masked with participant-chosen pseudonyms, and uploaded to NVivo 12 for analysis.

FINDINGS

For the purposes of this chapter, only the semi-structured interviews and self-compassion scales were analyzed in the findings and discussion. Qualitative data sources (i.e., semi-structured interviews) were first analyzed using a set of external codes (Graue & Walsh, 1998) such as "self-compassion" and "stress." Through the constant-comparative method (Merriam & Tisdell, 2016, p. 208) and triangulation of multiple data sources—both quantitative and qualitative—internal codes were developed (Graue & Walsh, 1998) such as "self-compassion works" and "self-compassion helps my students." The collective analysis of these data sources yielded two themes: (a) Self-compassion works for preservice teachers, and (b) Self-compassion changed the way these preservice teachers reacted to traumatized students.

Self-Compassion Works for Preservice Teachers. Qualitative and quantitative findings indicate that the preservice teachers in this study felt less stressed over time and associated this with practicing self-compassion. In the space of three semesters, these preservice teachers' self-compassion scores increased significantly with a p-value of .013 and a large Cohen's D effect size of .77 (see Table 4.1). Such an increase is highly correlated with high job satisfaction (Barnard & Curry, 2012) and reductions in feelings of stress, empathy fatigue, and burnout (Barnard & Curry, 2012; Duarte et al., 2016; Finlay-Jones et al., 2015). This finding mirrors other studies that indicate self-compassion practices may significantly increase one's self-compassion ratings over time (Neff & Germer, 2013).

In analyzing how self-compassion practice appeared to work for them, these preservice teachers explained this process through the three elements of self-compassion—mindfulness, self-kindness, and common humanity (Neff, 2011).

Elaine attributed her ability to be mindful in challenging situations with students to her self-compassion practice when she said:

> It's never like, "oh my gosh, she's getting on my nerves. She's such a bad student," It's like "oh my gosh, what's going on? I know her past; I know where she comes from—did something happen?" I really try to take away the negative, and I'm not as negative as I used to be, which I think might be because of [the] self-compassion thing.

To Elaine, the ability to step back in a challenging situation to understand the broader implications of her students' lives is emblematic of her developing mindfulness, and ultimately, self-compassion practice (Neff, 2011).

Bob reflected on her experiences of what it felt like to practice self-compassion and how it evolved over time when she said:

> At first it felt a little bit forced. Like I was trying to just say nice things to myself. But after a while … I just felt happier … I was like "we're going to say nice things to ourselves, this is so exciting!" That really helped. I think it also helped my inner voice say nicer things. I get tempted so many times a day to say, "oh this day stinks. I'm not going to have a great day. These kids aren't listening to me."… Just telling myself "it's okay just take it slowly—you're doing great."… I feel like that really helped.

Bob's reflection of the evolution of her self-compassion practice shows that although being kind to oneself (i.e., self-kindness) can be challenging (Neff, 2011), with time and practice, she was excited to do it and felt it helped her confidence as a developing teacher.

Nicole shared an insight emblematic of common humanity when she described a vulnerable moment with the other preservice teachers:

> I started crying in front of everyone [and it] made them all feel vulnerable—we all started sharing and pouring our hearts out to each other after that … I think that really bonded us because we allowed ourselves to be vulnerable … it's okay to be vulnerable.

To Nicole, this was a moment of common humanity (Neff, 2011) in which she and her cohort allowed themselves to be vulnerable by connecting over the shared (i.e., common) challenges they experienced in their training.

Combined, these findings indicate that practicing self-compassion benefited these preservice teachers in the moment and influenced their work with students (as Elaine and Bob said). Further, they believed being more self-compassionate could protect them from burnout in the future. As Anna said:

> I think it can definitely help fight against the burnout feeling.… [B]eing aware of what's going on, objectively helps you keep going. If you're always wrapped up in the emotions, you're dealing with parents, you may be having a challenging time with students or your administration, you're always feeling so much stress versus taking a few minutes out of the day to just take a step back from that intentionally.

These preservice teachers' statements indicate that they felt self-compassion was important to their development as teachers and believed it could protect them from burnout in the future. Their beliefs echoed the lived experiences of professional caregivers in studies in which it was found that higher levels of self-compassion are connected to reductions in burnout and increases in job satisfaction (Barnard & Curry, 2012; Neff & Germer, 2019).

Self-Compassion Changed the Way These Preservice Teachers Reacted to Traumatized Students. In her second interview (as a first-year teacher), Quinn extended her perceptions of self-compassion to how it impacts students when she said,

> I think the number one thing [about] the self-compassion thing [that] has been really helpful, not only in helping my own morale and my own mental wellbeing while teaching, has also been the fact that it really has affected the way that I treat students and the way that I encourage students to think about themselves. I think it ties in really nicely with the growth mindset ideas that people have.

Here, Quinn reflected that her self-compassion practice extends beyond just herself—that she can now be a teacher that encourages students to develop these skills themselves. Many of the other participants, now first year teachers, echoed Quinn's sentiments. For example,

Bob said:

> I actually talked to my student about [self-compassion] because he was very upset one day that his parents had said something to him and it was pretty harsh. And I was like, "woah, okay." I'm not going to step in and be like, "your parents are wrong," I'm going to say like, "Nope, sometimes people say things and you are allowed to disagree with what they're telling you." And I told him about self-compassion and … I said, "look in the mirror and just talk to yourself." And I was so surprised to how he responded to that, he genuinely was listening. And he genuinely was like, "okay." And he walked me through it and gave me goosebumps. I started crying. We were both crying—it was crazy.

These findings indicate that practicing self-compassion throughout their teacher education program was important to them and extended to their interactions with students as they began their teaching careers. Now, as teachers, they seemed to believe that their students, particularly students experiencing incredible stress—including trauma—benefited from having such practices modeled and taught to them in their classrooms (Jennings, 2019).

Limitations and Issues of Trustworthiness. This research is limited in terms of transferability because, as a case study, I, the researcher, investigated a particular phenomenon in a particular context with a limited number of participants (Thomas, 2016; Yin, 2018). To "increase the 'credibility' or trustworthiness of [my] findings (Merriam & Tisdell,

2016, p. 244), I triangulated multiple sources of data (p. 244) and member checked with participants (p. 246).

These preservice teachers' increases in self-compassion and reductions in stress may be due in part to the fact that they gained experience over time. However, given that they explicitly linked these benefits to self-compassion practice during both rounds of interviews indicates the powerful role these practices appeared to play in their development as teachers.

CONCLUDING THOUGHTS AND SCHOLARLY SIGNIFICANCE

Children in public elementary schools deserve expert teachers, however, nearly half of all teachers leave before gaining high levels of expertise (Djonko-Moore, 2016; Fantilli & McDougall, 2009). With burnout being one reason that teachers exit the classroom (Ryan et al., 2017), it seems that teacher educators should prioritize equipping preservice teachers with the skills to manage the stressors of teaching, particularly when supporting traumatized children. Imbedding self-compassion in teacher education programs, as indicated by the findings of this study, may be one way to do that. Jennings (2019) noted the importance of such practices in order that teachers do not enter a "burnout cascade" (p. 114) as a result of supporting traumatized students when she wrote,

> Regularly engaging in mindful awareness and compassion practices can be an excellent part of a self-care routine, not only for building our own inner resources, but for bringing greater awareness to bodily sensations that give us clues to our needs. With practice, we can begin to notice the early stages of our emotional exhaustion, before it turns into a burnout cascade … a negative spiral of teacher and student reactivity. As we have seen, disruptive, chaotic environments can trigger trauma-exposed students, adding to the negative spiral and impairing everyone's learning.

Like any other skill, increasing one's self-compassion takes time but can be developed with practice (Neff & Germer, 2013). Without adequate time available to preservice teachers to develop these skills, beginning teachers may enter their first classrooms unequipped with the capability to withstand the stressors of teaching that exist beyond curriculum, instruction, and standardized testing. Teacher educators can show their commitment to the emotional needs of their program's preservice teachers by reserving a few minutes of class time to practice self-compassion rather than reminding them to do so on their own time (Brown et al., 2021).

This work extends the extant research on teacher attrition and burnout (e.g., Ingersoll, 2001; Ryan et al., 2017) by providing an in-depth case study of the experiences of preservice teachers who addressed their stress during their training—before the effects of empathy fatigue and burnout were felt. Furthermore, this study extends previous work by researching the benefits of potential solutions to pre- and in-service teachers' experiences of stress, burnout, and attrition (Hirshberg, 2017; Jennings et al., 2017; Roeser et al., 2013). Finally, this work points to how self-compassion practices may influence teachers to be less reactive when working to support traumatized students in their classrooms by avoiding triggering practices that negatively impact students, classroom climate, and teachers themselves (Jennings, 2019).

ACKNOWLEDGMENTS

The author would like to acknowledge that this study was funded in part by The University of Texas at Austin's College of Education Graduate Student Research Award. Additionally, the content of this chapter (e.g., literature review, data, table, etc.) comes from the author's doctoral dissertation (Barry, 2021a) and has been adapted from conference papers (Barry, 2020; Barry, 2021b). There are no conflicts of interest to report. The author would like to thank Dr. Christopher Brown, Dr. Allison Skerrett, Dr. Catherine Riegle-Crumb, Dr. Kristin Neff, and Dr. Maleka Donaldson for their invaluable feedback and support that strengthened the quality of his work.

REFERENCES

Adams, R. (2013, May 1). *Headteacher killed herself after six months in job, coroner rules*. The Guardian. https://www.theguardian.com/education/2013/may/01/headteacher-kills-herself

American Psychiatric Association. (2013). Diagnostic and statistical manual of mental disorders (5th ed.).

Amrani, P. (2010). *Loving-kindness: Self-compassion, burnout and empathy among therapists* (Doctoral dissertation). Retrieved from UMI. (3420446)

Barnard, L. K., & Curry, J. F. (2012). The relationship of clergy burnout to self-compassion and other personality dimensions. *Pastoral Psychol, 61*, 149–163.

Barry, D. P. (2020, December). *Letters to myself: Self-compassionate letter writing as a way to mitigate preservice teachers' experience with stress and burnout* [Paper presentation]. The annual meeting of the Literacy Research Association's virtual conference.

Barry, D. P. (2021a). *Self-compassionate letter writing as a potential way to mitigate feelings of stress, empathy fatigue, and burnout among preservice teachers* [Unpublished doctoral dissertation]. The University of Texas at Austin.

Barry, D. P. (2021b, April). *Self-compassion practice "definitely help[ed] fight againstthe burnout feeling" according to first year teachers* [Paper presentation]. AERA annual meeting (virtual conference).

Benzo, R. P., Kirsch, J. L., & Nelson, C. (2017). Compassion, mindfulness, and the happiness of healthcare workers. *EXPLORE, 13*(3), 201–206.

Bishop, S. R., Lau, M., Shapiro, S. L., Carlson, L. E., Anderson, N. D., Carmody, J., & Devins, G. (2004). Mindfulness: A proposed operational definition. *Clinical Psychology: Science and Practice, 11*, 230–241.

Brown, C. P., Barry, D. P., Ku, D., Puckett, K. (2021). Teach as I say, not as I do: How preservice teachers made sense of the mismatch between how they were expected to teach and how they were taught in their professional training program. *The Teacher Educator, 56*(3), 250–269.

Corey, G., Muratori, M., Austin, J. T. I., & Austin, J. A. (2018). *Counselor self-care*. http://ebookcentral.proquest.com

Creswell, J. W., & Plano Clark, V. L. (2018). *Designing and conducting mixed methods research* (3rd ed.). SAGE.

Djonko-Moore, C. M. (2016). An exploration of teacher attrition and mobility in high poverty racially segregated schools. *Race Ethnicity and Education, 19*(5), 1063–1087. https://doi.org/10.1080/13613324.2015.1013458

Duarte, J, Pinto-Gouveia, J., & Cruz, B. (2016). Relationships between nurses' empathy, self- compassion and dimensions for professional quality of life: A cross-sectional study. *International Journal of Nursing Studies, 60*, 1–11.

Dunn, A. H. (2018). Leaving a profession after it's left you: Teachers' public resignation letters as resistance amidst neoliberalism. *Teachers College Record*, 34.

Fantilli, R. D., & McDougall, D. E. (2009) A study of novice teachers: Challenges and supports in the first years. *Teaching and Teacher Education, 25*, 814–825.

Finlay-Jones, A. L., Rees, C. S., & Kane, R. T. (2015). Self-compassion, emotion regulation and stress among Australian psychologists: Testing an emotion regulation model of self- compassion using structural equation modeling. *PLos ONE, 10*(7), e0133481https://doi.org/10.1371/journal.pone.0133481

Gaikhorst, L., Beishuizen, J., Roosenboom, B., & Volman, M. (2017). The challenges of beginning teachers in urban primary schools. *European Journal of Teacher Education, 40*(1), 46–61.

Germer, C. K., & Neff, K. D. (2019). *Teaching the mindful self-compassion program: A guide for professionals*. Guilford Press.

Germer, C. K.. & Neff, K. D. (2017). *Mindful self-compassion handout booklet*. Center for Mindful Self-Compassion.

Graue, M. E., & Walsh, D. J. (1998). *Studying children in context: Theories, methods, and ethics*. SAGE.

Hirshberg, M. H. (2017). *Well-being training for preservice teachers* (Publication no. 10622669) [Doctoral dissertation, University of Wisconsin-Madison]. ProQuest Dissertations Publishing.

Ingersoll, R. M. (2001). Teacher turnover and teacher shortages: An organizational analysis. *American Educational Research Journal, 38*(3), 499–534. https://doi.org/10.3102/00028312038003499

Jennings, P. A. (2019). *The trauma-sensitive classroom: Building resilience with compassionate teaching*. W. W. Norton & Company.

Jennings, P. A., Brown, J. L., Frank, J. L., Doyle, S., Oh, Y., Davis, R., Rasheed, D., DeWeese, A., DeMauro, A. A., Cham, H., & Greenberg, M. T. (2017). Impacts of the CARE for teachers program on teachers' social and emotional competence and classroom interactions. *Journal of Educational Psychology, 109*(7), 1010–1028. https://doi.org/10.1037/edu0000187

Kabat-Zinn, J. (1994). *Wherever you go, there you are: Mindfulness meditation in everyday life.* Hyperion.

Kelly, A. L., & Berthelsen, D. C. (1995). Preschool teachers' experiences of stress. *Teaching & Teacher Education, 11*(4), 345–357.

Klocker, N. (2007). An example of 'thin' agency: Child domestic workers in Tanzania. In R. Panelli, S. Punch, & E. W. Robson (Eds.), *Global perspectives on rural childhoods and youth: Young rural lives* (pp. 83–94). Routledge.

Kneebone, E., & Raphael, S. (2011). *City and suburban crime trends in metropolitan America.* Brookings.

Kulgren, I. K. (2012, March 2). *Do most child abuse reports come from people required to report?* PolitiFact Oregon. https://www.politifact.com/oregon/statements/2012/mar/02/laurie-monnes-anderson/do-most-child-abuse-reports-come-people-required-r/

Merriam, S. B., & Tisdell, E. J. (2016). *Qualitative research: A guide to design and implementation* (4th ed.). Jossey-Bass.

Montero-Marin, J., Zubiaga, F., Cereceda, M., Demarzo, M. M. P., Trenc, P., & Garcia- Campayo. (2016). Burnout subtypes and absence of self-compassion in primary healthcare professionals: A cross-sectional study. *PLoS ONE, 11*(6), 1–17.

Neff, K. D. (2011). *Self-compassion.* William-Morrow.

Neff, K. D., & Germer, C. K. (2013). A pilot study and randomized controlled trial of the mindful self-compassion program. *Journal of Clinical Psychology, 69*(1), 28–44.

Raes, F., Pommier, E., Neff, K. D., & Van Gucht, D. (2011). Construction and factorial validation of a short form of the Self-Compassion Scale. *Clinical Psychology & Psychotherapy, 18*, 250–255.

Roeser, R. W., Schonert-Reichl, K. A., Jha, A., Cullen, M., Wallace, L., Wilensky, R., Oberle, E., Thomson, K., Taylor, C., & Harrison, J. (2013). Mindfulness training and reductions in teacher stress and burnout: Results from two randomized, waitlist-control field trials. *Journal of Educational Psychology, 105*(3), 787–804. https://doi.org/10.1037/a0032093

Ryan, S. V., von der Embse, N. P., Pendergast, L. L., Saeki, E., Segool, N., & Schwing, S. (2017). Leaving the teaching profession: The role of teacher stress and educational accountability policies on turnover intent. *Teaching and Teacher Education, 66*, 1–11.

Sciamanna, J. (2020). *2018 report shows an increase in child abuse.* CWLA. https://www.cwla.org/child-maltreatment-2018-report-shows-an-increase-in-child-abuse/

Shapiro, S. L., Astin, J. A., Bishop, S. R., & Cordova, M. (2005). Mindfulness-based stress reduction for health care professionals: Results from a randomized Trial. *International Journal of Stress Management, 12*(2), 164–176.

Siegel, R. D. (2010). *The mindfulness solution.* The Guilford Press.

Simos, M. (2013, March 27). Policies lead to teacher burnout. *The Adelaide Advertiser*, p. 29.

Sinclair, S., Kondejewski, J., Raffin-Bouchal, S., King-Shier, K. M., & Singh, P. (2017). Can self-compassion promote healthcare provider well-being and compassionate care to others? Results of a systematic review. *Applied Psychology: Health and Well-Being, 9*(2), 168–206.

Stebnicki, M. A. (2015). *The professional counselor's desk reference* (2nd ed.). http://ebookcentral.proquest.com

Thomas, G. (2016). *How to do your case study* (2nd ed.). SAGE.

Westervelt, E. (2016, September 15). *Frustration. burnout. attrition. It's time to address the national teacher shortage.* NPR Ed. https://www.npr.org/sections/ed/2016/09/15/493808213/frustration-burnout-attrition-its- time-to-address-the-national-teacher-shortage

Wrobel, M. (2013). Can empathy lead to emotional exhaustion in teachers? The mediating role of emotional labor. *International Journal of Occupational Medicine and Environmental Health, 26*(4), 581–592.

Yin, R. K. (2018). *Case study research and applications: Design and methods* (6th ed.). SAGE.

Yong, Z., & Yue, Y. (2007). Causes for burnout among secondary and elementary school teachers and preventive strategies. *Chinese Education and Society, 40*(5), 78–85.

CHAPTER 5

EQUIPPING AND EMPOWERING THE NEXT GENERATION OF TEACHERS

Building Trauma-Informed, Inclusive Pedagogical Practices and Resiliency for Transformational Education

Grace Fantaroni and Heather Bertrand
Point Loma Nazarene University

ABSTRACT

According to the National Child Traumatic Stress Network (2018), it is estimated in the United States, one in every four children has been exposed to a traumatic event that has influenced the child's learning or behavior in the classroom. Kim and Cho (2014) claimed teacher education programs must require preservice teacher candidates to explore and develop constructive and reflective competencies for classroom practice with all students, including those who may have experienced trauma. As schools are now the epicenter of social-emotional development, extensive planning of curriculum and fieldwork opportunities at the preservice program level must allow new educators purposeful preparation of pedagogical, intellectual, and psychological classroom skill sets and components (Kim & Cho, 2014; Paccione-Dyszlewski, 2016).

Developing Trauma-Informed Teachers: Creating Classrooms That Foster Equity, Resiliency, and Asset-Based Approaches: Research Findings From the Field, pp. 71–91
Copyright © 2023 by Information Age Publishing
www.infoagepub.com

This chapter provides an overview of changes and implementation of trauma-informed practices the School of Education at a private university has initiated for preservice and graduate special education teachers. Background and current research are provided with descriptions of two different class and program changes. One addition is a four-hour seminar class focused on trauma that corresponds with a special education foundation class for preservice teachers. The other class is a revision of a graduate course for new special education teachers as part of a Master of Arts in Special Education. Some promising results as well as future plans for research are included.

This chapter provides an overview of changes and implementation of trauma-informed practices the School of Education at a small private university has initiated for preservice and graduate special education teachers. Background and current research are provided first, followed by a description of class and program changes. One is the addition of a seminar class focused on trauma that corresponds with a special education foundation class for preservice teachers. The other is a revision of a graduate course for new special education teachers as part of a Master of Arts in Special Education. Survey results are explored as well as future plans for research are included.

BACKGROUND/HISTORICAL CONTEXT

According to the National Child Traumatic Stress Network (2018), it is estimated in the United States, one in every four children has been exposed to a traumatic event that has influenced the child's learning or behavior in the classroom. Trauma is defined as a single or multiple series of events or situations experienced and perceived as life-threatening physically or emotionally, often resulting in an undesirable impact on an individual's overall cognitive, academic, social-emotional, and behavioral functioning (Substance Abuse and Mental Health Services Administration [SAMHSA], 2018). Kim and Cho (2014) claimed teacher education programs must require preservice teacher candidates to explore and develop constructive and reflective competencies for classroom practice with all students, including those who may have experienced trauma. As schools are now the epicenter of social-emotional development, extensive planning of curriculum and fieldwork opportunities at the preservice program level must allow new educators purposeful preparation of pedagogical, intellectual, and psychological classroom skill sets and components (Kim & Cho, 2014; Paccione-Dyszlewski, 2016).

Students who present with disability and trauma are illuminated in the literature as a significantly overrepresented and underrepresented population. Sullivan and Knutson (2000) shared that many individuals with disabilities have known histories of abuse but often underreporting or lack of recognition actually occurs. Additionally, their experiences of traumatic abuse may be further complicated by the impact of various circumstances including deprivation due to poverty and lack of resources, lack of social relationships and supports, insufficient coping skills, as well as any other comorbid conditions related to their medical, physical, or psychiatric status (Keesler, 2014). The myriad of factors contributing to overall student development leads to a need for students to be diagnosed, placed and served correctly to avoid overrepresentation or underrepresentation not only in special education but regarding trauma statistics. Bullock et al. (2017) discussed the critical role educators play in the lives of their students, and reiterated the importance of exemplary preparation to effectively assume their respective roles and support appropriate representation of each student, and increasingly when trauma is involved.

Adverse Childhood Experiences Theory. In 1998, researchers with the Center for Disease Control and Kaiser Permanente published a landmark research study that linked traumatic experiences during critical development to increased health issues and challenges in adult life (Felitti et al., 1998). Findings from the study were that childhood adversity, including three categories of abuse and four categories of household dysfunction, causes harm to whole child developmental cognitive, social, and emotional milestones which may result in internal physiological changes during adolescence and beyond, and prompted further exploration on the impact of traumatic experiences on an individual's overall well-being over time (Schickedanz et al., 2018). The Felitti et al. (1998) has prompted continuous research across fields including public health, medicine, nursing, social services, and criminal justice systems to increase understanding of the impact of trauma on overall health and well-being between birth and adulthood (Lynch et al., 2013) which has led to the theory of contemporary trauma.

Trauma Theory. Early work within trauma theory had been noted by Jean-Martin Charcot in the late 19th century (Libbrecht & Quackelbeen, 1995). Stemming from continued research development throughout the past century and current ACEs research (Al-Shawi & Lafta, 2015; Lynch et al., 2013; McGavock & Spratt, 2014; Walker & Walsh, 2015), trauma theory has developed to encompass the unique and individualized perceptions of experiences and a desire to develop individualized support for resilience needs after exposure to a traumatic event (Cavanaugh, 2016; Dods, 2015; Perfect et al., 2016; Strom et al., 2016). Trauma theory focuses on mental and physical health outcomes through a new lens of "what happened to you" instead of previous misguided assumptions of "what is wrong with you" (American Academy of Pediatrics, 2014). Thus, contemporary trauma theory reflects an informed shift in mindset in how responses should be provided to support individuals after traumatic events and focuses on healing and resilience to overcome adversity (Goodman, 2017).

Trauma-Informed Practices Framework. Trauma-informed practices have been developed from guiding principles that seek to promote an understanding of the impact of trauma, recognize the symptoms of trauma, and cater appropriate responses to individualized needs due to exposure to traumatic experiences (SAMHSA, 2014). Through extensive study across multiple social science fields of the impact of trauma, and the exploration of structures connected to overcoming the impact of trauma, SAMHSA (2014) have outlined a framework of six guiding principles (intra), which aid in informing resilience beyond trauma. The guiding principles focus on individual support, rooted in choice, collaboration, empowerment, safety, and trustworthiness for all students while promoting recovery and resilience for those impacted by trauma (Keesler et al., 2017; SAMHSA, 2014). The additional framework also seeks to consider cultural, historical, and gender issues represented in their student populations (Zakszeski et al., 2017), albeit using an asset-based approach. Dis/ability critical race theory (DisCrit) is an important lens to view trauma of systematic racism and inequalities through the intersectionality of race and disability (Annamma et al., 2012), however, in this chapter, an asset based individualized of trauma is reviewed.

PRESERVICE CALIFORNIA TEACHER EXPECTATIONS

In response to the growing literature regarding the impact of trauma and students in schools, the California Commission on Teacher Credentialing executed new Teacher Performance Expectation (TPE) requirements for novice education teachers and teacher preparation programs (California Commission on Teacher Credentialing, 2016). TPEs outline state-approved standard requirements for preservice educators to be introduced to, practice, and be assessed as part of the certification. As part of the requirements of the new standards, TPE 2.4 outlines that certified educators must "Know how to access resources to support students, including those who have experienced trauma, homelessness, foster care, incarceration, and/or are medically fragile." Subsequently, in 2018, with the anticipation of similar program standards being developed for education specialists, the faculty developed universal, program coursework for general educators and education specialist programming to meet the preservice teacher needs in areas of diversity and inclusion for all students.

The Point Loma Nazarene University (PLNU) School of Education follows the university mission "to teach, to shape, to send," and focuses on a learning community which "exists to develop high-performing, reflective educators of noble character who impact the lives of learners." Within this community, the School of Education focuses on equipping candidates with the all-encompassing knowledge, skills, and dispositions demonstrated by educators to inspire candidates to seek continuous development and competence across diverse environments. This transformative focus is illuminated in course development of content and fieldwork opportunities to ensure all students' needs are met in all classroom environments where PLNU educators continue to grow, develop, and empower themselves and their students.

Using the lens of Universal Design for Learning (UDL) and backgrounds in special education, faculty set out to prepare educators to teach *ALL* students who walk into a classroom. All of our revisions were thoughtfully created, not only for state required content but with pedagogical approaches based on using the foundation of increasing critical conscience (Byrd, 2012; Rochester 2019), Mezirow's transformative learning theory (1997), and the six guidelines of trauma-informed practices for use within educational environments, creating safe environments, instilling trustworthiness and transparency between teachers and students, increasing peer support, empowering students through allowing voice and choice within the classroom, accessing community resources for students and families, and understanding how cultural, historical, and gender bias may impact classroom performance (SAMHSA, 2014).

PROGRAM COURSEWORK

Preservice Trauma-Informed Teaching Approaches

As aforementioned, teacher candidates complete coursework developed to grow their knowledge, skill sets, and practices in supporting students who have experienced various adverse traumas as well as those with varied learning needs due to a diagnosed disability. Each course builds upon inclusionary practices on multi-tiered systems of support (MTSS) for individualized student academic, behavior, and social-emotional needs, UDL lesson development and implementation, and classroom behavioral support including positive behavior interventions and supports (PBIS) and the structures involved in each practice.

Trauma-Informed Practices Seminar. In 2018, the university created EDU 6017A, a four-hour seminar course, that required *all* teaching candidates (general and education specialist) to establish the knowledge, skills, and dispositions which align to contemporary issues and challenges in California's teaching/learning systems related to student trauma and PBIS.

The course offers introductory, foundational information to teacher candidates through providing guided models of practice surrounding realizing the impact of trauma, recognizing the signs and symptoms of trauma, and responding fully through the integration of knowledge and practices to support resilience (SAMHSA, 2018).

The SAMHSA (2014) outlines a guiding model of trauma-informed practices for use within broad fields of study, including educational environments in support of children who have experienced traumatic events. The model components drive the 4-hour EDU6017A program seminar curriculum and focus on classroom pedagogy related to six principles of trauma-informed approaches (SAMHSA, 2014).

Utilizing an interdisciplinary focus grounded in educational learning/teaching theory and pedagogy, candidates explore personal and professional planning practices of self-assessment, missional, or life purpose development. Resilience establishes a capacity to successfully adapt to perceived challenges that may impact individual functioning, survival, and continued development (Masten & Barnes, 2018). The capacity of an individual's ability to positively adapt to challenges greatly depends on consistent, nurturing interactions and relational connections to others, providing teachers with an opportunity to play a critical role in student resilience development (Masten & Barnes, 2018).

The seminar course components discuss the implementation of classroom support structures which focus on creating safe environments, instilling trustworthiness and transparency between teachers and students, increasing peer support, empowering students through allowing voice and choice within the classroom, accessing community resources for students and families, and understanding how cultural, historical, and gender bias may impact classroom performance. Upon completion of professor-led exploration of foundational trauma-informed concepts including realizing the prevalence of trauma among children, recognizing potential signs or symptoms associated with trauma experiences, and providing framework structures for responding to trauma in the classroom, candidates apply new knowledge to develop skills in providing an outline of supports which may benefit a specific grade and content level of students within their potential classroom. Activities related to the course allow students an opportunity to research and develop a trauma-informed support plan for classroom implementation and research related to understanding what trauma resources are available within the school campus community.

The trauma-informed classroom support plan requires teacher candidates to establish an initial, yet flexible, plan based on potential student needs which include rules and roles of the teacher, staff, students, and parents in supporting the development of social-emotional learning capacities within the classroom structures. Such structures include practices for teaching students about bullying prevention, social-emotional skill development, and establishing a classroom community conducive to empowering students to have a voice and choice within the environment. Core social-emotional skills addressed in seminar and student reflective practices include student self-awareness, self-management, responsible decision-making, relationship skills, and social awareness (Collaborative for Academic, Social, and Emotional Learning, 2020).

As one out of five students report being bullied in school or by school peers, the act of being bullied can be considered a traumatic adverse experience (Pacer's National Bullying Prevention Center, 2020). Additionally, youth who engage as a bully often seek control by any means possible often as a result of adverse experiences (Pacer's National Bullying Prevention Center, 2020). As bullying frequently manifests in classrooms, teacher candidates engage in a bullying module review as part of the course objectives and provide reflective feedback on new insights within bullying prevention and intervention. Stopbullying.gov (2019) provides a model for candidate review of practices including prevention at school, building safe environments, appropriate research-based responses to bullying on the school campus, and supporting all students involved.

Furthermore, to better understand the demographics and individual needs and supports available for students outside of their classroom environment, teacher candidates research and develop a local database of awareness of trauma and bullying resources aimed at providing local resources for teachers, students, and families. Based on statewide demographics, teacher candidates focus on collecting information on a variety of student and family needs including refugees and immigrant's supports, foster care supports, homeless supports, medically fragile or special needs supports, and bullying supports and resources. This deep dive of their surrounding communities seeks to provide knowledge of the schools' students and neighborhoods, identifying students' assets and strength and the possible advantages or preconceived notions teaching at the school may bring (Piñeros & Quintero, 2006). Lastly, teacher candidates collect resource contact information, describe what the resource could do for or provide for students and families, as well as determine if resources can be sought individually or if students and families must be referred to increase their knowledge of community outreach and assistance available.

Foundations in Special Education. Finally, this seminar course is designed to be taken simultaneously with EDU6002, Foundations of Special Education, includes a fieldwork application component. The fieldwork is completed in special education classrooms hosted by veteran special education teachers and provide opportunities to observe diverse students and settings. This allows for teacher candidates to explore the concepts of trauma-informed structures being implemented, and the chance for the application that supports changes in preservice teachers' attitudes and skills with students in inclusive settings (Voss & Bufkin, 2011).

EDU6002, Foundations in Special Education, is a 3-unit course which includes face to face classes and an additional 20 hours of fieldwork in a special education classroom. In 2018–2019, a total of 795,047 students with IEPs were serviced in special education and general education classrooms across California state (California Department of Education, 2020). Nationally, the increase in students with disabilities spending 80% or more of the day learning in the general education classroom grew substantially from 2008–2017 (U.S. Department, 2019). Due to inclusionary practices, it became a critical need for all preservice educators to have a foundation of special education disability characteristics and best practices for learning support. Within best practices, preservice teachers are introduced to and practice necessary framework structure including MTSS, PBIS, and UDL in this course before refining practices throughout the remainder of their program. As candidates complete EDU6002 simultaneously with EDU6017A, the trauma-informed practices seminar, preservice teachers receive critical foundational information about disability and trauma characteristics and development of an understanding to individualize support for students early on in his/her program. Typically, as the first line of response for student concerns, it was imperative candidates were provided hands-on practical concepts around the use of both academic and behavior MTSS, tiers and interventions, ideally to reduce the overidentification of students with behavioral challenges in special education. This may occur when students with learning and behavioral challenges present as needing special education interventions when more precise understanding and information on the impact of trauma may mitigate the need for these services (Bradley Williams et al., 2017; Gottlieb & Weinberg, 1999; Sciuchetti, 2017). The Federal Advisory Committee on Juvenile Justice (FACJJ) supported by the Office of Juvenile Justice and Delinquency Prevention (OJJDP), supported this idea when they called for more policy and research examining the disproportionality of youth where trauma symptoms and exposure were overlooked and instead given behavioral disorders diagnoses related to criminal behavior (FACJJ, 2015).

As a part of MTSS, PBIS structures that impact classroom systems and settings, or student skill sets, are reviewed through lecture and discussion in class, and candidates are then asked to apply structure and supports through the development of a classroom management support plan. Additionally, candidates become familiar with the Pre-Referral Intervention Manual 4th edition (McCarney & Wunderlich, 2014). Candidates are asked to identify specific student academic or social behaviors observed in their fieldwork setting and connect potential intervention supports for positively rectifying such behaviors. Candidates develop an intervention plan which describes the behavior being targeted, the intervention being modeled and practiced with the student, and a progress monitoring plan to evaluate the effectiveness of the intervention.

Finally, the university developed a UDL lesson plan template that was approved by the state of California to be used on the cumulative Teacher Performance Assessment (TPA) at the end of the candidate's program. UDL's three core components for successful lesson planning includes representation, engagement, and expression (Center for Applied Special Technology [CAST], 2021).

In EDU6002, students are guided through the components established within the lesson plan template, including instructional practices, and receive a plethora of support in outlining sections for candidates to reflect on students' special education disability characteristics, English language development needs, and the impact of adverse experiences to determine where lesson plan barriers may present. Barriers to learning pertain to how content is being represented, how students engage in the content, and how students express what they are learning or have learned.

Teacher candidates utilize the UDL template to mitigate the outlined barriers. Within each component within the UDL process, candidates provide reflective, differentiated support for all students based on their individual needs for representation, engagement, and expression within each lesson they develop. Table 5.1 outlines a section of the UDL lesson plan template where a candidate will explain the lesson instruction, discuss the teacher procedures for the instruction, outline potential student barriers, and support to mitigate barriers. Table 5.2 provides an example of a lesson plan section completed by a preservice teacher candidate.

Teacher candidates continue to utilize the UDL lesson plan template throughout program coursework as they develop their UDL competencies and instructional pedagogy. At the completion of the teacher preparation program, teacher candidates must engage in a performance assessment. The university currently uses the California TPA to evaluate teacher candidates in each TPE established by the state and embedded in the teacher preparation program (Commission on Teacher Credentialing, 2018b). As part of the TPA deliverable, teacher candidates are assessed as they use background knowledge and learner characteristics to plan instruction and provide assessment-driven instruction (Commission on Teacher Credentialing, 2016). Each assessment requires teacher candidates to discuss instructional and assessment strategies and supports for students who present with academic, emotional, or behavioral needs in the classroom due to exceptional life experiences (California Teacher Performance Assessment, 2020). Such life experiences may reflect individual student challenges in the home, community, or school as a result of various adverse needs including bullying, illness, parental loss, parental separation or

Table 5.1

UDL Lesson Plan Template Excerpt Example

Lesson Element Guided Practice	Teacher Procedures	Barriers	UDL Multiple Means
Guided Practive of concept of skill development strategies	Did you list what the teacher will be doing? Is there a time frame	Is there at least one potential barrier for each domain listed here?	Is there at least one specific solution for each potential barrier listed here? (Describe in detail, not just with the support number and title, how the solution mitigates the barrier.)
Student Activities: What will the students do?		Representation	Representation
Student Grouping: How will they be grouped?		Engagement	Engagement
Are Student Activities listed that describe: What will the students do with a group or guided by the teacher?		Expression	Expression

Note: This portion of the UDL lesson plan shows the template with guided notes for students to complete the lesson element of "guided practice," teacher procedures, barriers, and UDL multiple means of support

divorce, parental incarceration, perceived trauma, homelessness, or socio-economic status. Adverse needs may additionally be exacerbated as a result of the student being an English language learner, migrant, immigrant, or a student in foster care (California Teacher Performance Assessment, 2019).

Advanced Special Education Graduate Coursework

Advanced Special Education Assessment and Analysis of Behavior. In 2019, a 3-unit graduate course, GED 6022: Advanced Special Education Assessment and Analysis of Behavior, was restructured to include additional learning on topics such as behavior beliefs, PBIS, and trauma in various experiences as well as evidence-based interventions and social-emotional learning (Taylor et al., 2017). The students enrolled all have special

Table 5.2

Example of Completed UDL Lesson Plan Template Section

INSTRUCTION:

Instructional Stratagies: Describe the concept or skill development strategies (including modeling). Describe your plan for instruction in the order in which it will be implemented (with approximate times for each step).	(12 minutes) Teacher will model filling out their own chart with the students on the Smart Board. The teacher will guide the students through their own example of guessing how many M&Ms there are and deciding if they are close or not based upon the teacher's criteria. Students will then find Mode, Median, and Mean respectively of teacher-created examples, and finally with their own data, filling in their table. The teacher will be doing all of these steps one at a time with students.	Students may not know what a good answer looks like, so they may shut down. Students may find Mean, Median, and Mode dry. Students may be intimidated by writing down long answers, or may prefer not to write their answers down.	The teacher will model what an acceptable answer looks like and check for understanding by circulating the room and asking the students if they have questions. Examples have cloze components and MAZE components that allow students to pick the correct answer without having to worry about a language component. Each question will also be read the whole class and done whole class. The teacher or staff will ask the students to say their answers verbally and come up with an answer. Then, either staff or students can write their answers down in the spaces provided, or, circle the correct binary answer.

Note: This portion of the UDL lesson plan shows a student response to developing the lesson element of "instruction" based on a math standard, teacher procedures, barriers, and UDL multiple means of support.

education credentials with varying levels of experience and knowledge of disabilities, programs, and supports. A textbook is not used, instead applicable and direct sources, articles, and supports are linked for new teachers to bookmark and reference in the future. As a fully online course, this class is required as part of the Master of Arts in Special Education offered at the authors' university. To support learning in an online environment, students are randomly placed in groups of three or four which stay consistent throughout the entire course for students to make connections and bounce ideas off of each other as part of their assignments.

As beginning special education teachers are navigating their first couple of years learning to implement behavior plans, writing IEPs, and creating meaningful lessons for their students in special education, they are also called into early assessments and intervention conversations when schools may have student concerns. The importance of comprehensively reviewing student backgrounds and cumulative records to consider extrinsic factors such poor school attendance, cultural differences, language barriers, and trauma are emphasized to ideally reduce the disproportionality and over identification of populations in special education.

Baglivio et al. (2017) found discrepancies in identification in their study examining racial and ethnic differences in behavioral diagnoses of over 10,000 juvenile offenders assigned to residential programs. They discovered Black males were more likely to have a diagnosis of conduct disorder (CD), which is entirely defined by continual behavioral symptoms of violating the social standards and rules (Burke et al., 2002). According to the 5th edition of the *Diagnostic and Statistical Manual of Mental Disorders* (DSM-5), a diagnosis of CD includes deficiencies in social, academic, or work-related functioning over at least 12 months with at least one impairment in the last six months (American Psychiatric Association, 2013). In the aforementioned study of juvenile offenders, the authors found that Black and Hispanic males were less likely to be diagnosed with ADHD than their White peers even though the authors controlled for factors such as traumatic experiences. Overall, however, the study found that for male juvenile offenders, traumatic experiences, defined by the ACE scores, amplified the probability of diagnoses for oppositional defiant disorder (ODD) and attention deficit hyperactivity disorder (ADHD) (Baglivio et al., 2017). In the 41st Annual Report to Congress on the Implementation of the Individuals with Disabilities Education Act, Black or African American students were more likely to receive special education services under the disability categories of autism, emotional disturbance, intellectual disability, other health impairment, specific learning disability, multiple disabilities and developmental delays than all other racial or ethnic groups combined for students ages 6 through 21 (U.S. Department of Education, 2019).

Understanding how trauma may impact students with a disability is another crucial but overlooked area of need (Hoover & Kaufman, 2018). Students with the educational disability diagnosis of emotional and behavioral disorders, other health impairment (primarily ADHD), specific learning disabilities, and intellectual disability are more likely to be suspended than any other of the disability categories (Losen et al., 2015). Novice teachers may not have the skills to address the behavior and social-emotional supports for their students experiencing both trauma and a diagnosed disability. During the 2016–2017 school year, 340 out of every 10,000 students under the category of emotional disturbance received out of school suspension or expulsions for more than 10 days. This is at least 2.5 times greater than the 131 students out of 10,000 students under all other disability categories that had suspension or expulsions for over 10 days. The risk of students ages 3 to 21 under the disability of emotional disturbance had almost twice the rate of in-school suspension for more than 10 cumulative days (104 out of 10,000) in comparison to all other disability categories (64 out of 10,0000) (U.S. Department of Education, 2019). This not only impacts the climate of the school but heavily affects students long term. Students who have been suspended or expelled are three times more likely to drop out of school (U.S. Department of Education, 2010). In 2016–2017, 17.1% of students with disabilities dropped out of school and a larger percentage of those were students with the diagnosis of emotional disturbance among all other disabilities (U.S. Department of Education, 2019). These startling statistics were the basis of creating and revising content for the course GED 6022.

This course was also redesigned to consider Mezirow's transformative learning theory and practices (1997). Based on this theory, students are asked to consider their own thoughts about problem behavior. One of their very first assignments is to take a short survey to determine their beliefs about discipline based upon the hypothesis that although teachers may have varying backgrounds and ideas, one discipling style tends to be dominantly practiced (Wolfgang & Glickman, 1986). The 12-question survey from Wolfgang (2009), asks students to choose between two statements in which they identify the most. From the scoring key, the students find their answers agreeing more with one discipline approach over the others. The three categories are human relations-listening approach, confronting-contracting approach, and rules/rewards-punishment approach to discipline. Each approach has distinctive characteristics of how individuals view their role as teachers, behavioral approaches, and how behavior may be able to change. While there is not a right or wrong answer, this self-awareness of beliefs and how they influence behavior is often eye-opening and part of the activation step of Mezirow's transformative learning theory (1997).

Students read and reflect on the influence of teacher beliefs in their instruction and review or refresh their understanding of PBIS. In another purposeful transformational activity, the students match the age of a typical student between 4–12 years of age to their developmental traits, based upon Chip Wood's (2017) text on creating developmentally responsive classrooms. This confusing task again acts as an activating event as students identify current assumptions and engage in critical reflection, core components of transformative learning (Cranton, 2002).

Individually and then in groups, students create appropriate developmental responsive supports for different age groups. Once students have a new understanding of how typical or age-appropriate students may behave corresponding with appropriate supports, information on additional factors that may influence behavior is provided. These factors include environmental pollution, such as the lead crisis in Flint, Michigan leading schools to be overwhelmed by special education needs (Mitchell, 2019), the increase in opioid use which led to more kids in foster care (Neilson 2019), and an overview of trauma and how trauma changes children's brains (Flannery, 2016). In addition, special consideration is given regarding the triple trauma refugees may endure in their home country, during their journey and/or in refugee camps and resettlement in a new country. The changing demographics and increasing student diversity create the need for additional cultural competency and trauma informed decision making during MTSS discussions (Levi, 2009). Within the first couple days in a new country, refugee children are enrolled in their neighborhood school, often without knowledge of the English language, school resources and expected behaviors. Many refugees are resettled in the local area of this university and in fact, home to more new arrivals than in all other counties in California (Aguilera, 2017). With this new and sometimes shocking information, students add to their list of developmental responsive classroom supports and begin to build a reference library.

In addition to practical and integrated academic and behavioral assessment instruction, students design and implement academic and behavior intervention plans into their classrooms. Student groups create reflective digital graphic organizers and examples of support on self-determination theory, social-emotional learning, and restorative practices. After readings and presentations are provided on the topic of growth mindset and resilience, students create an infographic of positive messages to display in their classrooms. In another assignment, students reflect upon their own resilience and success as a special education teacher and provide additional tips for new teachers on a discussion board. These responses focus on themes of self-care, finding a supportive community/team of teachers, continual learning, and keeping a positive mindset. The final culminating project asks students to create and record their professional development presentations, highlighting, summarizing, and demonstrating their new learning and serves as a reflective evaluation tool for both teachers and students.

PRELIMINARY RESEARCH

Students enrolled in the most recent section of GED 6022 were asked to complete a pre and post survey that contained twelve statements to which students could respond on a 5 point Likert-type scale (1 = I am a novice in this area, 2 = This information has been introduced to me and I am learning, 3 = I am beginning to practice the concepts in real-world interactions and experiences, 4 = My understanding is fully observable in my interactions and practices and 5 = I could coach or teach someone else these concepts). The survey questions and self-assessment levels of performance were adapted from Multnomah County's (2020) *Defending Childhood: Protect, Heal, Thrive* document which used SAMHSA's *Concept of Trauma for Guidance for Trauma Informed Approach* developed in 2014 and *The Heart of Teaching and Learning* from 2001 for development. The SAMHSA guided approach was coordinated and prepared by the Trauma and Justice Strategic Initiative through support of the U.S. Department of Health and Human Services and the Office of Policy, Planning and Innovation.

Composite scores were separated into groups based on pre-class or post-class survey responses and calculated to determine mean scores. The mean scores were compared to determine whether statistically significant differences in response scores existed using a two-tailed, unpaired, unequal variance *t*-test. Table 5.1 displays all twelve survey statements with corresponding pre- and post-mean scores *(m)*, standard deviation *(sd)*, *t*-test *(t)* and *p* values. Due to the small sample size, as only eight students completed both pre- and post-surveys, the following results (Table 5.1) should be viewed cautiously but optimistic.

Future Research. Plans for future research include increasing the sample size by continuing to collect pre- and post-survey results when this class is offered again. Current research is also being conducted within the EDU 6017A seminar course with special education teacher candidates on implementing trauma-informed strategies and resources in classrooms with students with disabilities (Bertrand, 2021). Future research will examine the same constructs with general education populations. While this research aims to confirm coursework meets our desired outcomes, creating and transforming teachers ready to teach diverse learners with a trauma-informed lens, additional outcomes should be explored. In a review of professional development practices, Phuong et al. (2018), identified a need for research to measure the effect of teacher's new learning to influence student success in their own classrooms. While these are topics of interest to the authors, as further research on the effect of student outcomes is desired, it will be critical to consider exceptional trends in education including the over or under identification of students with disabilities and trauma needs. Additionally, potential incorporation of the DisCrit should be explored further by teacher certification program institutions.

Table 5.1

Results of the t-Test of Differences in Composite Scores in Pre/Post Survey Responses

	Pre-survey		Post- survey			
Survey Statements	**M**	**SD**	**M**	**SD**	**t**	**p**
1. I understand the impact of trauma on brain science.	2.25	0.707	3.125	0.641	2.593	0.021**
2. I realize my own assumptions and biases regarding students who have experienced adverse trauma.	2.5	0.926	3.375	0.518	2.333	0.040**
3. I realize the interactions of trauma and race.	2.625	1.060	3.5	0.535		0.063
4. I recognize the varied abilities of children/students to self-regulate and to perceive safety.	2.75	0.886	3.625	0.518	2.411	0.034**
5. I respond to students through a personal self-regulated process.	2.875	0.991	3.5	0.534		0.145
6. I respond to children/students in a strength-process.	2.625	1.188	3.5	0.926		0.124
7. I respond to student routines consistently as a support for children/students who may have experienced trauma.	2.75	0.707	3.625	0.744	2.411	0.030**
8. I incorporate opportunities to build self-regulation skills within a community of care.	2.625	0.744	3.625	0.518	3.121	0.008**
9. I use a variety of Positive Behavior Intervention Supports (PBIS) strategies to promote positive behavior.	2.875	1.126	3.875	0.835		0.065
10. I regularly reflect on classroom spaces and children/student feedback in regards to physical spaces.	3	0.926	3.875	0.835		0.067

(Table continued on next page)

Table 5.1 (Continued)

Results of the t-Test of Differences in Composite Scores in Pre/Post Survey Responses

Survey Statements	Pre-survey		Post- survey			
	M	*SD*	*M*	*SD*	*t*	*p*
11. I regularly provide children/ students opportunities for helpful participation, meaningful work, and to share positive aspects of their identity.	2.875	1.126	3.625	0.518		0.118
12. I consistently remain aware of classroom environments and responses may contribute to re-traumatization.	2.571	1.195	3.5	0.756		0.069

Note: **indicates significantly significant *p* <0.05 values.

REFERENCES

Aguilera, E. (2017). *San Diego welcomes more refugees than any other California county.* CalMatters. https://calmatters.org/justice/2017/07/san-diego-welcomes-refugees-california-county/

Al-Shawi, A. F., & Lafta, R. K. (2015). Effect of adverse childhood experiences on physical health in adulthood: Results of a study conducted in Baghdad city. *Journal of Family and Community Medicine, 22*(2), 78–84.

American Academy of Pediatrics. (2014). *Adverse childhood experiences and the lifelong consequences of trauma.* http://www.aap.org/traumaguide

American Psychiatric Association. (2013). *Diagnostic and statistical manual of mental disorders* (5th ed.). American Psychiatric Publishing.

Annamma, S. A., Connor, D., & Ferri, B. (2013). Dis/ability critical race studies (DisCrit): theorizing at the intersections of race and dis/ability. *Race Ethnicity and Education, 16*(1), 1–31. https://doi.org/10.1080/13613324.2012.730511

Baglivio, M. T., Wolff, K. T., Piquero, A. R., Greenwald, M. A., & Epps, N. (2017). Racial/ethnic disproportionality in psychiatric diagnoses and treatment in a sample of serious juvenile offenders. *Journal of Youth and Adolescence, 46,* 1424–1451. https://doi.org/10.1007/s10964-016-0573-4

Bertrand, H. (2021). *Novice special education teachers and trauma-informed training* [Unpublished doctoral dissertation, Grand Canyon University]. Phoenix, AZ.

Bradley Williams, R., Bryant-Mallory, D., Coleman, K., Gotel, D., & Hall, C. (2017). An evidence-based approach to reducing disproportionality in special education and discipline referrals. *Children and Schools, 39*(4), 248–251. https://doi.org/10.1093/cs/cdx020

Bullock, L. M., Zolkoski, S. M., Lusk, M. E., & Hovey, K. A. (2017). Educators' perceptions of school-based factors that impact their effectiveness in working with students with challenging behaviors: A pilot investigation. *World Journal of Education, 7*(3), 92–102.

Burke, J. D., Loeber, R., Mutchka, J. S., & Lahey, B. B. (2002). A question for DSM-V: Which better predicts persistent conduct disorder—delinquent acts or conduct symptoms? *Criminal Behaviour and Mental Health, 12*, 37–52.

Byrd, D. (2012). Social studies education as a moral activity: Teaching towards a society. *Educational Philosophy and Theory, 44*(10), 1073–1079.

Commission on Teacher Credentialing. (2016). *Teacher performance expectations.* https://www.ctc.ca.gov/docs/default-source/educator-prep/standards/adopted-tpes 2016.pdf

Commission on Teacher Credentialing. (2018a). *Preliminary education specialist teacher credential program requirements.* https://www.ctc.ca.gov/docs/default-source/educator-prep/sped-summary-Concerns-and-authorization.pdf

Commission on Teacher Credentialing. (2018b). *Redeveloped CalTPA.* https://www.ctc.ca.gov/educator-prep/tpa-california

California Department of Education. (2020). *Special Education—CalEDFacts.* https://www.cde.ca.gov/sp/se/sr/cefspeced.asp

California Teacher Performance Assessment. (2020). *CalTPA.* http://www.ctcexams.nesinc.com/TestView.aspx?f=HTML_FRAG/CalTPA_TestPage.html

Cavanaugh, B. (2016). Trauma-informed classrooms and schools. *Beyond Behavior, 25*(2), 41–46. https://doi.org/10.1177/107429561602500206

Center for Applied Special Technology. (2021). *Universal design for learning guidelines.* Retrieved from https://www.cast.org/impact/universal-design-for-learning-udl

Collaborative for Academic, Social, and Emotional Learning. (2020). *SEL: What are the core competence areas and where are they promoted?* https://casel.org/sel-framework/

Cranton, P. (2002). Teaching for transformation. *New Directions for Adult and Continuing Education, 2002*(93), 63. https://doi-org.pointloma.idm.oclc.org/10.1002/ace.50

Darling-Hammond, L., Wei, R., Andree, A., Richardson, N., Orphanos, S. (2009). *Professional learning in the learning profession: A status report on teacher development in the United States and abroad.* National Staff Development Council. https://edpolicy.stanford.edu/sites/default/files/publications/professional-learning-learning-profession-status-report-teacher-development-us-and-abroad_0.pdf

Dods, J. J. (2015). Bringing trauma to school: The educational experience of three youths. *Exceptionality Education International, 25*(1), 112–135.

Federal Advisory Committee on Juvenile Justice. (2015). *Recommendations to the President, Congress, and OJJDP administrator.* http://www.facjj.org/annualreports/FACJJ_2015_Cover_letter_and_recommendations_FINAL.pdf? ed2f26df2d9c416fbddddd2330a778c6=oxvooxixv-oanpoana

Felitti, V. J., Anda, R. F., Nordenberg, D., Williamson, D. F., Spitz, A. M., Edwards, V., Koss, M. P., & Marks, J. S. (1998). Relationship of childhood abuse and household dysfunction to many of the leading causes of death in adults: The adverse childhood experiences (ACE) study. *The America Journal of Preventative Medicine, 14*(4), 245–258. https://doi.org/10.1016/s0749-3797(98)00017-8

Flannery, M. E. (2016). *How trauma is changing children's brains: Understanding how severe stress affects students in the important first step in creating trauma-sensitive classrooms.* National Education Association. https://www.nea.org/advocating-for-change/new-from-nea/how-trauma-changing-childrens-brains

Goodman, R. (2017). Contemporary trauma theory and trauma-informed care in substance use disorders: A conceptual model for integrating coping and resilience. *Advances in Social Work, 18*(1), 186–201. https://doi.org/10.18060/21312

Gottlieb, J., & Weinberg, S. (1999). Comparison of students referred and not referred for special education. *Elementary School Journal, 99*(3), 187. https://doi.org/10.1086/461922

Hoover, D. W., & Kaufman, J. (2018). Adverse childhood experiences in children with autism spectrum disorder. *Curr Opin Psychiatry, 31*(2), 128–132. https://doi.org/10.1097/YCO.0000000000000390

Keesler, J. M. (2014). A call for the integration of trauma-informed care among intellectual and developmental disability organizations. *Journal Of Policy and Practice In Intellectual Disabilities, 11*(1), 34–44.

Keesler, J. M., Green, S. A., & Nochajski, T. H. (2017). Creating a trauma-informed community through university-community partnerships: An institute agenda. *Advances in Social Work, 18*(1), 39–52. https://doi.org/10.18060/21298

Kim, H., & Cho, Y. (2014). Pre-service teachers' motivation, sense of teaching efficacy, and expectation of reality shock. *Asia-Pacific Journal of Teacher Education, 42*(1), 67–81.

Levi, T. K. (2019). Preparing pre-service teachers to support children with refugee experiences. *Alberta Journal of Educational Research, 65*(4), 285–304.

Libbrecht, K., & Quackelbeen, J. (1995). On the early history of male hysteria and psychic trauma. Charcot's influence on Fraudian thought. *Journal of the History of the Behavioral Sciences, 31*(4), 370–384. https://doi.org/10.1002/1520-6696(199510)31:4<370::AID-JHBS2300310404>3.0.CO;2-6

Losen, D. J., Ee, J., Hodson, C., & Martinez, T. E. (2015). Disturbing inequities: Exploring the relationship between racial disparities in special education identification and discipline. In B. J. Losen (Ed.), *Closing the school discipline gap: Equitable remedies for excessive exclusion* (pp. 107–117). Teachers College, Columbia University.

Lynch, L., Waite, R., & Davey, M. P. (2013). Adverse childhood experiences and diabetes in adulthood: Support for a collaborative approach to primary care. *Contemporary Family Care, 35*(4), 639–655. https://doi.org/10.1007/s10591-013-9262-6

Masten, A. S., & Barnes, A. J. (2018). Resilience in children: Developmental perspectives. *Children, 5*, 1–16. https://doi.org/10.3390/children5070098

McGavock, L., & Spratt, T. (2014). Prevalence of adverse childhood experiences in a university population: Associations with use of social services. *British Journal of Social Work, 44*(3), 657–674. https://doi.org/10.1093/bjsw/bcs127

Mezirow, J. (1997). Transformative learning: Theory to practice. *New Directions for Adult and Continuing Education, 74,* 5–12. https://doi.org/10.1002/ace.7401

Mitchell, C. (2019). *In Flint, Schools overwhelmed by special education needs in aftermath of lead crisis.* Education Week. https://www.edweek.org/teaching-learning/in-flint-schools-overwhelmed-by-special-ed-needs-in-aftermath-of-lead-crisis/2019/08

Multnomah County. (2020). *Defending childhood: Protect, heal, thrive.* https://traumainformedoregon.org/resource/multnomah-county-defending-childhood-website/

McCarney, S. B, & Wunderlich, K. C. (2014). *Pre-referral intervention manual* (4th ed.). Hawthorne.

National Child Traumatic Stress Network. (2018). *About child trauma.* https://www.nctsn.org/what-is-child-trauma/trauma-types

Ncilson, S. (2019). *More kids are getting placed in foster care because of parents' drug use.* National Public Radio. https://www.npr.org/sections/health-shots/2019/07/15/741790195/more-kids-are-getting-placed-in-foster-care-because-of-parents-drug-use

Paccione-Dyszlewski, M. (2016). Trauma-informed schools: A must. *The Brown University Child and Adolescent Behavior Letter, 32*(7), 1–8. https://doi.org/10.1002/cbl.30139

Pacer's National Bullying Prevention Center. (2020). *Bullying statistics.* https://www.pacer.org/bullying/resources/stats.asp

Perfect, M. M., Turley, M. R., Carlson, J. S., Yohanna, J., & Saint Gilles, M. P. (2016). School-related outcomes of traumatic event exposure and traumatic stress symptoms in students: A systematic review of research from 1990 to 2015. *School Mental Health, 8*(1), 7–43. https://doi.org/10.1007/s12310-016-9175-2

Phuong, T. T ., Cole, S. C., & Zarestky, J. (2018). A systematic literature review of faculty development for teacher educators. *Higher Education Research & Development, 37*(2), 373–389. https://doi.org/10.1080/07294360.2017.1351423

Piñeros, C., & Quintero, A. (2006). Conceptualizing as regards educational change and pedagogical knowledge: How novice teacher-researchers' proposals illustrate this relationship. *Issues in Teachers' Professional Development, 7*(1), 173–186.

Rochester, P. R. (2019). Facilitation of student resilience through educator development of critical conscience. *European Journal of Educational Sciences,* 130–138.

Schickedanz, A., Halfon, N., Sastry, N., & Chung, P. J. (2018). Parents' Adverse childhood experiences and their children's behavioral health problems. *The American Academy of Pediatrics, 142*(2), 1–11. https://www.doi.org/10.1542/peds.2018-0023

Sciuchetti, M. B. (2017). Addressing inequity in special education: An integrated framework for culturally responsive social emotional practice. *Psychology in the Schools, 54*(10), 1245–1251.

Substance Abuse and Mental Health Services Administration. (2018). *Trauma-informed approach and trauma-specific interventions.* https://www.samhsa.gov/nctic/trauma-interventions

Substance Abuse and Mental Health Services Administration. (2014). *Concept of trauma and guidance for a trauma-informed Approach.* https://store.samhsa.gov/product/SAMHSA-s-Concept-of-Trauma-and-Guidance-for-a-Trauma-Informed-Approach/SMA14-4884

Sullivan, P. M., & Knutson, J. F. (2000). Maltreatment and disabilities: A population-based epidemiological study. *Child Abuse and Neglect, 24,* 1257–1273.

Stopbullying.gov. (2019). *How to prevent bullying.* https://www.stopbullying.gov/prevention/how-to-prevent-bullying

Strom, I. F., Schultz, J., Wentzel-Larsen, T., & Dyb, G. (2016). School performance after experiencing trauma: A longitudinal study of school functioning in survivors of the Utoya shootings in 2011. *European Journal of Psychotraumatology, 7,* 1–11.

Taylor, R. D., Oberle, E., Durlak, J. A., & Weissberg, R. P. (2017). Promoting positive youth development through school-based social and emotional learning interventions: A meta-analysis of follow-up effects. *Child Development, 88*(4), 1156–1171. https://doi.org/10.1111/cdev.12864

U.S. Department of Education. (2010). 29th annual report to Congress on the implementation of the Individuals with Disabilities Education Act, 2007 (Vol.1). Washington, D.C. https://www2.ed.gov/about/reports/annual/osep/2007/parts-b-c/29th-vol-1.pdf

U.S. Department of Education. (2019). *41st Annual Report to Congress on the implementation of the individuals with Disabilities Education Act.* Washington, D.C. https://sites.ed.gov/idea/files/41st-arc-for-idea.pdf

Voss, J. A., & Bufkin, L. J. (2011). Teaching all children: Preparing early childhood preservice teachers in inclusive settings. *Journal of Early Childhood Teacher Education, 32*(4), 338–354. https://doi.org/10.1080/10901027.2011.622240

Walker, A. J., & Walsh, E. (2015). Adverse childhood experiences: How schools can help. *Journal of Child and Adolescent Psychiatric Nursing, 28,* 68–69. https://doi.org/10.1111/jcap.12105

Wolfgang, C. H. (2009). *Solving discipline and classroom management problems* (7th ed.). Wiley & Sons.

Wolfgang, C. H., & Glickman, C. D. (1986). *Solving discipline problems: Strategies for classroom teachers* (2nd ed.). Allyn and Bacon.

Wood, C. (2017). *Yardsticks: Child and adolescent development ages 4–14* (4th ed.). Center for Responsive Schools.

Zakszeski, B. N., Ventresco, N. E., & Jaffe, A. R. (2017). Promoting resilience through trauma-focused practices: A critical review of school-based implementation. *School Mental Health, 9*(4), 310–321. https://doi.org/10.1007/s12310-017-9228-1

CHAPTER 6

RESTORATIVE PRACTICES AS TEACHER PREPARATION FOR BUILDING SKILLS TOWARD PERSONAL RESILIENCY AND APPLYING TRAUMA-INFORMED PRACTICES

Lorna Hermosura and Molly Trinh Wiebe
The University of Texas at Austin

ABSTRACT

This qualitative study investigates the relationship between participation in a teacher preparation Restorative Practice course and building skills toward personal resiliency and applying trauma-informed practices. Data for this study are students' final reflective essays from a teacher preparation Restorative Practices course. The general inductive approach was used to analyze the data. Findings indicate that students' participation in the course specifically enabled students to experience mindset shifts that align with building personal resiliency and applying trauma-informed practices including: increased empathy, compassion, and care for others; increased understanding, awareness, and insight of others; and increased self-awareness, confidence, and personal growth. In addition, this study demonstrates the convergence of trauma-informed practices and restorative practices and the efficacy of combining the two approaches.

Developing Trauma-Informed Teachers: Creating Classrooms That Foster Equity, Resiliency, and Asset-Based Approaches: Research Findings From the Field, pp. 93–108
Copyright © 2023 by Information Age Publishing
www.infoagepub.com

From the first time I participated in a [Restorative Practice] Circle, I felt humanized and respected by my peers in a way I had never felt with what was, at the time, essentially just a group of strangers. As a participant of the Circle, I felt a sense of belonging with my peers that I likely would not have experienced had it not been for the experience of the circle. As the weeks went by, I learned more about myself than I ever did just by getting to be honest with my core-self and the core-selves of others.... These weekly circles helped me learn that there is a common sort of humanity amongst all my peers. I learned that I am not alone and neither are my peers. Our experiences were so much more interconnected than they seemed at the surface.

—Omara, University Senior

Trauma-informed schools are those that adopt practices to intentionally create educational environments that respond to the needs of trauma-exposed students. This is achieved by incorporating principles, practices, and programs that contain elements of safety, trust, empowerment, collaboration, and recognition of cultural, historical, and gender issues (Overstreet & Chafouleas, 2016; Substance Abuse and Mental Health Services Administration [SAMHSA], 2014). Transforming a school to become trauma-informed requires fundamental mindset shifts regarding schooling among school personnel. Indeed, organizational theory identifies changing mindsets as key to successful systemic change (Blasé et al., 2014; Joseph & Reigeluth, 2010; Senge, 1990). However, our collective mindset about schooling is entrenched in antiquated models and can thus be difficult to change (Tyack & Cuban, 1995). Mindsets, or mental models, are "deeply ingrained assumptions, generalizations, or even pictures or images that influence how we understand the world and how we take action. Very often we are not consciously aware of our mental models or the effects they have on our behavior" (Senge, 1990, p. 8).

Teacher preparation programs have a unique opportunity to support mindset shifts toward trauma-informed practices among teacher candidates before they enter the profession. We assert that integrating into the teacher preparation curriculum a Restorative Practice (RP) course using an experiential learning design both supports students to develop personal resiliency skills and prepares them to thoughtfully apply trauma-informed practices in their future. We present our qualitative research on students' final reflective essays from a teacher preparation RP course and our findings that the experiential component of the course enabled student mindset shifts that align with trauma-informed practices toward building resiliency. Study findings reveal that students who completed the course experienced: personal transformation, increased emotional intelligence, establishment of meaningful relationships, and motivation for their future lives and careers. Specifically, students reported: increased empathy, compassion, and care for others; increased understanding, awareness, and insight of others; and increased self-awareness, confidence, and personal growth.

RESTORATIVE PRACTICES AS TRAUMA INFORMED PRACTICES

The nationwide movement toward trauma-informed schools is indicative of the growing recognition of the prevalence of students with trauma exposure and the potential for school-based interventions to improve student academic and behavioral outcomes. Due to the global COVID-19 pandemic the experience of trauma has undoubtedly increased among school children throughout the United States. Evidence of promise for trauma-informed practices in schools continues to accrue such that the 2015 reauthorization of the Elementary and Secondary Education Act authorized the use of federal education funds toward trauma-informed training and services within schools. In Texas, the 2019 legislative session passed a bill (SB 11) mandating the planning and implementation of trauma-informed practices in all public schools statewide.

Restorative practices are principles, methods, and approaches rooted in Indigenous practices that proactively and responsively prioritizes relationships, community building, and self-reflection while repairing harm and holding those accountable when harm is caused. One of the fundamental practices in RP is the circle, a structured practice designed to facilitate relationship- and community-building (Boyes-Watson & Pranis, 2015). In an RP circle, participants sit together in the form of a circle and the circle facilitator guides the RP circle process, which includes voicing and agreeing upon shared values (Boyes-Watson & Pranis, 2015). The bulk of the RP circle is dedicated to each participant having time to respond to a discussion prompt that is curated by the facilitator to either build relationships and community or, in the case of rule infractions, to repair harm and come to consensus regarding accountability measures (Boyes-Watson & Pranis, 2015). While the circle is structured for each participant to take a turn to respond to the prompt, one fundamental RP circle value is that participants have the choice to pass on their turn with no need for explanation and no judgement from the group.

The RP circle is a fundamental point of convergence with all six key principles of a trauma-informed approach: (1) empowerment, voice, and choice; (2) historical, cultural, and gender issues; (3) safety; (4) trustworthiness and transparency; (5) peer support; and (6) collaboration and mutuality (SAMHSA, 2014). Specifically, the Circle practice provides a structure for participants to see each other and be seen as well as to hear each other and be heard. As such, the RP circle is a modality for empowerment, voice, and choice and peer support. In addition, the Circle Values promote emotional safety that opens the door for participants to express the historical, cultural, and gender dimensions of their own identity thus challenging possible assumptions and stereotypes held about them. Ongoing participation in circles can lead to deeper sharing, vulnerability, and transparency contributing to feelings of trustworthiness and mutuality and the opportunity for peer support and collaboration.

Omara's reflection in the opening quote speaks to the power of RP circles. Her statement illustrates how continual engagement in RP circles created a sense of belonging and mutual respect. For Omara, community-building circles provided a time and space to engage in self-reflection as well as a window into her peers' lived-experiences. More importantly, it ruptured the notion of individuality; and in turn, sparked insights regarding collectivity, connection, and shared experiences among her peer-group.

THE TEACHER PREPARATION RESTORATIVE PRACTICE COURSE

The teacher education program at the study site includes a strong focus on equity, social justice, and asset-based pedagogies and requires successful completion of the RP course for specific teaching credentials. As part of teacher candidate preparation, students participate in a three semester-long student teaching internship series. The internship provides teacher candidates with opportunities to gain real-world teaching experiences including lesson planning, teaching, and classroom management. Teacher candidates also engage in coursework focused on examining education from critical and humanizing perspectives as well as the sociocultural factors that influence learning.

The teacher preparation RP course objective is to increase knowledge about RP and its implementation through the exploration of the following topics: (1) models of education discipline policies and practices; (2) how those models have adversely affected students' social and emotional development and academic trajectories; and, (3) how restorative practices could serve as an alternative model to address discipline in schools. The RP course design includes weekly readings on RP theory and practice along with reading reflections; in-class lectures; a weekly in-class experience of RP circles; a field-component in which students apply RP theories, practices, and processes; and a final reflective paper. Significant course time is dedicated to the RP circle experience. During one class day each week, all students participate in an in-class RP circle. At the start of the semester, the instructor facilitates the in-class RP circles. As the semester progresses, two students co-facilitate the week's in-class RP circle until all students have had a turn at co-facilitating the RP circle in class. On the days that they are not co-facilitating the in-class circle, students are circle participants along with the instructor.

Providing teacher candidates with this semester-long opportunity to both directly experience RP and to engage in independent inquiry around RP invites reflection upon one's own mindset toward education, toward self, and toward others. The circle experience particularly illuminates the interpersonal and didactic nature of education and makes clear the notion that each person is an instrument of change and so the mindset that they operate from—including any assumptions that are made about others—can empower or impede their students' path toward learning and growth. In these ways, engaging teacher candidates with RP supports them to build their own resiliency and to thoughtfully apply trauma-informed practices.

THEORETICAL FRAMEWORK

The teacher preparation RP course curriculum is designed to focus on theory and continual practice and as such, is rooted in experiential learning theory (ELT) which allows students to experience the tenets of RP as they learn them. ELT is a framework composed of a four-stage learning cycle (Kolb et al., 2001, p. 228):

- Concrete Experience (CE)—immediate, tangible, felt experience
- Abstract Conceptualization (AC)—thinking and analyzing
- Reflective Observation (RO)—observing and reflecting
- Active Experimentation (AE)—acting

These four stages are nested within two distinct modalities: CE and AC are nested under Grasping Experience, and RO and AE are nested under Transformative Experience. *Grasping Experience* is where the learner engages with new information through experiencing the "concrete, tangible, felt qualities of the world"; whereas others may process new information through "symbolic representations" (Kolb et al., 2001, p. 228). *Transformative Experience* is where the learner processes new experiences through observing and reflecting or engages in active participation. According to Kolb et al. (2001), these modalities are dialectical in that they afford the learner the decision-making power to choose which modality to apply in a given situation as they immerse and process new experiences.

In the teacher preparation RP course, the CE stage is facilitated through students' participation in weekly class readings, class lectures, and RP circles. The AC stage is facilitated through reading reflection assignments. The RO stage is facilitated through participation in circles and reflection assignments. The AE stage is facilitated through the in-class RP circle co-facilitation assignment and the field-based assignment to independently facilitate an RP circle within the greater community.

In order to determine the development of resiliency within teacher candidates completing the RP course, we utilize the BRiTE framework developed by Mansfield et al. (2016). The BRiTE framework identifies five central components that contribute to developing personal resiliency: (B) building/understanding resilience, (r) relationships, (i) well-being, (t) motivation, and (e) emotions (pp. 18–19). Specifically,

- Building/Understanding Resilience: Resilience as a dynamic, multifaceted process where individuals mobilize personal and contextual resources and use coping strategies to enable resilience outcomes. This includes intrapersonal growth and intrapersonal validation.
- Relationships: Social competence (for building relationships, support networks, and working collaboratively), setting boundaries, communication.
- Well-Being: Seeking renewal work life balance, time management.
- Motivation: Efficacy, value, sense of purpose, sense of vocation, initiative, high expectations, problem solving, professional learning, goal setting, help seeking, reflection, persistence.
- Emotions: Emotional competence, optimism, empathy, hope, courage, humor, emotion regulation, mindfulness.

METHODOLOGY

This research study examines the learning outcomes of a teacher preparation RP course as they relate to personal resiliency and preparation to thoughtfully apply and integrate trauma-informed practices in educational settings. The study is guided by the following research questions:

- RQ1: In what ways does the teacher preparation Restorative Practice course build resiliency skills in students?
- RQ2: In what ways does the teacher preparation Restorative Practice course build skills toward thoughtfully applying and integrating trauma-informed practices (e.g., safety, trust, empowerment, collaboration, and recognition of cultural, historical, and gender issues)?

DATA COLLECTION AND ANALYSIS

Data for this study are artifacts from a fall 2020 teacher preparation RP course taught at the study university in the Department of Curriculum and Instruction within the College of Education. Course enrollment consisted of 16 students: 12 of whom were females and four were males; 13 of whom were upper-level undergraduate students and 3 were masters-level graduate students. The data are the 16 students' final reflective essays which were initially collected for course evaluation purposes and are being used here to investigate the research questions. As such, the data are considered to be secondary (Glaser, 1963; Heaton, 2008). While secondary data analysis is commonly applied to quantitative data, its application to qualitative data is relatively new (Heaton, 2008) even as an abundance of secondary data is ripe for analysis in this age of constant amassing of data (Andrews et al., 2012; Johnston, 2017). In the case of this study, the use of secondary data is appropriate as it provides the researchers a view of students' organic reflections, growth, and learning based on their participation in the teacher preparation RP course.

Data were analyzed using a systematic procedure for analyzing qualitative data known as the general inductive approach (GIA; Thomas, 2006). In accordance with Straus and Corbin's (1998) interpretation of inductive analysis, GIA allows the data to speak for itself rather than using start codes and thus imposing expectations of what will emerge from the data. In addition, GIA is consistent with grounded theory as well as qualitative analysis methods as it involves the three tasks of analysis defined by Miles and Huberman (1994): data reduction, data display, and conclusion drawing and verification. However, unlike Miles and Huberman's inductive analysis methods, GIA includes a defined, systematic set of coding procedures and unlike grounded theory, GIA findings are presented as a description of the most important themes rather than as an emergent theory generated by the themes (Thomas, 2006).

The authors followed GIA procedures to analyze the data and to ensure trustworthiness. First, data were gathered and cleaned as necessary (e.g., several data sets required reformatting). Then, the authors independently read and reread the texts closely to identify and assign codes and themes. Next, the authors came together to review overlapping codes and uncoded text as well as to reach consensus on overall codes and themes. Finally, revisions and refinements were conducted to emerge with a cohesive analysis.

RESEARCHER POSITIONALITY

Disclosing researcher positionality identifies the similarities and differences that a researcher has with the research subjects and influences the manner in which the research subjects are represented within a study (Merriam et al., 2001). Both authors are women of color and daughters of immigrant parents who survived war in their home countries. The authors have both experienced secondary trauma as well as their own personal traumas, which include lived experiences and educational histories in navigating systemic barriers and systems of institutional power and privilege. These positionalities inform the authors' interest in the use of restorative and trauma-informed practices in educational settings and their belief in the transformative potential of educational experiences.

FINDINGS

This study is an analysis of final reflective essays written by 16 students enrolled in a Fall 2020 teacher preparation Restorative Practices course toward the investigation of the following two research questions: *In what ways does the teacher preparation Restorative Practice course build resiliency skills in students?* and *In what ways does the teacher preparation Restorative Practice course build skills toward thoughtfully applying and integrating trauma-informed practices?*

Application of the general inductive analysis method ultimately yielded 216 phrases which were assigned to 19 codes and organized into four thematic findings: *Finding 1: Personal Transformation, Finding 2: Emotional Intelligence, Finding 3: Meaningful Relationships,* and *Finding 4: Future Motivation.* Each of these findings are elaborated upon below with data samples included.

Finding 1: Personal Transformation

Students disclosed that regular engagement in RP circles as both participant and facilitator contributed to: personal growth and increased self-awareness; an increased willingness to challenge their own thinking and an increased openness; increased confidence, leadership, and bravery; and personal validation. These were labeled as personal transformation. Student quotes from the data include:

- *… being vulnerable through sharing my sincere feelings and past experience that carry different sides of traumas would no longer seem shameful to me.* —Carol, Graduate Student
- *From being a facilitator of circles, I gained a lot of confidence as a leader. It was my first experience leading a practice that asked others to be vulnerable. I discovered not only how much I enjoyed it but how I have the*

authority and power to create a positive restorative circle with my peers.
—Evelyn, Senior

- *This class has challenged my thinking in regards to education, relationships, and harm. Oftentimes, I find myself thinking that education is just about earning a degree. However, I now believe that a degree has little significance if I have not built meaningful connections with individuals who were present along the way.* —Jack, Junior

- *Through the experience of participating in circles led by my classmates weekly, I learned that I am an active listener and that it is vital that I feel comfortable and safe when discussing serious topics with my peers. Being a part of this class changed me as a person, and made me see for myself the truly incredible impact that circles can have on individuals and groups.* —Heather, Sophomore

- *Listening to my peers reflect on their situations and share their experiences was relieving. It was nice to know that others are going through similar issues and are having the same doubts that I had through the semester.* —Miranda, Junior

Finding 2: Emotional Intelligence

According to Salovoy and Mayer (1989), emotional intelligence is defined as "the ability to monitor one's own and others' feelings and emotions, to discriminate among them and to use this information to guide one's thinking and actions" (p. 189). Student reflections indicated that participating in RP circles resulted in their increased capacity for empathy, compassion, and care for others. In addition, students stated that their awareness, understanding and insight of others was also increased. Student quotes from the data include:

- *I realized that my ability to hear, respect, and learn from others who hold opposing opinions permanently enhanced. The individual which I embodied at the beginning of the semester would be unrecognizable in comparison to the person I have become.* —Addison, Senior

- *The circle helped me realize that compassion isn't remotely easy and if I want to honor the intrinsic values of the circle, then I have to put aside my own feelings and recognize that everyone's true self is "good, wise and powerful" (Boyes-Watson & Pranis, 2015, p. 1).* —Madison, Graduate Student

- *Each circle made me more aware of the experiences of others and allowed for me to be vulnerable. The most important thing I learned in each restorative activity was that everyone has their own starting point in life, as well as their own pace.* —Beth, Junior

- *As a participant I was able to learn about myself with others and I also took away a lot of lessons from listening to others and their experiences.* —Mia, Junior

- *Being able to take time out of our day and learn more about each other provided insight into who my classmates were and their perspectives and experiences ... I have to say I learned a lot from other people's struggle.* —Selena, Senior

Finding 3: Meaningful Relationships

Students recognized that in-class RP circles enabled the establishment of meaningful relationships with their class peers, an outcome that was more valued and unexpected given that all class meetings occurred via remote video conferencing during the COVID-19 pandemic. Students used words such as relationships, connection, trust, and community to describe the significance of these relationships. Student quotes from the data include:

- *My relationships with my peers were closer than they would have been otherwise, specifically due to the fact that we met exclusively online due to COVID-19. We learned about each other's backgrounds, racially-tied experiences, traumas, and much more by simply being willing to meet and open up to one another over time.* —Carrie, Senior

- *Participation in these circles helps to bring people together by allowing us to learn about one another and share our experiences, thus building relationships that otherwise might not exist.* —Damien, Graduate Student

- *Restorative practices have helped me to be able to trust those that I do not know.* —Orion, Senior

- *... the positive effects that circles have on building meaningful relationships and fostering a communicative and healthy environment can truly be seen by anyone participating in them.* —Yara, Junior

- *Through circles, I have had the opportunity to really connect and relate to each of my peers on a deeper and personal level. Without having Circles, these connections would not have formed.* —Addison, Senior

Finding 4: Future Motivation

In their reflections, students applied their experience with RP circles, the skills that they gained, and the insights that the experience afforded to their future lives and careers. They indicated motivation to integrate the skills they learned and the experiences they had into the future lives and careers. Student quotes from the data include:

- *As a stressed senior at the university, being a part of a restorative circle was a moment to breathe in my otherwise hectic and extravagantly overwhelming weeks. I often came to class tired, unenthusiastic, and was often struggling with my own mental health. There were days where I could not even show my face but still felt safe and welcome enough to listen and communicate with the only people I would speak with that day. This is the kind of life-altering environment I want us to create at [future workplace] … —*Carrie, Senior

- *My entire perspective shifted and I now consider restorative practices to be one of my core passions as well as something that I implement in my daily life and approach to people. The skills and tools that are gained through practicing the values and engaging openly with a community are things that can be taken with you and incorporated into various elements of one's life. —*Evelyn, Senior

- *My experiences being enrolled in mainstream schooling and studying restorative practices while pursuing my undergraduate degree, now being introduced to my experiences extensively working with speech, language, and hearing-impaired children, bring a new perspective to my career … that otherwise would have been left unthought. —*Yara, Junior

- *As a facilitator, I learned that it is of the utmost importance to make sure that all participants are comfortable with participating, including allowing passes on questions when necessary. —*Damien, Graduate Student

- *In taking RP and working through the course, I realize now more than ever that I must never lose sight of pedagogy and my own philosophy in the face of experience. I want education to be a practice of freedom, a practice that restores, brightens, and celebrates my students—their identities, their efforts, and their stories. —*Madison, Graduate Student

DISCUSSION

The purpose of this research was to determine if participation in a teacher preparation RP course led to building skills toward personal resiliency and applying and integrating trauma-informed practices. The data substantiates that it does. The findings indicate that students enrolled in the fall 2020 teacher preparation RP course experienced personal transformation, increased emotional intelligence, meaningful relationships, and inspired motivation for their future lives and careers. Participation in the course specifically enabled students to experience mindset shifts that align with trauma-informed practices including: increased self-awareness, confidence, and personal growth; and increased empathy, compassion, understanding, and awareness of others.

Regarding Research Question 1 and building skills toward personal resiliency, we juxtapose the research findings with the BRiTE framework's five central components that contribute to developing personal resiliency: (B) Building/Understanding Resilience, (R) Relationships, (i) Well-Being, (t) Motivation, and (E) Emotions (Mansfield et al., 2016). In doing so, we see a close alignment that indicates that students' experience of the course contributed to their building personal resiliency skills. Specifically, *Finding 1: Personal Transformation* aligns with the Building/Understanding Resilience and Wellbeing components of the BRiTE framework. *Finding 2: Emotional Intelligence* aligns with the Emotions component. *Finding 3: Meaningful Relationships* aligns with the Relationships component of the framework. And *Finding 4: Future Motivation* aligns with the Motivation component.

The following reflection illustrates how the RP circle's established community values coupled with the regular practice of listening and sharing as a circle participant supported resiliency building skills as they relate to the intrapersonal growth aspect of Building/Understanding Resilience along with Wellbeing and Emotions within the BRiTE framework:

> *We started with a foundation of values that we agreed upon as a class, which lead to our vulnerability as a whole. I am not a vulnerable person. I struggle with opening up and examining my emotions. I tend to keep my weaknesses and struggles hidden to make myself feel that I am stronger than I truly am. I understood myself more in this class because I sorted through the pains and struggles I had. I didn't push them to the side and move on like I always have. This growth mindset that I developed from this class made me reflect on previous issues that I have had in my educational experiences.* —Sean, Senior

The following student's reflection demonstrates how regular participation in RP circles supported the intrapersonal validation aspect of the BRiTE framework's Building/Understanding Resilience, particularly with his linguistic identity, as well as Motivation, especially as it relates to his new-found confidence in his 'accent' and in embodying his full self:

I saw myself grow in such a way that I can say it made my life better. I learned so much about what I value and what matters. Being in a circle also opened up my confidence. For the first time in a while, I was unable to keep myself from switching accent…. Because of this circle I decided that I will make my native accent a part of my presentation. —Orion, Senior

Regarding Research Question 2 and building skills toward applying and integrating trauma-informed practices, we turn to SAMHSA's six key principles of a trauma-informed approach: (1) empowerment, voice, and choice; (2) historical, cultural, and gender issues; (3) safety; (4) trustworthiness and transparency; (5) peer support; and (6) collaboration and mutuality (2014). Juxtaposing our research findings with these six key principles, we again see a close alignment that indicates that students' participation in the RP course indeed built skills toward applying and integrating trauma-informed practices. Specifically, *Finding 1: Personal Transformation* aligns with: empowerment, voice, and choice; and trustworthiness and transparency. Further, *Finding 2: Emotional Intelligence* and *Finding 3: Meaningful Relationships* align with: historical, cultural, and gender issues; safety; peer support; and collaboration and mutuality.

In the following example, the student discloses that participation in RP circles provided a place of safety, voice, empowerment, mutuality, and peer support—all of which are principles of a trauma-informed approach:

As a student, we face many struggles, trying to figure out our passion, dealing with social injustice, personal problems, etc. and we usually aren't given a space to discuss these hardships with others in a safe space where we can support each other. It made a huge difference in my mental health, and made me feel like I wasn't alone, and that others in my direct community were experiencing hard times just like me. It also helped me to make friends by finding commonalities between myself and my classmates. —Heather, Sophomore

In this portion of the same student's reflection, she acknowledges her increased awareness of historical and cultural issues as a result of the course readings, which also aligns with trauma-informed principles:

Before participating in this class, I was almost entirely unaware of the severity of racial injustice in public schools and how it has led to thousands of minority youth dropping out or being removed from school and ending up incarcerated mainly as a result of zero-tolerance policies. After taking this class, my eyes have been opened to how much work our society needs to become truly equal, equitable, and provide the best chance for every child to have a successful future. —Heather, Sophomore

CONCLUSIONS

This study demonstrates that a teacher preparation RP course that is designed using experiential learning theory is an effective modality toward preparing future teachers to be resilient and to be equipped to apply and integrate trauma-informed practices in their future careers. As noted at the start of this chapter, changing mindsets is key to systemic change. The findings of this research study demonstrate that indeed, students who engaged in the teacher preparation RP course experienced meaningful mindset changes regarding schooling, their own role in education, and the value of the perspectives of others. Those specific mindset changes were in the areas of: personal transformation, emotional intelligence, meaningful relationships, and future motivation. The BRiTE resiliency framework (Mansfield et al., 2016) and SAMHSA's (2014) trauma-informed principles were used to verify that the self-reported changes are aligned with increased personal resiliency and trauma-informed approaches. Furthermore, the students' reflections collectively demonstrated the power of the experiential learning, that is, of studying RP philosophy while engaging in community-building RP circles. The experiential learning model allowed for retrospection, development of meaningful relationships, and a deeper knowing of themselves and others. Therefore, including in teacher preparation programs a course focused on learning and experiencing Restorative Practices invokes an increase in tendencies that support integrating trauma-informed practices, including: empathy, compassion, self-awareness, and confidence.

Further, this study demonstrates both the empowering and transformative impact of combining restorative practices with trauma-informed practices as well as the convergence of the two approaches. While the discipline of the impact of trauma on later life outcomes, specifically *adverse childhood experiences* (Felitti et al., 1998), has its origins in the medical field and has been embraced by the mental health field and the discipline of restorative practices has its origins in Indigenous practices and has been adopted within the justice field, the two approaches converge in both their humanizing philosophical orientations and the nature of the populations that they serve.

Limitations and Implications for Future Research

It is important to emphasize that these findings were based on university students engaging in a consecutive weekly experience of participating in restorative circles, facilitating restorative circles, and engaging in theoretical materials and lectures over the course of a 16-week semester. Although this chapter and book address teacher candidate development, there is a need for training among existing teachers and practitioners in the field who likely do not have the same luxury of time as teacher candidates. As such, research on minimum training dosage and impact could provide useful information for the design of professional development opportunities that can accommodate the needs of professionals already in the field.

REFERENCES

Andrews, L., Higgins, A., Andrews, M. W., & Lalor, J. G. (2012). Classic grounded theory to analyse secondary data: Reality and reflections. *Grounded Theory Review, 11*(1), 12–26.

Blase, K. A., Fixsen, D. L., Sims, B. J., & Ward, C. S. (2015). *Implementation science: Changing hearts, minds, behavior, and systems to improve educational outcomes.* Frank Porter Graham Child Development Institute, University of North Carolina at Chapel Hill.

Boyes-Watson, C., & Pranis, K. (2015). *Circle forward: Building a restorative school community.* Living Justice Press.

Felitti, V. J, Anda, R. F., Nordenberg, D., Williamson, D. F., Spitz, A. M., Edwards, V., Koss, M. P., & Marks, J. S. (1998). Relationship of childhood abuse and household dysfunction to many of the leading causes of death in adults: The adverse childhood experiences (ACE) study. *American Journal of Preventative Medicine, 14*(4), 245–258.

Glaser, B. G. (1963). Retreading research materials: The use of secondary analysis by the independent researcher. *American Behavioral Scientist, 6*(10), 11–14.

Heaton, J. (2008). Secondary analysis of qualitative data: An overview. *Historical Social Research/Historische Sozialforschung,* 33–45.

Johnston, M. P. (2017). Secondary data analysis: A method of which the time has come. *Qualitative and Quantitative Methods in Libraries 3*(3), 619–626.

Joseph, R., & Reigeluth, C.M. (2010). The systemic change process in education: A conceptual framework. *Contemporary Educational Technology, 1*(2), 97–116.

Kolb, D. A., Boyatzis, R. E., & Mainemelis, C. (2001). Experiential learning theory: Previous research and new directions. In R. J. Steinberg & L. Zhang (Eds.), *Perspectives on thinking, learning, and cognitive styles* (pp. 227–248). Routledge.

Mansfield, C. F., Beltman, S., Broadley, T., & Weatherby-Fell, N. (2016). Building resilience in teacher education: An evidenced informed framework. *Teaching and Teacher Education, 54,* 77–87.

Merriam, S. B., Johnson-Bailey, J., Lee, M. Y., Kee, Y., Ntseane, G., & Muhamad, M. (2001). Power and positionality: Negotiating insider/outsider status within and across cultures. *International Journal of Lifelong Education, 20*(5), 405–416.

Miles, M. B., & Huberman, A. M. (1994). *Qualitative data analysis: An expanded sourcebook* (2nd ed.). SAGE.

Overstreet, S., & Chafouleas, S. M. (2016). Trauma-informed schools: Introduction to the special issue. *School Mental Health, 8*(1), 1–6.

Salovey, P., & Mayer, J. D. (1989). Emotional intelligence. *Imagination, Cognition and Personality, 9,* 185–211. http://dx.doi.org/10.2190/DUGG-P24E-52WK-6CDG"

Senge, P. (1990). *The fifth discipline: The art and practice of organizational learning.* Doubleday.

Strauss, A., & Corbin, J. (1998). *Basics of qualitative research techniques.* SAGE.

Substance Abuse and Mental Health Services Administration (SAMHSA). (2014). *SAMHSA's concept of trauma and guidance for a trauma-informed approach* (HHS Publication No. 14-4884). https://ncsacw.samhsa.gov/userfiles/files/SAMHSA_Trauma.pdf

Thomas, D. R. (2006). A general inductive approach for analyzing qualitative evaluation data. *American Journal of Evaluation, 27*(2), 237–246.

Tyack, D. B., & Cuban, L. (1995). *Tinkering toward utopia.* Harvard University Press.

CHAPTER 7

REFLECTIONS IN CRISIS

Teachers' Empowerment, Empathy and Social Justice

Lisa L. Minicozzi and Devin Thornburg
Ruth S. Ammon School of Education, Adelphi University

ABSTRACT

The chapter explores whether and how trauma-informed practices within a social justice framework might be important for the education of diverse populations they serve as well as a way to understand the roles that their own traumas and biases can play in their teaching, both in-person and remotely. The authors worked with 24 in-service teachers and 35 teacher and leader education students since the pandemic resulted in the closure of most schools and institutions of higher education in this metropolitan region of the Northeastern U.S. Emerging research, anecdotes from class discussions, and voices from the field are included to offer readers contextual understanding. The research methodology in this work involves Appreciative Inquiry within Communities of Practice in both preservice and in-service programs. Themes of trauma-informed strategies, community, student engagement and equity are explored. The chapter concludes with suggestions and new ways to think about how pedagogical experiences aligned to trauma-informed practices will contribute to the development of a comprehensive teacher education preparation, responsive to trauma.

Developing Trauma-Informed Teachers: Creating Classrooms That Foster Equity, Resiliency, and Asset-Based Approaches: Research Findings From the Field, pp. 109–125
Copyright © 2023 by Information Age Publishing
www.infoagepub.com

Prior to COVID-19, nearly half of all children in the U.S. were exposed to at least one social or family experience leading to trauma-related stress (Johns Hopkins Bloomberg School of Public Health, 2014) and most of those children were in communities of color and poverty. With the pandemic, the uncertainty, and stresses that teachers and soon-to-be teachers face are geometrically more challenging. This chapter provides new ways of thinking about teacher preparation in the United States, responding to the complexities of teaching and learning in a post Pandemic world.

The chapter explores whether and how trauma-informed practices within a social justice framework might be important for the education of diverse populations they serve as well as a way to understand the roles that their own traumas and biases can play in their teaching, both in-person and remotely. Emerging research, anecdotes from class discussions, and voices from the field are included to offer readers contextual understanding. The chapter concludes with suggestions and new ways to think about how pedagogical experiences aligned to trauma-informed practices will contribute to the development of a comprehensive teacher education preparation, responsive to trauma (Thomas et al., 2019).

The Pandemic Context

The research described in this chapter builds on the recent conclusions of Gherardi et al. (2020) that trauma and toxic stress are pervasive and impact the majority of people but disproportionately people of color, the poor and those of marginalized identities. Through the early weeks of the pandemic in the United States, it was apparent that communities of color and poor—particularly older adults—were at greater risk of COVID infection, serious illness, and death. The disparities in information and health care—let alone increases in food insecurity (e.g., García & Weiss, 2020) and the conditions to remain socially distant in overcrowded spaces—were glaring (e.g., Centers for Disease Control and Prevention [CDC], 2020). In school districts in many areas of the nation, the disparities for those serving higher-need and marginalized communities in the resources they have had to address schooling is also apparent (Alliance for Quality Education, 2020).

The inequities in health care and educational resources have only added to the trauma and stress that these communities disproportionately experience. A joint communication from the National Child Traumatic Stress Network and Teaching Tolerance (Learning for Justice, 2020), for example, wrote about the conditions where children have had a history of exposure to traumatic events, making them especially vulnerable to changes in schedule, routine, and expectations that has occurred since spring 2020.

Students who have special needs, families who have lost income or jobs, students with family members who are at risk of viral infection by age or occupation, and students who are less supervised are groups of particular concern for trauma during the pandemic.

In March 2020, nearly all of over 55 million U.S. school children under the age of 18 stayed home, with 1.4 billion out of school or childcare across the globe (Cluver et al., 2020; National Center for Education Statistics [NCES] 2019a; U.S. Census Bureau, 2019). Not only did these children lack daily access to school and the basic supports schools provide for many students, but they also lost out on group activities, team sports, and recreational options such as pools and playgrounds. Added to this has been the huge disparity in access to technology, internet, and/or family know-how for those schools seeking remote learning as part of the only solution for their students. The differences by race/ethnicity, income, and location with lack of access or devices mirror those found with school achievement; more than double the percentage of Black, Latinx and Indigenous students lack internet access in comparison to White students (Future Ready Schools, 2020).

Teachers in these communities were already facing extreme barriers—such as lower pay, threats to physical safety, and a lack of trusting relationships. More recently, in a nationwide poll of educators, the National Educational Association (NEA, 2020) found that 28% said the pandemic has caused them to consider early retirement or leave the profession. Interestingly, that number includes a considerable number of novice teachers—one in five teachers with less than 10 years experience.

For teachers, the sense of isolation and loneliness that may arise from the challenges of the pandemic can cause responses akin to teacher burnout, where they experience emotional exhaustion, depersonalization and lower sense of efficacy and empowerment (Leiter & Maslach, 2016; Skaalvik & Skaalvik, 2014). Not only are teachers now working alone at home, but they are working on tasks about which they may or may not feel competent. Teachers who are experts in in-classroom instruction are learning that different skill sets, and methods are required for delivering instruction online.

Primary trauma, trauma experienced firsthand, is not the only trauma that will impact teachers. Secondary traumatic stress is the emotional distress that results when a teacher hears about and is witness to the traumatic experiences of other individuals, such as their students. As teachers hear about their students' experiences with a lack of food, inequitable or intermittent access to the internet, their desire to demonstrate care and commitment can lead teachers to experience secondary traumatic stress, also known as compassion fatigue.

Research Framework

The program backgrounds discussed here are situated in a metropolitan university's Early Childhood Special Education, Childhood Education and Educational Leadership programs. The voices of in-service teachers also contribute to the research findings and shared learning experiences of all participants. While social justice has been part of our core values in our curriculum and preparation of our preservice teachers, we have not had previous opportunities to explore this framework as related to trauma-informed practices. The research framework involved embedding social justice into coursework and field experiences as a lens for building knowledge of trauma, shifting perspectives and creating emotionally healthy school cultures, and supporting self-care for educators (Thomas et al., 2019). This framework requires the creation of conditions to encourage self-reflection—including the relatively recent work on implicit bias—but also about their own experiences of trauma that make it more difficult to create safe spaces for students.

Due to COVID-19, the urgency for preservice and in-service teachers to connect, virtually, with both students and colleagues alike was profound. As teacher educators, we recognize that learning is often situated within a social context and requires reflection to deepen understanding and foster professional growth. This research explores preservice and in-service teachers' understandings of how their participation in communities of practice (CoP) supported their own professional development with trauma-informed practices. Employing the CoP framework helped to explore teachers' experiences during COVID-19 and to understand how their concept of equity/social justice and self-reflection developed as a shared experience or learning partnership (see, e.g., Lave & Wenger, 1991; Wenger-Trayner, 2015).

CoPs have been found to be a powerful support for innovation in schools using a social justice lens for a variety of programs, including language education (King, 2019), place-based education (Scanlan & Park, 2020), and inclusive education (Mortier, 2018). An increasing number of studies linking CoP to trauma-informed practices have emerged, most notably in health care systems globally and in school communities in the U.S. that seek to include parents (Lawson & Alameda-Lawson, 2012) and as part of an overall initiative by school leaders in trauma-informed schools (Stokes & Brunzell, 2020).

This notion of CoP certainly had a resurgence pre-pandemic with the expansion of technology and the internet across professional settings. However once schools were forced to shutter the doors, teachers began creating organic virtual CoPs to cope with their "new normal." In doing so, the teachers and teacher leaders found informal communities to share knowledge, develop skills, and support one another's socioemotional well-being.

MATERIALS AND METHODS

Participants from two graduate level classes and ongoing (weekly) professional development sessions from March through December 2020, serve as the basis for exploration around about the following questions:

1. How has the pandemic affected you personally and professionally, in your learning and/or teaching?
2. What are the biggest challenges you have faced as a result?
3. How has the move to either hybrid or fully remote models of learning and teaching affected your practices as an educator?
4. Are there valuable lessons to be gained from the last year and what might those be?
5. Given the challenges educators face having to do with equity in both policy and practices, what do you think we might do towards addressing social justice and access in the communities we serve?

This qualitative approach in the work here can best be described as exploring the field of study ecologically, reflecting the contextual aspects of culture, pedagogy, and history as well as seeing the interconnections among professional disciplines as well as the educational systems and the communities that system serves. Growing out of the tradition of ethnography, qualitative studies of trust are derived from a research tradition that encompass ethnographic inquiry and are field based, conducted in schools and communities where people "live," and use descriptive detail to build toward general patterns or explanatory theories (e.g., Richardson, 2000). There are other components to this work, including that it is undertaken by those who are in daily contact with the people they are studying over long periods of time who, ultimately, are both participants and observers of the research.

To value their views, they bring to bear and discover what has been successful in efforts to reach and connect with students in remote learning, the authors sought to explore the concept through the use of "Appreciative Inquiry." This is an approach to action research that looks at change in an organization—or school—contextually. It sets out to discover what has been successful in the past to build on for a positive future, addressing challenges that are currently faced (Cooperrider & Srivastva, 1987).

Research Collaborators

Together, the authors worked with 24 in-service teachers and 35 teacher and leader education students since the pandemic resulted in the closure of most schools and institutions of higher education in this metropolitan region of the Northeastern United States. Together, the authors worked with 3 distinct groups of educators: 24 in-service teachers, 28 school leaders, and 7 educational leader candidates to explore the implications of teaching & learning through a global pandemic. The in-service teachers are currently in urban schools, pre-K–12, in a range of subject areas. They were together for the purposes of professional development in one of three (and overlapping) topics involving remote learning, social-emotional learning, and culturally responsive teaching during the spring and fall 2020. As a group, they represented diverse backgrounds, including seven who identified as Black, six as Latinx, and three as Asian. Eight were bilingual and were working with bilingual populations in their schools. All came from the metropolitan area being served by the schools. Participants' teacher education experience ranged from 2–15 years and held faculty ranks from assistant teacher, nontenured leave replacement, to tenured teaching status.

The teacher education students were enrolled in classes in early childhood and childhood education at a university in fall 2020. The majority of these students identified themselves as White and grew up in suburban school districts that were fairly homogeneous. Those in the Educational Leadership program were a cohort of seven aspiring school leaders and were more diverse in demographic and professional backgrounds, including teachers and other school professionals in this urbanized region of the United States.

Implementation of CoP

Within the first two weeks of school closures (as early as March 2020) educators began contacting us about forming "support groups" to navigate remote learning. In some cases, the request was for professional development sessions on use of technology in remote learning and/or social-emotional learning strategies with students. It became clear, however, that the need was greatest for teachers to be in support of one another's efforts and challenges as the spring months continued.

Initially, the teachers who were part of the study, began meeting online through informal ways to simply "check-in" and build a sense of social community during a time of social isolation and loneliness. As one of the teacher leader's remarked, "I can't tell you how helpful this is to hear about how other schools are handling these issues ... we are literally flying the plane as we are building it."

During the first several weeks of mandatory school closures, teachers engaged in what can be referred to as "crisis-teaching"—whereby teachers urgently met with their students and tried to provide stability and some continuity of instruction. Teachers were essentially challenged by not knowing what to do and expressed, "what do I do ... how can I plan when I can't even reach my students?" One veteran in-service teacher continually asked, how do I do something that is pedagogically credible within the confines of remote learning ... what's beyond the reach?"

Through the educator prep cohort-based programs, teachers built positive communities, learning networks and pedagogical knowledge. A primary value of creating these CoPs is shared knowledge. Participants regularly commented on the benefits of having a "group" to brainstorm ideas with and gain "support." Since these communities continued over several months, members had a sustained learning opportunity and reliable community to share responsibility and build resilience.

It was not clear at first whether teachers were meant to hold classes during scheduled days and times. School and community leaders struggled to provide clear guidance during many of the transitions between face to face and distance learning. The level of uncertainty and lack of consistency plagued teachers daily, often leaving them feeling undervalued and unsupported. Early on, administrators were sending mixed messages about teacher-student interactions, while some schools were able to swiftly adjust to Zoom or Google Meet class sessions, others were building asynchronous learning classrooms. This lack of consistency and structure contributed to stress for both the teachers and students. As each gained greater comfort with distance learning technologies, interest began to focus on the importance of having guided interactions to support student learning and socioemotional well-being. Teachers soon realized that implementing even a small classroom (online) routine could alleviate stress and provide students with a sense of safety.

Of the preservice teachers, many shared concerns about how these virtual interactions would eventually shape their own teaching identities. During one class meeting, the teachers expressed concern about teaching in a post-pandemic world. One commented by stating, "we can't be naive to say that everything will go back to normal and we can't just assume that when we take the mask off, we will go back to teaching as it was pre-pandemic." It seemed that the preservice teachers wanted the time to continually reflect and together, with their classmates, identify lessons learned. Wenger and Wenger-Trayner's (2015) components of CoP were used to identify appropriate cohorts.

FINDINGS

Using an appreciative inquiry approach (Whitney & Trosten-Bloom, 2010) for gathering narratives from teachers, identified areas worth noting; trauma-informed strategies, building bridges with community outreach, fostering student engagement and issues focused on educational equity. These were all framed within the perspectives of social justice and the personal experiences of trauma that are used throughout the chapter.

Trauma-Informed Strategies

By creating CoP within graduate level education courses, the authors found that preservice students, in particular, were able to develop empathy skills, gain foundational knowledge (understanding the nature and impact of trauma), and sustain meaningful relationships. By placing trauma-informed practices within the context of CoP it provided the necessary space for reflection, collective healing, and joint inquiry to shift teachers' perspectives and begin to re-think educational priorities. The descriptions of resilience look at the teachers' personal, community and professional attributes that allowed growth throughout the challenges of teaching through Global pandemic. As one teacher noted, "I looked forward to this meeting time each week because it was for me ... a sanctuary ... and a time to learn."

The Appreciative Inquiry method used was to engage in conversations with a purpose across boundaries of race/ethnicity, economic status, or location, asking others what positive aspects of remote learning in supporting their students. Analysis of the conversations with students, teachers and leaders would have broad cultural implications. Critical to these capacities is the self-reflection of the researcher to understand how those within a given cultural group are perceiving her or him or them in the role or position.

The cultural lens that was used was intended to ensure that participants feel free to speak, participants' views are represented accurately, and a comfortable environment is created in which participants can speak openly (Burnette et al., 2014). Part of the lens includes cultural sensitivity through sharing the research findings with participants after they are complete as well as qualitative content analysis to ensure authenticity of codes or themes were coming from the data without preconceived notions or categories (Wardale et al., 2015).

A young woman from a high-needs community herself who was originally from Jamaica, talked about the challenges that her family and neighbors are facing and how that must be for teachers. "The trauma that people have suffered is huge and it adds to the stress in their lives being Black, immigrants, poor. But their pride sometimes gets in the way of knowing that they are scared or overwhelmed." Participants in this CoP relied on one another to scaffold understanding and learn new ways to support all students and families during such a challenging time. A teacher in an urban school noted, "while trauma is part of what is happening in the families, they don't want to see it like that or use that language ... it's more about supporting strengths than talking about trauma."

Community

As Fay et al (2020) outlined, schools are a source of community resilience (along with the economy and health care system). However, teachers can see the community as a source of strengthening resilience in the school, as well. Mirroring the notions of cultural assets supporting the school, there is a dynamic connection that can be made among schools, families, and communities in the strengthening of each to respond to the trauma resulting from the pandemic and prior to this, to inequities in resources and access to them.

A member of the educational leadership cohort commented, "the school must be working together with the community in this crisis, which means being responsive to the community's needs." Two additional themes warranted exploration in greater depth here as the experiences of those involved in classes and workshops frequently echoed these, across setting and beliefs.

Student Engagement

In this region, public schools had replaced attendance figures in brick-and-mortar settings with online engagement of students. Yet the definition for accountability purposes involves submission of online assignments as the key metric rather than any social or interpersonal aspect of learning. Teachers then became virtual truant officers and the "work" or "online assignments" became the currency of doing school.

Time and again, students of color from underserved communities faced increased barriers to learning during the pandemic, including lack of Wi-Fi, reliable technological devices, and food insecurity. Teachers surveyed for our project all estimated that about two thirds of their students were regularly attending or engaging in virtual learning. One teacher likened the experience to "coaxing participation to the indifferent" he further stated, "we had so little buy- in because of the immediacy of the closure ... kids didn't even know what to expect." We heard from many of the participants how difficult it was to virtually connect with portions of their students. "Some weeks go by and then I realize I haven't seen or spoken to (student name)."

Both teacher education students and in-service teachers benefited from social interactions during learning and being able to support ways in which students can engage with one another, as well. A recurring theme for the communities of practice was student engagement. Teachers often shared stories revealing small ways they were able to connect with their students. "I just came to the realization that if I call them on their cell phones before my class, they will more likely show up." During one meeting session, participants collaborated on strategies to improve student engagement and engaged in a rich discussion about the different types of student engagement - emotional, cognitive, and behavioral. Ultimately, the participants found that trying to help students foster a positive disposition toward remote learning was a top priority.

A student in the educational leadership program offered these comments: "Engagement with students. Last year my son was sent a list of daily activities, and from March–June he had only 3, 20-minute live sessions with his class."

Another student in that same program provided an urban perspective: "students and teachers are not required to have their cameras on so we have no way of being mandated reporters. It's been an ongoing problem in my school ... we don't know if students are engaging in maladaptive behaviors."

Equity

The challenge here is that the lack of technological equity for students (specifically, not having the devices for learning, not having the internet access, and/or not having the knowledge or the family knowledge to use what they have) that has been tied to race and economic class in both research and practice has another disparity in the social realm. Unlike other countries, the U.S. seems particularly, often exclusively, focused on student academic progress through the pandemic. But what about their social growth? This was a theme picked up by the in-service teachers surveyed.

A significant insight has been the lack of "social equity," bridging social justice and social-emotional learning. There are issues of equity in an area that has been largely ignored or dismissed in the field and even more so with teachers, involving the impact of social connection, of being with one another in a social setting. Students who attend affluent school districts have had more opportunity for social interaction offline if only because the spaces school provides are more ample and safer. At the height of the pandemic, students in private schools, for example, were much more likely to be attending face-to-face classes or were, at least, given the opportunity to do so.

As one in-service teacher commented,

> we all knew educational inequity existed but so many of my students were left without the necessary technology … which creates more inequity…many students are receiving different types of education based on what they have available to them in terms of resources … it's just not fair and I struggle with understanding how this can still happen.

During one class meeting of in-service and preservice early childhood teachers, the conversation revolved around feelings of "helplessness and longing." During the class, cohort members openly discussed how much they missed seeing and interacting with their young learners—especially "longing" for the human touch of the children under their care. Research has shown that children need responsive care and opportunities to build healthy attachments to their caregivers (Carlson, 2006). What about the adults? The lack of human interaction and ability to offer a student a pat on the back, high-five in the air, or hug, took an emotional toll on the teachers we surveyed. Many commented on the "unnaturalness" of not being able to hug their preschool or kindergarten age students, during this very difficult time.

As the pandemic unfolded, for example, schools had to prioritize continuous instruction and technology access with the output of grades. This, in itself, represented an issue of equity. Would freezing previous grades and replacing letter grades with pass-fail be equitable solutions (Townsley & Wear, 2020)? The CoP participants felt this keenly in their daily contact with students in the remote classrooms.

IMPLICATIONS

The following represents suggestions for teacher educators to build teacher candidates' self-efficacy for trauma-informed social justice education based on the themes and related literature about the challenges to equity before and after the pandemic. Pedagogical experiences aligned to trauma-informed practices are explored that can contribute to the development of a comprehensive teacher education preparation, responsive to trauma (Thomas et al., 2019). Considerations must take on a social-justice and equity lens when looking at the challenges faced by teachers and students. Education leaders and policy makers need to recognize the resource inequities that already exist in order to be able to assess and distribute support moving forward.

School leaders are strongly urged to consider the critical role teachers play in recognizing the symptoms of trauma and treating it at the classroom level. There is a clear need to prioritize social-emotional learning, for both students and teachers alike. The pandemic has ravaged so many communities, disproportionately impacting those of color. Teachers desperately need the skill set to address the emotional needs of their students and teachers should be given the appropriate resources to mitigate these challenges. Many of the teachers discussed the overwhelming stress they felt on a daily basis, trying to put together lessons remotely while attending to the emotional needs of their students and respective families. Some shared individual coping strategies, but as a collective voice, teachers interviewed seemed to be calling for a more comprehensive school-wide commitment to creating healthier and emotionally supportive work environments, for teachers and students alike.

Drawing on the work of Darling-Hammond and Oakes (2019), teacher preparation programs should look to "deepen learning" and engage students in critical discussions to scaffold candidates' developing competencies. Through this research project, the authors found the need to support both in-service and preservice educators with opportunities for collaboration, engagement, and professional learning. All participants welcomed the experiences for reflection and to further develop their skills and understanding of equity and social justice.

Trauma-informed social-emotional learning (SEL) efforts must be a priority for teacher preparation programs. Schools of education need to build educator capacity for socioemotional learning. In doing so, teacher candidates will be better prepared to foster safe, supportive, and equitable learning environments that give students the opportunity to feel supported, cared for, and nurtured to reach their potential

The experience of those interviewed, is that their learning from one another is a critical part of their professional growth. Making the extra effort to create those spaces through coursework, to have students and teachers interact and build on each other's experiences among themselves, is a very important part of this work.

Providing educators with foundational knowledge in trauma-informed practices will be a likely first step for programmatic reviews in the following months. That being said, actually developing ways for teachers to integrate such practices into their teaching pedagogies to better understand student trauma will begin the initial work of creating emotionally healthy schools. Schools of education could be leveraged here to provide training and offer support within school district partners to contribute to an interdisciplinary approach to having a resilient and healthy P–12 student populace.

School leaders have an opportunity to build trusting relationships and create school cultures that evoke agency, community, and collective efficacy. The teachers interviewed for this project all felt a lack of trust and uncertainty, sometimes from their administrators and most recently from parents and public sentiment. Throughout these several months, the teachers felt devalued and at odds with what initially motivated them to become teachers, the ability to make a difference and have "purpose." These emotions obviously have broad implications for the teachers.

In order to build resilience in students, there is a need to start with the teachers, providing authentic self-care experiences, mental health resources, and shared decision-making opportunities, just to name a few, could promote resilience in teachers. The concept of resilience is regularly used in a range of disciplines, associated with both strength and flexibility. In the context of disasters, it can be defined as "coping ability, the ability to bounce back, pull through or adapt to the disruption of a crisis" (Sellnow & Seeger, 2013, p. 123). Although teacher resilience lacks a widely agreed-upon definition (see, e.g., Beltman et al. 2011; Schelvis et al. 2014). There is evidence that teacher resilience includes positively working through adversity, ability to show empathy with challenging students, enacting a growth mindset—optimism toward the future. Possible next steps for deepening the commitment to trauma-informed practices within a social justice framework in teacher education programs, hopefully building empathy and empowerment to candidates and partner teachers may include the following:

- Varied program curricula to address trauma-informed teaching principles (this would include foundational knowledge as well as interdisciplinary pedagogical practices)
- Field-based learning opportunities to build understanding of trauma-informed practices (teacher candidates working with restorative justice models of practice in partner schools)
- Teacher trainings and professional development in resilience building
- Creation of CoP between mentor teachers, university faculty and preservice teachers
- Redesign of teacher education courses to include trauma-informed pedagogies. Specific content may include: childhood trauma and how it can impact brain development, learning, and behavior regulation, adverse childhood experiences (ACE) study, and the implications for learning and long-term effects on America's students. the effects poverty may have on learning and how educators can create safe and supportive environments

- Offer ongoing workshops focused on the intersection of race, social justice, and trauma (required workshop series for all preservice candidates)
- Offer site visits and workshops at model partner schools embodying a holistic, healthy school culture
- Embed research projects for candidates to explore the impact of trauma on all members of the school community and how it affects student and adult behavior in schools
- Collaborate with the educational leadership program to develop and design best practices on how schools and educators can address the needs of children and educators affected by trauma

Given the fact that mastery experiences provide the most effective way of gaining self-efficacy, field experiences need to include mastery level competencies to expand and challenge personal beliefs while providing growth opportunities for preservice teachers. Rethinking field experiences to enact more *learning by doing* and less participant observation could better prepare preservice teachers for the challenges and dilemmas of teaching in a post-pandemic culture. Having authentic field-based learning CoP that are linked to trauma's impacts on learning, and how teachers may be responsive to those needs would greatly benefit preservice teachers. Preservice teachers need the foundational knowledge, practicum related experiences and the time and space to reflect on their teaching.

Emerging research suggests that teachers who are given opportunities to actively collaborate and co-design their teaching practices through trauma-informed positive education principles, felt empowered as professionals to meet the complexities of teaching and learning (Brunzell et al., 2019). What is also striking about Brunzell and his colleagues' work is how their methodology of appreciative inquiry mirrored the research here but they were working with current teachers. This research effort was to bring a similar framework to teacher education candidates, as well, and the conclusion is that the two populations of future and current educators benefit from a trauma-informed social justice approach and believe that it will be relevant in the times after the pandemic has ended.

REFERENCES

Alliance for Quality Education. (2020, September). *Set up to fail: How Cuomo's school cuts target New York's black and brown students.* Public Policy and Education Fund of New York. https://tinyurl.com/y7mmfp5h

Beltman, S., Mansfield, C. F., & Price, A. (2011). Thriving not just surviving: A review of research on teacher resilience. *Educational Research Review, 6*(3), 185–207. https://10.1016/j.edurev.2011.09.001

Brunzell, T., Stokes, H., & Waters, L. (2019). Shifting teacher practice in trauma-affected classrooms: Practice pedagogy strategies within a trauma-informed positive education model. *School Mental Health, 11,* 600–614. https://doi.org/10.1007/s12310-018-09308-8

Burnette, C. E., Sanders, S., Butcher, H. K., & Rand, J. T. (2014). A toolkit for ethical and culturally sensitive research: An application with indigenous communities. *Ethics and Social Welfare, 8*(4), 364–382.

Carlson, F. M. (2006). *Essential touch: Meeting the needs of children.* NAEYC.

Centers for Disease Control and Prevention. (2020). *Covid-19 in racial and ethnic minority groups. (COVID-19).* https://www.cdc.gov/coronavirus/2019-ncov/need-extra-precautions/racial-ethnic-minorities.html

Cluver, L., Lachman, JM., Sherr, L., Wessels, I., Krug, E., Rakotomalala, S., Blight, S., Hillis, S., Bachman, G., Green, O., Butchart, A., Tomlinson, M., Ward, C. L., Doubt, J., & McDonald, K. (2020). Parenting in a Time of COVID-19. *The Lancet, 393*(10231), E64. https://doi.org/10.1016/S0140-6736(20)30736-4

Cooperrider, D. L., & Srivastva, S. (1987). Appreciative inquiry in organizational life. In W. Pasmore & R. Woodman (Eds.), *Research in organization change and development* (Vol. 1). JAI Press.

Darling-Hammond, L., & Oakes, J. (2019). *Preparing teachers for deeper learning.* Harvard Education Press.

Fay, J., Levinson, M., Stevens, A., Brighouse, H., & Geron, T. (2020). *Schools During the COVID-19 Pandemic: Sites and sources of community resilience* [White Paper]. Harvard University, Edmond J. Safra Center for Ethics. https://ethics.harvard.edu/files/center-for-ethics/files/20schoolsduringpandemic2.pdf

Future Ready Schools. (2020). *New analysis shows students of color far more likely to be cut off from online learning,* Alliance of Excellent Education. https://futureready.org/new-analysis-shows-students-of-color-far-more-likely-to-be-cut-off-from-online-learning-data-from-education-and-civil-rights-groups-show-that-nearly-17-million-students-nationally-fall-into-homework-g/

García, E., & Weiss, E. (2020). *A policy agenda to address the teacher shortage in u.s. public schools. The sixth report in 'the perfect storm in the teacher labor market' series.* Economic Policy Institute. https://www.epi.org/publication/a-policy-agenda-to-address-the-teacher-shortage-in-u-s-public-schools/

Gherardi, S. A., Flinn, R. E., & Jaure, V. B. (2020). Trauma-sensitive schools and social justice: A critical analysis. *Urban Review, 52,* 482–504. https://doi.org/10.1007/s11256-020-00553-3

Johns Hopkins Bloomberg School of Public Health. (2014, December 8). *Nearly half of U.S. kids exposed to traumatic social or family experiences during childhood.* Science Daily. https://www.sciencedaily.com/releases/2014/12/141208105318.htm

King, B. W. (2019). *Communities of practice in language research: A critical introduction.* Routledge.

Lave, J., & Wenger, E. (1991). *Learning in doing: Social, cognitive, and computational perspectives. Situated learning: Legitimate peripheral participation.* Cambridge University Press. https://doi.org/10.1017/CBO9780511815355

Lawson, M. A., & Alameda-Lawson, T. (2012). A case study of school-linked, collective parent engagement. *American Educational Research Journal, 49,* 651–684.

Learning for Justice. (2020, March 23). *A trauma-informed approach to teaching through coronavirus.* https://www.learningforjustice.org/magazine/a-trauma-informed-approach-to-teaching-through-coronavirus

Leiter, M. P., & Maslach, C. (2016). Latent burnout profiles: A new approach to understanding the burnout experience. *Burnout Research, 3*(4), 89–100.

Mortier, K. (2020) Communities of practice: A conceptual framework for inclusion of students with significant disabilities, *International Journal of Inclusive Education, 24*(3), 329–340.

National Educational Association. (2021, June 17). *Educators ready for all, but a teacher shortage looms.* https://www.nea.org/advocating-for-change/new-from-nea/educators-ready-fall-teacher-shortage-looms

National Center for Education Statistics (NCES), U.S. Department of Education. (2019a). Table 216.20. Number and Enrollment of Public Elementary and Secondary Schools, by School Level, Type, and Charter, Magnet, and Virtual Status: Selected Years, 1990–91 Through 2017–18. https://nces.ed.gov/programs/digest/d19/tables/dt19_208.20.asp

Richardson, L. (2000). Writing: A method of inquiry. In N. K, Denzin & S. Lincoln (Eds.), *Handbook of qualitative research.* SAGE.

Scanlan, M., & Park, H. (2020). The learning of stakeholders in a community school: A narrative history of Gardner Pilot Academy, *Journal of Education for Students Placed at Risk, 25*(2), 146–163

Skaalvik, E. M., & Skaalvik, S. (2014). Teacher self-efficacy and perceived autonomy: Relations with teacher engagement, job satisfaction, and emotional exhaustion. *Psychological Reports, 114*(1), 68–77.

Townsley, M., & Wear, N. L. (2020). *Making grades matter: Standards-based grading in a secondary PLC at Work®.* Solution Tree.

Schelvis, R. M. C., Zwetsloot, G. I. J. M., & Wiezer, B. & N. M. (2014). Exploring teacher and school resilience as a new perspective to solve persistent problems in the educational sector. *Teachers and Teaching, 20*(5), 622–637. https://www.tandfonline.com/doi/abs/10.1080/13540602.2014.937962

Sellnow, T. L., & Seeger, M. Q. (2013). *Theorizing crisis communication.* Wiley and Sons.

Stokes, H., & Brunzell, T. (2020). Leading trauma-informed practice in schools. *Leading & Managing, 26*(1).

Thomas, M. S., Crosby, S., & Vanderhaar, J. (2019). Trauma-informed practices in schools across two decades: An interdisciplinary review of research. *Review of Research in Education, 43*(1), 422–452.

U.S. Census Bureau. (2019). *CPS historical time series tables on school enrollment: Table A-1. School enrollment of the population 3 years old and over, by level and control of school, race, and Hispanic origin: October 1955 to 2018.*

Wardale, D., Cameron, R., & Li, J. (2015). Considerations for multidisciplinary, culturally sensitive, mixed methods research. *Electronic Journal of Business Research Methods*, *13*(1), 37–48.

Wenger, E., & Wenger-Trayner, B. (2015). *Communities of practice. A brief introduction.* http://wenger-trayner.com/introduction-to-communities-of-practice/

CHAPTER 8

COLLABORATIVE PROFESSIONAL DEVELOPMENT SUPPORTING TRAUMA-INFORMED PRACTICES

Linking Preservice Teacher Candidates with Behavioral Interventionists

Regina Rahimi
Georgia Southern, Armstrong Campus

Vanessa Keener
Savannah-Chatham Public Schools

Delores D. Liston
Georgia Southern, Statesboro Campus

Amee Adkins
Georgia Southern, Armstrong Campus

ABSTRACT

This chapter details a pilot collaborative professional development (PD) experience to enhance understanding of trauma-informed pedagogy (TIP). We engaged eight professional behavioral interventionists (BIs) in an urban school district with three teacher candidates (TCs) at a comprehensive state

Developing Trauma-Informed Teachers: Creating Classrooms That Foster Equity, Resiliency, and Asset-Based Approaches: Research Findings From the Field, pp. 127–147
Copyright © 2023 by Information Age Publishing
www.infoagepub.com

university. Through this PD experience, the TCs gained first-hand exposure to the work of the BIs as they implemented TIP in their work with teachers. These collaborative relationships deepened TCs understanding of the symbiotic relationships between professional roles of teachers and BIs in schools. TCs and BIs gained knowledge about the challenges and areas of expertise of each other's work in schools. Further, it is anticipated this introduction to school and local resources will increase the capacity for these TCs to identify support resources and work collaboratively with a team, starting from their first hire in a school system. Lastly, we hope through this project that participants can employ the knowledge and understanding of TIP to support student success in the schools. As a pilot study, this project is limited in scope but the results warrant replicating it on a larger scale.

OPPORTUNITIES/CHALLENGES FACED BY TEACHER PREPARATION PROGRAMS

As we seek opportunities to enhance our teacher preparation programs to support student learning, we must develop teacher candidates' understanding of how adverse childhood experiences can impact their students' social, behavioral, and educational outcomes. With pressure to focus on many other aspects of student and learning development, universities and teacher preparation programs have been tasked with finding creative ways to incorporate TIP into coursework (Cole et al., 2013). TIP promises to equip our TCs to support the social- emotional needs of their students while preparing them to handle the academic and behavioral challenges they will face.

This chapter serves to highlight a project that brought together university faculty, teacher candidates (TCs), and behavioral interventionists (BIs) from a local, urban school district to examine TIP, share strategies for implementing restorative discipline, and detail effective classroom management practice.

This collaborative project provided investigation into TIP while providing "real world" exposure for TCs through a voluntary PD opportunity. This chapter details the development and implementation of the model and our findings from pairing school district BIs and three TCs in study around topics related to TIP. We share these experiences as consideration for others interested in such work, noting that this is a pilot project with a limited number of participants.

THEORETICAL FRAMEWORK/RESEARCH GROUNDING WORK

Much attention has been directed to trauma-informed practice (TIP), with the field of education most recently entering the discussion (Alexander,

2019; Blaustein & Kinninburgh, 2010; Blodgett, 2013; Craig, 2016; Olson, 2014; Perry, 2014). While the origins of trauma-informed practice came from the healthcare field, with development in behavioral health, it has found a welcome place in understanding student behavior and learning in classrooms. As this important approach is making its way into education, clearly it also needs to become a part of our teacher preparation programs. There exists a great deal of research documenting the impact of childhood trauma and stress on brain development, cognitive functioning, and school performance (Burke et al., 2011; Delaney-Black et al., 2002; Pechtel & Pizzagalli, 2011; Streeck-Fischer & van der Kolk, 2000). The implications for teachers and teacher-candidates are clear: TIP holds promise for addressing the student needs caused by adverse childhood experiences (ACES), as proven by treatments in the fields of psychiatry, psychology, and social work (Amaro et al., 2007; Azeem et al., 2011; Huntington et al., 2005; Rivard et al., 2005). While the application of the principles of trauma-informed care is relatively new to the field of education, there has been some evidence that these practices applied in academic settings have a positive impact (Alexander, 2019; Stevens, 2012). Understanding the implications of the impact of ACES and other principles undergirding TIP provides a fresh perspective for educational professionals (Centers for Disease Control and Prevention, 2019).

The project outlined in this chapter links the emerging field of TIP and classroom practices, particularly in how educational professionals and TCs view their role in shaping classroom experiences for students who may have experienced trauma. While managing classroom behavior and engaging students in instruction is a significant aspect of an educator's role, only recently that there has been theory emerged that aligns classroom management practices so clearly with social emotional well-being (Gay, 2010; Jones & Kahn, 2017; Ladson-Billings, 1995, 2014; Meyer & Evans, 2012; Teasley, 2014; Thornsborne & Blood, 2013). In line with TIP, these frameworks highlight the impact social and emotional environments of schools and classrooms have on students' well-being (Berman et al., 2018).

Additional research suggests that preservice teachers often feel least prepared to teach children with challenging behaviors due to a general lack of confidence in classroom management (Dorado et al., 2016; Eisenman et al., 2012; McCormack, 2001). Indeed, the framework of trauma-informed practice enables teachers and teacher candidates to develop greater insight into these challenging student behaviors and approaches better suited to address students' needs successfully. The goal of our work has been to educate and support our participants in this study in understanding the tenets of trauma-informed practice, to support their approaches to understanding student behavior and learning, and to improve their capacity to offer the appropriate supports and interventions students need to be successful.

PROGRAM BACKGROUND

Curriculum and Pedagogies Utilized to Integrate Trauma-Informed Practices

In the fall of 2018, three faculty members in a College of Education from a large university in the Southeastern United States, each from distinctive backgrounds (nursing, curriculum theory/social work, and secondary teacher preparation), came together over an interest in the emerging field of trauma-informed practice. When the project was initiated, it was suspected that many educators had not yet learned much about TIP in education. Our first goal was to develop a survey for area practicing teachers to assess the level of teachers' knowledge and understanding of trauma-informed practice. This survey (in an abbreviated form—see Appendix A) sought explicitly to determine what teachers observed or knew about adverse childhood experiences, identified the interventions they have used, and assessed their current knowledge of trauma-informed theory. The results of this survey informed a direction for this experience.

A total of 515 educators completed the electronic survey, indicating deep interest in this topic. The findings from this survey clearly indicated that there was a great need for professional development (PD) on trauma-informed practice and pedagogy. General findings from that study served to shape our work in this project: teachers feel unprepared to deal with the social and emotional issues faced by their students; educators perceive a rise in "traumatic events" facing our youth such as poverty; teachers are unaware of topics such as: ACES, culturally relevant and TIP pedagogies, symptoms, and triggers of trauma, and wrap- around services; and teachers desire PD and information helping students who have experienced trauma (Rahimi et al., 2021). The results from our study served to confirm earlier findings (Alisic et al., 2016; Blodgett & Dorodo, 2016; Conley et al., 2014; Dods, 2013; Kenny, 2004; Marquez-Flores et al., 2016; Reker, 2016; Thomas et al., 2019; Yoon, 2000) that support the need for PD to provide emotional and pedagogical support and resources for teachers in understanding TIP.

One of the participants in the original survey, who leads a team of BIs (behavioral interventionists) in the local school district, became a co-researcher on this project. Her role as director of specialized instruction helped generate the concept of connecting the BIs with much teaching experience to this current study and preservice teachers.

The BIs' role in the schools is primarily to provide coaching and support to P–12 teachers regarding classroom management, de-escalation of challenging behaviors, and implementation of social emotional learning (SEL). By participating in the study, we aimed for the BIs to gain greater knowledge of TIP helping them to educate and support teachers with whom they work in the schools. Bringing together BIs and TCs represented a collaborative opportunity for both groups of participants to focus on challenging classroom behaviors through TIP.

In the fall of 2019, we began the project which linked BIs working in an urban school district with TCs in their junior year as teacher candidates. The benefit to the teacher candidate was an opportunity for a unique and tailored PD experience as they had the opportunity to shadow and learn from BIs in public schools. The benefit for BIs was to gain new information regarding the framework of TIP for addressing their work with challenging students while also serving as mentors for the TCs.

PROJECT DESIGN, METHODOLOGY, AND DATA COLLECTION

Based upon findings from our initial survey of educators (see Appendix A), the planned activities for this project included a 10-week PD series consisting of weekly one hour PD sessions. We addressed topics related to TIP, SEL, and instructional practices.

The collaborative PD project entailed two phases. During the first phase the TCs, BIs, and the researchers for this project (district personnel and university faculty) met for one hour each week for six weeks to discuss TIP. Evidenced by their responses on a pre-assessment and through focus groups, the TCs and BIs held an emerging understanding regarding the basics of TIP and social-emotional learning (Gresham, 2017), the ACES and related studies (Alexander, 2019; Finkelhor et al., 2015; Kavanaugh, 2016; Trayser, 2016), and the essential characteristics of a trauma-informed school (Alexander, 2019; Finkelhor et al., 2015; Kavanaugh, 2016). The goal of the first phase was to ensure that all involved would develop enhanced knowledge and perspective of TIP and a repertoire of resources to aid with working in classroom settings with students who have experienced trauma.

Following this training, phase two engaged TCs in "shadowing" the BIs throughout the semester as they implemented TIP with teachers/students. The shadowing portion of the project was intended to provide the opportunity to debrief strategies and principles from the PD sessions through direct application of theory presented in a variety of P–12 grade levels.

We evaluated the effectiveness of the project through data collected via pre- and post-assessments with qualitative value (see Appendix B) and focus group interviews (see Appendix C). The interviews were transcribed and reviewed by the researchers. Using a content analysis approach the researchers looked for themes and coded the data accordingly. Participants were given an opportunity to "member check" (Patton, 2002) the results to assure the validity of the data.

FINDINGS, OUTCOMES, AND LESSONS LEARNED

Behavioral Interventionists

Their pre-assessment data and focus group responses indicated the BIs' had some understanding of ACES, some knowledge of chronic stressors and complex trauma (Herman, 1997) and some strategies for classroom teachers to consider addressing the needs of students who have experienced trauma. The data reviewed below represents the BIs' responses from the pre-assessment and the initial focus group. They reflect three categories: BIs working knowledge of trauma (pre-project), expectations for this professional development experience, and other insights into related experiences the BIs have encountered with TIP work in the schools.

The behavioral interventionists participating in this project revealed a spectrum of understanding. Their knowledge ranged from one BI who said, "I have not had any training or workshops on trauma and have just begun reading about it. I believe it affects and produces behaviors in young children that may look like other things such as autism," to a more complex understanding provided by another BI participant, such as, "Trauma can shape a child's understanding, decision making process and relationships throughout life, ultimately affecting adult life." The range was also evident when we asked the BIs to provide a general definition of trauma at the onset of this experience. The BIs articulated a range of understanding and perception of the concept of trauma as reflected in their general definitions. "Any adverse or significantly negative experience that changes the way a person thinks, functions, or behaves." Another offered, "Trauma is something that physically and emotionally impacts a child's success in life." A third BI offered, "Trauma as it relates to children involves an experience that left a negative impact. It could be direct or indirect.... Could involve the death of a loved one for example. Involves how the brain develops and changes." These early definitions provided us with insight into the BIs' knowledge, and we knew that they had already begun thinking of how trauma impacts children's lives.

The BIs noted that trauma affects different individuals in different ways, can manifest itself differently over time, and often influences children's experiences of the learning environment. One stated, "it affects the brain. Can affect behavior and learning, can get stuck in fight or flight mode."

Another noted that when trauma impacts the brain the "child's ability to understand/react to their surroundings" is affected. And a third contributed, "This may or may not interfere with their relationships, learning, emotional attachment, and physical development." These statements indicated they had basic definitions of trauma and a general understanding of the variety of ways that trauma affects children and adolescents coming into this project. The designers (and researchers) knew that throughout this experience we could leverage their understanding in working with the TCs to enhance the working knowledge they had currently on the topic.

Next, our initial data allowed us to note the BIs' expectations for PD. During this time, the BIs' responses highlighted hopes to learn new strategies and understand the preparation of preservice teachers. One BI noted, "Hopefully will learn some new strategies to share with my teachers. I would like to learn more about trauma and ways to help my teachers be successful with those students in their classrooms." The project designers were excited by this response as we were hoping to focus largely on strategies and approaches to help classroom teachers specifically. Another BI with similar interest remarked, "It may change my approach in working with classroom teachers in terms of modeling how to implement and use various strategies and interventions. I am very interested and excited to expand my knowledge of trauma-informed schools, the ACEs study and brain development." Others remarked on wanting to learn more about TIP and "newer interventions" to "bring back into our teachers and students."

It was also interesting to see the interest the BIs had in working directly with preservice teachers in a collaborative capacity. One BI noted, "They [preservice TCs] may have fresh ideas from their classes in education and classroom management is fluid over time. They will be critical in creating a community of teachers who understand the connection between trauma and behavior in children." Another noted, "I hope to learn more about current methods of classroom management compared to what I know as a special educator. I look forward to learning from them and gaining understanding of how new teachers are trained … I would like to improve my skills as a mentor." One of the BI participants articulated the possible reciprocal benefit of pairing seasoned professionals with preservice teachers. "It will be a good way for the teacher candidate to gain experience and learn techniques as it relates to classroom management. It will also give a fresh outlook for us to learn their thoughts and ideas." We were encouraged at the outset by the positive approach taken by this group working with this model.

The focus group also allowed participants to engage in more general discussion regarding their work with students and teachers of students who have experienced adverse experiences. During their discussion a few significant points emerged. First, one BI noted, "Sometimes I just get so overwhelmed. I don't even know where to start. It's so bad." The BIs noted that the variety of roles in the school generates independent silos of operations where teachers operate separately from counselors and social workers, whereas administrators (and some teachers) approach schools from an "academics first" perspective. One BI noted, "school is focused on academics, but the students are not prepared because of trauma." The BIs also said that this focus on academics-first can blind personnel to the trauma that students experience in their day-to-day lives. According to one of the BIs:

> I offered to do a training with a—one of my schools, and she's [the administrator] like, "They don't have trauma. They're fine." I'm like, "Okay. Well, this young man just saw his stepdad shot six times, and this one's going through this, and this one's going through this," but they don't even see the relevance of it. They're like, "No, we don't need trauma training."

Overall, this freeform discussion revealed frustrations among the BIs over the disconnects they observe between teachers and administrators whose focus on "academics first." This was expressed succinctly by one BI who stated, "We need trauma strategies, not classroom management." As part of the curriculum for this project, we added a segment on trauma-informed schools to help the BIs advocate for more school-wide approaches to TIP.

Findings from post assessments indicated that the BIs gained some new insight and ideas for working with classroom teachers who may have traumatized students. One area that was noted was an increased knowledge of brain-based learning. One BI noted, "you're teaching to the brain and brains are different and need a varied amount of input. Another added, "That's what stood out to me, the fact that the brain can change and what an impact trauma has on that and how important it is that we learn how to teach those babies." Another BI contributed, "also about recovery and the aspects of the brain and how consistent interactions can have positive impact on re-programming the brain." A second noted area of growth was an increased knowledge of adverse childhood experiences and the impact of trauma on behavior and mental health. One BI noted, "It doesn't take a lot. It adds up so quickly. I think the society and the societal aspects of kids today in their lives, it's just different. I think they check off a lot of boxes [ACEs] fast. That's what you're dealing with. It explains where her anxiety comes from…. She (one of her students) truly has boxes checked there."

We also noted an improved understanding of the importance of SEL and mindfulness, "it should be a priority because those of us who know behavior know that you're not gonna get anywhere else if that's not taken care of first, and that academics is important, but that [social emotional learning] should come first." Another BI added, "It helps the administrators too …

with the social-emotional learning curriculum.... It's amazing, no fights [in the school] ... It makes a difference when they see that it's making a difference." One BI noted, "It's hard to relax in a room full of people when you're thinking about some of the things that come into your mind while you're trying. Cause some of the traumatic things or the upsetting things come to you." Another BI added, "Some people can't be left—they can't be left alone with their own silence." One BI commented:

> I taught some mindfulness techniques. Now, there are two teachers—and only two—who have mindfulness classrooms this year. They've done their light. They've got the infusers. They do the mindfulness in between transitions. They take that time and that effort. They're putting into place, and it has been life changing for those two teachers. They said their classroom is—it's completely different.

Finally, the BIs expressed increased comfort and interest in utilizing TIP in their work with teachers in the schools. When asked, *how prepared do you feel about utilizing trauma-informed practices in your work with classroom teachers?* one BI responded, "We can always learn more. I want and need more. I think all of us do. This is my first experience with any of it, but I definitely will seek more opportunities." "There's a lot of stuff that the counselors were told that never gets to the teacher that works with that kid every single day. A lot of it they can't, but a lot of it is trauma," noted one BI. "It's important to know that know that this child does have extreme trauma," added another BI. "This is what you need to do. Can't tell you what the trauma is, but this is what you need to do," added a third BI. One BI pointed out that TIP has many benefits for their work, "Cause once you have some knowledge, it makes you more empathetic, more compassionate."

One BI also suggested that during our in-class sessions, it would be helpful to have opportunities to work through "scenarios to work through the implementation of the potential strategies." Content had relied on the shadowing to provide that theory-practice connection. Overall, the BIs felt that it was worth their time in enhancing their knowledge and understanding of TIP.

Additionally, the BIs indicated that developing relationships between preservice teachers and BIs was in-itself a substantial outcome of the experience. The BIs noted that when they were shadowed, it was a "great experience." One BI remarked on her work with the teacher candidate in the field, "One of the [teacher] candidates, she did come to part of a mindset training in the field one day, which was great. She got to see and hear some of that. I love that." We recognize more in-depth shadowing would have enhanced the project a great deal, as the BIs noted how beneficial their experience with the TCs was.

Teacher Candidates

The three teacher candidates who participated in this voluntary professional development project were in their junior year preparing to become secondary teachers. Each of these participants expressed enthusiasm for learning about trauma-informed practice and adding to their knowledge base as they are preparing to become professional educators. Prior to the series, we interviewed the TCs to gauge their understanding of trauma-informed practices. Not surprisingly, they had some vague notions of trauma.

Based on the TCs pre-assessments and focus group responses, they started this experience with little to no knowledge of ACES, trauma and its impact on student learning, behavior, and performance.

We asked what they hoped to gain from the experience. The TCs expressed strong interest in shadowing the behavioral interventionists and, as one TC said, I would like to "walk away with strategies and resources that inform my own decisions . . . strategies to help with students who have been traumatized." Another TC shared hopes to learn about the role BI had in the classroom, working with the teacher, and helping traumatized students adjust. The TCs were enthusiastic and curious during the in-class meetings. They used discussion time to ask pointed questions of the behavioral interventionists regarding challenging behaviors they work with in the schools and how the course material (TIP) informed that work.

In a focus group conducted with the TCs following the project, we asked the TCs about their perceptions of the experience and their current level of knowledge of trauma-informed practice. They responded that they had heightened self-awareness of trauma. One TC noted, "I've always been a very empathetic person," and now when someone behaves in an antisocial way, she finds herself drawn to the question, "Why would that person have done that?" This TC noted the PD series alerted her to her ability to "de-escalate without having to add fuel to the fire." In one of our sessions this same TC shared she had observed a clinical supervisor (classroom teacher) to whom she previously was assigned aggravate tense situations with students through his authoritarian response. She noted that she now views teachers' behaviors and classroom environment as a potential source of stress for traumatized students. As the TCs reflected on what they learned, common themes emerged, including how they plan to respond differently to traumatic experiences, how trauma-informed practice is an extension of what they have learned about classroom management, and the advantages of being proactive in establishing a welcoming environment. The work with the BIs helped the candidates to reframe some of what they were observing. For instance, one TC shared her experience in another classroom where the classroom teacher responded to students falling asleep by banging a tambourine over their heads. "At first, I thought it was funny, but now I don't think it's funny at all." This TC reported that this professional development project led her to ask herself, "What is going on in his house? Why is this kid so tired all the time?" and "How can I work to not re-traumatize them?" We are hopeful that the TCs will take this newfound knowledge to build on as they matriculate throughout their program and into their professional practice.

Rarely do TCs have opportunities to interact with professional behavioral interventionists in the schools. The teacher candidates appreciated the practical examples and real-life situations that the BIs brought to this experience. One TC reflected, "It's different hearing someone actually doing it." The discussions that took place between the respective groups relating to how trauma from adverse childhood experiences manifests itself in classrooms was important in demonstrating the need and the promise of TIP.

IMPLICATIONS OF THE WORK AND PLANS TO CONTINUE DEVELOPING AND ENHANCING THIS WORK

As was revealed through this study, providing a PD experience for teacher candidates focusing on TIP can have impact their understanding of school and classroom practices, the principles of TIP, related approaches, and working through a TIP lens in their classrooms. Further, such a model provides TCs with direct access to educational professionals who work with some of the most challenging behaviors presented in schools and their application of TIP through this work. We hope that TCs benefit from this project in the long term, having emerging knowledge of school and local resources and developing relationships with local BIs which will allow these TCs to graduate from their teacher education program prepared to identify support resources and work collaboratively with a team at the outset of their professional practice. An area for future study will be whether such preparation assists with teacher retention, since it reduces the surprise, many new teachers experience when encountering challenging behaviors in the classroom (Dorado et al., 2016; Spooner et al., 2008).

This project has already served to provide practical implications. First, because of this work, we organized the first Trauma-informed Educational Symposium (TIES) in the summer of 2020 for teachers in the local, urban school district. Even amid the 2020 COVID-19 pandemic, over 100 teachers attended the virtual event. Professionals from the fields of juvenile justice, mental health, medicine, and social work provided presentations related to TIP. Second, as a direct result of this project, the BIs are now reconceptualizing their work to encapsulate a trauma-informed focus.

Their work should serve to provide a great scope of understanding of this pedagogical approach throughout the large, urban school district.

The researchers are continuing to develop TIP projects in the local school districts. This project has contributed to the implementation and support of TIP in teacher education programs and more collaborative PD opportunities. The insights provided in this chapter provide guidelines that may help other institutions and school districts develop collaborative PD opportunities.

REFERENCES

Alexander, J. (2019). *Building trauma-sensitive schools.* Paul H. Brookes Publishing.

Alisic, E., Boeije, H. R., Jongmans, M. J., & Kleber, R. J. (2012). Supporting children after single-incident trauma: Parents' views. *Clinical Pediatrics, 51*(3), 274–282. https://doi.org/10.1177/0009922811423309

Amaro, H., Chernoff, M., Brown, V., Arevalo, S., & Gatz, M. (2007). Does integrated trauma-informed substance abuse treatment increase treatment retention? *Journal of Community Psychology, 35,* 845–862. https://doi:10.1002/jcop.20185

Azeem, M. W., Aujla, A., Rammerth, M., Binsfeld, G., & Jones, R. B. (2011). Effectiveness of six core strategies based on trauma-informed care in reducing seclusions and restraints at a child and adolescent psychiatric hospital. *Journal of Child and Adolescent Psychiatric Nursing, 24*(1), 11–15. https://doi: 10.1111/j.1744-6171.2010.00262.x

Berman, S., Chaffee, S., & Sarmiento, J., (2018). *The practice base for how we learn: Supporting students' social, emotional, and academic development.* The Aspen Institute.

Blaustein, M., & Kinniburgh, K. M. (2010). *Treating traumatic stress in children and adolescents: How to foster resilience through attachment, self-regulation, and competency.* Guilford Press.

Blodgett, C. (2013). *Rising out of risk: Understanding the real time risk and response to ACEs in children.* http://www.courts.ca.gov/documents/A3_IT_TAKES_A_Community_Blodgett.pdf

Blodgett, C., & Dorado, J. (2016). *A selected review of trauma-informed school practice and alignment with educational practice.* Washington State University Extension, Child and Family Research Unit.

Burke, N., Hellman J., Scott, B., Weems, C., & Carrion, V. (2011). The impact of adverse childhood experiences on an urban pediatric population. *Child Abuse & Neglect, 35*(6), 408–413. http://doi:10.1016/j.chiabu.2011.02.006

Centers for Disease Control and Prevention. (2019). *Preventing adverse childhood experiences: Leveraging the best available evidence.* National Center for Injury Prevention and Control, Centers for Disease Control and Prevention.

Cole, S., Greenwald, J., Gadd, M. G., Ristuccia, J., Wallace, D. L., & Gregory, M. (2009). *Helping traumatized children learn: Supporting school environments for children traumatized by family violence.* Massachusetts Advocates for Children.

Cole, S., Eisner, A., Gregory, M., & Ristuccia, J. (2013). *Helping taumatized children learn: Creating and advocating for trauma sensitive schools*. Massachusetts Advocates for Children.

Conley, L., Marchant, M., & Caldarella, P. (2014). A comparison of teacher perceptions and research-based categories of student behavior difficulties. *Education, 134*, 439–451.

Craig, S. E. (2016). *Trauma sensitive schools: Learning communities transforming children's lives, K–5*. Teachers College Press.

Delaney-Black, V., Covington, C., Ondersma, S. J., Nordstrom-Klee, B., Templin, T., Ager, J., Janisse, J., & Sokol, R. J. (2002). Violence exposure, trauma, and IQ and/or reading deficits among urban children. *Archives of Pediatrics & Adolescent Medicine, 156*(3), 280–285. https://doi.org/10.1001/archpedi.156.3.280

Dods, J. (2013). Enhancing understanding of the nature of supportive school-based relationships for youth who have experienced trauma. *Canadian Journal of Education/Revue Canadienne de l'éducation, 36*(1), 71–95.

Dorado, J., Martinez, M., McArthur, L., & Lebovitz, T. (2016). Healthy environments and response to schools: A whole school multilevel prevention and intervention program for creating trauma informed, safe and supportive schools. *School Mental Health, 8*(1), 163–176.

Eismann, G., Edonns, S., & Cushman, C. (2012). Bringing reality to classroom management in teacher education. *The Professional Educator, 39*(1), 1–12.

Finkelhor, D., Shattuck, A., Turner, H., & Hamby, S. (2015). A revised inventory of adverse childhood experiences. *Child Abuse & Neglect, 48*, 13–21.

Gay, G. (2010). *Culturally responsive teaching* (2nd ed.). Teachers College Press.

Gresham, F. (2017). *Effective interventions for social-emotional learning*. Guilford Press.

Herman, J. (1997). *Trauma and recovery: The aftermath of violence from domestic abuse to political terror*. Basic Books.

Huntington, N., Jahn Moses, D., & Veysey, B. M. (2005). Developing and implementing a comprehensive approach to serving women with co-occurring disorders and of trauma. *Journal of Community Psychology, 33*(4), 395–410. https://doi.org/10.1002/jcop.20059

Jones, S., & Kahn, J. (2017). The evidence base for how learning happens: A consensus on social, emotional, and academic development. *American Educator, 41*(4), 16–23.

Kavanaugh, B. (2016). Trauma informed classrooms and schools. *Beyond Behavior, 25*(2), 41–26.

Kenny, M. (2004). Teachers' attitudes toward and knowledge of child maltreatment. *Child Abuse & Neglect, 28*, 1311–1319.

Ladson-Billings, G. (1995). Toward a theory of culturally relevant pedagogy. *American Educational Research Journal, 32*(3), 465–491. http://lmcreadinglist.pbworks.com/f/Ladson-Billings%20%281995%29.pdf

Ladson-Billings, G. (2014). Culturally relevant teaching 2.0 a.k.a the remix. *Harvard Educational Review, 84*, 74–84. http://piggottsclass.weebly.com/uploads/2/3/1/7/23179512/ladson-billings_culturally_relevant_pedagogy.pdf

Marquez-Flores, M., Marquez-Herndandez, V., & Granados-Gamez, G. (2016). Teachers' knowledge and beliefs about child sexual abuse. *Journal of Child Sexual Abuse, 25*(5), 538–555.

McCormack, A. (2001). The impact of an internship on the classroom management beliefs of preservice teachers. *The Professional Educator, 23*(2), 11–22.

Meyers, L. H., & Evan, I. M. (2012). *The teacher's guide to restorative classroom discipline.* Corwin.

Olson, K. (2014). *The invisible classroom: Relationships, neuroscience, and mindfulness in school.* Norton.

Patton, M. (2002). *Qualitative research and evaluation methods.* SAGE.

Perry, B. D. (2014). *The cost of caring: Secondary traumatic stress and the impact of working with high-risk children and families.* https://doi.org/10.1007/s12310-016-9175-2

Pechtel, P., & Pizzagalli, D. (2011) Effects of early life stress on cognitive and affective function: An integrated review of human literature. *Psychopharmacology, 214*(1), 55–70. https://doi:10.1007/s00213-010-2009-2

Rahimi, R., Liston, D., Adkins, A., & Nourez, J. (2021). Teacher awareness of trauma informed practice: Raising awareness in Southeast Georgia. *Georgia Educational Research Journal, 18*(2), 1.

Reker, K. (2016). *Trauma in the classroom: Teachers' perspectives on supporting students experiencing child traumatic stress* [Doctoral dissertation, Loyola University Chicago]. https://ecommons.luc.edu/luc_diss/2146

Rivard, J., Bloom, S., McCorkle, D., & Abramovitz, R. (2005). Preliminary results of a study examining the implementation and effects of a trauma recovery framework for youths in a residential treatment program. *Therapeutic Community: The International Journal for Therapeutic and Supportive Organizations, 26*(1), 83–96.

Spooner, M., Flowers, C., Lambert, R., & Algozzine, B. (2008). Is more really better? Examining perceived benefits of an extended student teaching experience. *The Clearing House, 81*(6), 263–270.

Streeck-Fischer, A., & van der Kolk, A. (2000). Down will come baby, cradle and all: Diagnostic and therapeutic implications of chronic trauma on child development. *Australian and New Zealand Journal of Psychiatry, 34*(6), 903–918.

Stevens, J. E. (2012). *Lincoln High School in Walla Walla, WA, tries new approach to school discipline—Suspensions drop 85%.* ACEs Too High. http://acestoohigh.com/2012/04/23/Iincoln-high-schooI-in-waIla-walia-wa-tries-new-approach-to-school-discipline-expulsions-drop-85/

Teasley, M. L. (2014). *Shifting from zero tolerance to restorative justice in schools. Children and Schools, 36*(3), 131–133.

Thomas, M. S., Crosby, S., & Vanderhaar, J. (2019). Trauma-informed practices in schools across two decades: An interdisciplinary review of research. *Review of Research in Education, 43*(1), 422–452. https://doi.org/10.3102/0091732X18821123

Thorsborne, M., & Blood, P. (2013). *Implementing restorative practices in schools: A practical guide to transforming school communities.* Jessica Kingsley.

Trayser, J. (2016). *The ACEs revolution: The impact of adverse childhood experiences.* Creating Space Independent Publishing Platform.

van der Kolk, B. (2014). *The body keeps the score.* Penguin.

Yoon, J. S. (2002). Teacher characteristics as predictors of teacher–student relationships: Stress, negative affect, and self-efficacy. *Social Behavior and Personality: An International Journal, 30(5),* 485–494.

APPENDIX A

Initial Survey (Abbreviated)

Participants were asked about their knowledge of and/or experience with students experiencing the following and their approach to and success with addressing the needs of the students.

Other questions related to their approaches to classroom management, and so forth.

APPENDIX B

Project Pre/Post Assessments

Trauma-Informed Pedagogy and Classroom Management: Pre-Assessment Survey

Teacher Candidates/Behavioral Interventionists

- What is your major? How long have you been teaching/serving as a behavioral interventionist?
- What is your understanding of "trauma" as it relates to childhood/adolescence?
- Have you ever read or studied any material related to the impact of childhood trauma on brain development?
- Have you ever read or studied any material related to the impact of childhood trauma on learning abilities?
- Have you ever heard of trauma-informed pedagogy?
- How would you define trauma-informed pedagogy? What would you say/think are the tenets or characteristics of this concept?
- Have you participated in professional development outside of your course of study as an education major?
- What do you know about theories of classroom management?
- What is your perceived approach to classroom management?
- Do you believe that understanding trauma-informed pedagogy may impact your understanding of classroom management? In what way(s)?

- What would you classify as "challenging classroom behaviors
  What is your perception of your preparedness in working with
  challenging classroom behaviors?
- How do you think the experience of working directly with behavioral interventionists/teacher candidates may impact your
  approach to classroom management?
- What do you hope to gain from this professional development
  experience?

Answer the following, without referencing any material:

1. Physiological changes to children's brains as well as emotional
   and behavioral responses to trauma have the potential to
   interfere with:

   A. School engagement, Children's learning & Academic
      success
   B. Physical development
   C. Cognitive and Social delays
   D. A & C only
   E. A, B, & C

2. Trauma experienced during childhood can have long lasting
   effects including elevated risk of mental and physical health
   problems, substance abuse, and criminal justice involvement in
   childhood and adulthood.

   A. True
   B. False

3. Which of the following is not considered to be an adverse
   childhood experience?

   A. Living in a household with a family member who is mentally
      ill
   B. Experiencing violence against one's mother
   C. Being suspended from school during elementary years
   D. Living with a family member who has been incarcerated

4. A student is frequently complaining about stomach pains
   and headaches in class and is frequently absent. Which of the
   following responses is trauma-informed?

A. The school nurse talks with the student's teacher and family and refers the child to outside services, as well as emphasizing the importance of feeling safe at school.
B. The student's teacher provides the student with breaks or a pass to see the nurse when she makes a complaint. The nurse lets the student rest before returning to class.
C. The child is referred to the school counselor to participate in social skills groups.
D. A social worker referral is made.

5. Identify the true statement regarding children who have experienced trauma:

   A. Children can be re-traumatized if they receive consequences for their behavior
   B. Punishment reduces behavioral problems
   C. Punitive measures after a violation can cause behavioral problems to be compounded

6. Children who have experienced trauma do not find it more challenging than their peers to pay attention.

   A. True
   B. False

7. Children who have been exposed to violence:

   A. Have difficulty responding to social cues or withdraw from social situations
   B. Bully others & are more aggressive
   C. Cannot form meaningful relationships
   D. A & B
   E. B & C
   F. A & C
   G. A, B, & C

8. Childhood maltreatment can reduce the size of several regions of the brain.

   A. True
   B. False

9. Children and adolescents in urban environments experience higher rates of exposure to violence.

   A. True
   B. False

10. What could be a symptom of children who have experienced trauma?

    A. Hyperactivity
    B. Delayed speech
    C. Changes in behavior
    D. Sensory sensitivity

11. Do you have any professional development experience regarding trauma?

    A. Only college level coursework
    B. Only trainings, conferences, or workshops
    C. Both college coursework and trainings, conferences, and workshops
    D. No professional development experience with trauma

12. How many educational texts, nonfiction books or journal articles have you read about trauma?

    A. 0
    B. 1–4
    C. 5–10
    D. 11–20
    E. More than 20

13. How often do you see public service announcements about trauma or mental health?

    A. Very rarely / almost never
    B. A few times a year
    C. Monthly
    D. Weekly
    E. Daily

14. How often do you read/watch a news story about trauma?

    A. Very rarely/almost never

    B. A few times a year
    C. Monthly
    D. Weekly
    E. Daily

APPENDIX C

Pre/Post Focus Group Questions

Focus Group Questions for Teacher Candidates

1. What is your current understanding/knowledge of the following topics?

    A. Brain-based learning
    B. ACES study
    C. De-escalation techniques
    D. Mindfulness
    E. Social-emotional learning
    F. Classroom management techniques
    G. Childhood poverty
    H. Childhood trauma

1. Given what you may already know about trauma-informed pedagogy, what information would you like to learn about this topic?

2. How comfortable are you hearing about topics related to trauma and childhood and adolescence in the context of learning?

3. What concerns you about this topic particularly?

4. How comfortable are you working collaboratively with a group of professional behavioral interventionists as they are learning about this topic too?

5. How comfortable are you in shadowing behavioral interventionists as they work with teachers in helping with challenging behavioral issues?

6. How prepared do you feel to work with challenging behavioral issues?

7. What concerns you about working in middle and high school settings?

8. How prepared do you feel about your classroom management techniques?

9. What do you hope to gain from this experience this term?

Focus Group Questions for Behavioral Interventionists

1. What is your current understanding/knowledge of the following topics?

    A. Brain-Based Learning
    B. ACES study
    C. De-escalation techniques
    D. Mindfulness
    E. Social-emotional learning
    F. Classroom management techniques
    G. Childhood poverty
    H. Childhood trauma

2. Given what you may already know about trauma-informed pedagogy, what information would you like to learn about this topic?

3. How comfortable are you hearing about topics related to trauma and childhood and adolescence in the context of learning?

4. What concerns you about this topic particularly?

5. How comfortable are you working collaboratively with a group of teacher candidates as they are learning about this topic too?

6. How comfortable are you in participating in the shadowing experience this semester?

7. How prepared do you feel to work with challenging behavioral issues?

8. What concerns you about working in middle and high school settings?

9. How prepared do you feel about your classroom management techniques?

10. What are the largest issues you have observed related to classroom management and new teachers?

11. How might training on trauma-informed practices help new teachers?

12. What do you hope to gain from this experience this term?

CHAPTER 9

MODELING TRAUMA-SENSITIVE CLASSROOM PRACTICES WITH PRESERVICE TEACHERS TO DEVELOP MENTAL HEALTH RESPONSIVENESS SKILLS

Linda K. Reece
University of North Georgia

ABSTRACT

Guiding principles in most teacher preparation programs include providing teacher candidates with meaningful classroom instruction in relevant content/academic areas that is paired with authentic, practical classroom experience under the mentorship of accomplished teachers. Over the past few decades, teacher preparation programs (TPP) broadened the scope of requisite teacher pedagogy to include competence and critical understandings in the areas of diversity—including language, culture, ableism, and sexual orientation—in order to more effectively meet the needs of all children in their classrooms. At the same time, statistics on mental illness and suicide rates of adolescents show dramatic increases, with exponentially rising rates due to remote learning and isolation during COVID. Very few TPPs require graduates to complete training, coursework, or field experiences in the area

Developing Trauma-Informed Teachers: Creating Classrooms That Foster Equity, Resiliency, and Asset-Based Approaches: Research Findings From the Field, pp. 149–168
Copyright © 2023 by Information Age Publishing
www.infoagepub.com

of mental health responsiveness. Teachers are often hesitant to reach out to students who may be experiencing mental illness, some teachers are unaware of the signs of mental illness, and some teachers are struggling to manage their own mental wellness or mental health issues. Mental Health Toolkit Training (Mental Health First Aid) workshops with pre-education students as part of a University-High School partnership provided these future teachers with the skills to respond to the mental health needs of their students. The training was also a starting point for these future teachers to become more aware of their own mental health and to advocate for increased mental health awareness with the creation of Mindfulness Spaces for self-care on campus.

Almost 25% of young people aged 11–17 report experiencing at least one depressive episode or anxiety attack significant enough to interfere with academic progress and personal relationships (Diaz et al., 2019; Jorm et al., 2010; Werner-Seidler et al., 2017). The National Child Traumatic Stress Network reported 52.5% of children *aged 2–5* had already experienced severe stressors as reported by caretakers and health services personnel (Banks & Meyer, 2017). According to the U.S. Centers for Disease Control and Prevention (CDC, 2019), suicide has become the second leading cause of death for children aged 14–17. Mental illness statistics vary by ethnicity and socioeconomic levels, as do the availability of support services. For example, Latinx students aged 11–17 report experiencing depression and anxiety at higher rates than do their white peers; at the same time, Latinx students are less likely to seek out mental health services than are their white peers. The reasons include a culturally based resistance in acknowledging mental illness as well as having less information about or access to available mental health resources (Dixon de Silva et al., 2020; Venta et al., 2019). Recent immigrants to the United States, often fleeing conflict or traumatic events in their home nations, are also more vulnerable to mental health issues at the same time they are also likely to have less access to and financial means for mental health services (Venta et al., 2019). In addition, numbers of students across all demographics reporting anxiety and depression due to social isolation during COVID remote learning have spiked in the past nine months (Sparks, 2020). CDC data showed mental health related emergency room visits between March and October 2020, among children aged 5–11 rose 25%; visits for children aged 12–17 rose 31% (CDC, 2020; Sparks, 2020).

Direct instruction and opening dialogue on mental health awareness and self-care practices delivered through health classes and curricula is one way to address mental health with school-aged students (Howard, 2019; Jorm et al., 2010). States mandating some form of mental health awareness and education in middle and secondary health curriculum standards report lower statistics with regard to suicide than states without specific mental health policies in place (Spera & Monnet, 2020; Stratford et al.,

2020). The goal for mental health curricula is to inform students about mental illness and to talk with them about available resources (Diaz et al., 2019).

While most classroom teachers feel prepared to talk about mental health as an academic standard, far fewer teachers feel comfortable approaching individual students experiencing mental health and/or substance abuse issues (Ball et al., 2016). Training teachers as "mental health first responders" that is, preparing them to recognize the signs of mental illness, respond appropriately, and connect students safely with the appropriate help, is now offered as professional learning in many U.S. school systems (Becker-Blease, 2017; Jorm et al., 2010; Osayande et al., 2018). Unfortunately, mental health awareness and responsiveness training do not currently exist in national teacher certification standards (Brown et al., 2019; Council for the Accreditation of Educator Preparation, 2013).

All teacher preparation programs (TPP) at a regional institution of higher education (IHE) in Georgia currently follow a Professional Development School (PDS) model with teacher candidates completing immersive field experiences to effectively meet the needs of children from diverse linguistic, cultural, socioeconomic, and academic backgrounds (Reece & Nodine, 2014; Reece et al., 2016). Because of the purposeful focus on inclusivity and diversity in teacher education that is a central component with Professional Development School partnerships, adding mental health responsiveness training would likely be welcomed by K–12 PDS partners.

There currently exists no training, coursework, or field-related experience in mental health for teacher certification in Georgia (Georgia Professional Standards Commission, 2016); therefore, the 2019 collaboration between this IHE and a local high school providing mental health training was a first for university students and faculty. Mental health training and field experiences occurred at The HUB, a wraparound service program for student mental health support located on site at an ethnically diverse high school, where 86% of students qualify for free and reduced lunches (Georgia Department of Education, 2020). Services available through The HUB include academic support (tutoring); basic care needs (a clothing boutique, washers and dryers, and a food pantry); mental health services (professional counselors and social workers providing counseling sessions on site); small group discussions on student selected topics; and college application and admissions support. Pre-education students who participated in the mental health training and subsequently mentored high school students requested in class debriefing time to share their own experiences with mental illnesses including anxiety and depression. These students wanted to read more, talk more, and learn more to understand their own mental health needs and the needs of students they will be teaching. Their desire to connect mental health responsiveness with trauma-sensitive classroom practices led to course modifications based on Harris and Fallot's (2001) *Five Principles of Trauma-Informed Practice*—safety, trust, choice, collaboration, and empowerment. Conversations and readings on topics such as classroom management, testing, and communication with parents were processed through a trauma-sensitive lens. This chapter will explore how mental health responsiveness training and trauma sensitive-classroom skills are developed by pre-education students in an educational psychology course.

HISTORY OF TRAUMA-INFORMED PRACTICE (TIP) AND DEFINITION OF TERMS

Trauma is defined by the American Psychological Association (2015) as "an emotional response to a terrible event like an accident, rape or natural disaster. Immediately after the event, shock and denial are typical. Longer term reactions include unpredictable emotions, flashbacks, strained relationships and even physical symptoms like headaches or nausea" (p. 6). This definition includes individual experiences (abuse, neglect, exposure to violence), community-based experiences (high crime rates, isolation in unsafe neighborhoods), or even national events (United States following 9/11). Over the past two decades, human services systems have developed protocols based in research on the effects of trauma as well as best practices for guiding clients with trauma and/or ACEs (adverse childhood effects). This is known as *trauma-informed practice* (Courtois, 2002; Courtois & Gold, 2009; Fallot & Harris, 2009; Harris & Fallot, 2001).

Trauma-informed practice (TIP) has been adapted from its original design for mental health/trauma recovery work in a clinical, therapeutic setting (Fallot & Harris, 2009; Hanson & Lang, 2016) for use by teachers, counselors, and administrators in school settings (Brunzell et al., 2016; Cavanaugh, 2016; Courtois & Gold, 2009; Jennings, 2019). Harris and Fallot (2001) define *trauma informed* as first understanding "ways in which violence, victimization, and other traumatic experiences have impacted the lives of individuals" (as cited in Carello & Butler, 2015, p. 264) and subsequently implementing responsive practices in the clinical or educational setting (therapy, hospital, school) that support the needs of the individual and promote emotional wellbeing and healing. Most K–12 school professionals interacting with students on a daily basis are not mental health clinicians; rather they are teachers, support staff, guidance counselors, and administrators. The research and application of trauma-informed practices in this chapter is intended to instruct front-line education personnel—teachers, administrators, and staff—on responsiveness techniques that will increase student success and minimize the potential for re-traumatizing children who have experienced ACEs.

Trauma sensitive refers to teachers and other school professionals who have had training in mental health responsiveness and understand the complex and often challenging needs of the students in their classes who have experienced or are experiencing trauma (Harris & Fallot, 2001; Jennings, 2019; Mental Health First Aid, 2018). In public schools, most teachers already provide a level of emotional and academic support for struggling students. Creating trauma-sensitive classrooms may be seen as a natural extension of the emotional and academic support teachers provide on a daily basis (Brown et al., 2019).

Trauma-sensitive classrooms (and schools) require a commitment to creating safe spaces for students with increased responsiveness in managing the classroom environment to maximize inclusivity and prosocial support (Armstrong et al., 2015; Cavanaugh, 2016; Fallot & Harris, 2009; Glasper, 2020; Jennings, 2019; Keyes, 2002). In this chapter, *trauma sensitive* refers to specific beliefs and practices teachers and administrators use in creating safe classrooms where all students may thrive. The terms *trauma-informed practice* and *trauma-informed pedagog*y may be used interchangeably to unpack research findings across academic settings (counseling, schooling, alternative education settings). While there also may be overlap with the above terms and *trauma sensitive*, the latter will be used in direct reference to classroom practices. Use of Harris and Fallot's (2001) model for incorporating trauma-sensitive classroom activities and practices in EDUC 2130 was a good fit as the model's *5 Principles for Trauma-Informed Practice* (safety, trustworthiness, choice, collaboration, and empowerment) align with research-based best practices for teaching that foster inclusivity (Banks, 2002); relational caring (Noddings, 2013); and responsive classrooms where students are actively engaged in the learning process (Slavin, 2018).

SAFETY IN TRAUMA-SENSITIVE CLASSROOMS

Trauma creates a disruption in the child's sense of time, and memories of a traumatic event may come flooding back to the child, often at unexpected times (Shalka, 2015). Teachers informed about trauma a student has experienced may be inclined to think, "Well, I'll give her a little time and she'll be back to normal soon." Much of that statement is concerning and inaccurate as trauma survivors' progress is seldom linear. Well-intentioned teachers may inadvertently add pressure to students with trauma by indicating they should be "feeling better by now because." In contrast, teachers who create trauma-sensitive classrooms understand that each child's experience with trauma is different, just as each student's academic strengths and needs may be different. Joshua may startle at loud noises as a result of witnessing a shooting; Jose may not be comfortable with adults who stand close to him or touch him as a result of physical abuse; and Claire may "freeze" when the teacher asks students to pick partners as her recent trauma has left her overwhelmed and unable to participate socially. All three students have experienced trauma and all three display different trauma responses in school and classroom settings. While teachers are not expected to address issues of trauma as clinicians would, understanding the connection between emotional dysregulation and acting out behaviors among children who have experienced trauma is essential for teachers interested in establishing classroom culture that minimizes the potential for re-triggering students.

Self-regulation (e.g., the ability of one to regulate their impulses) is an essential requisite skill for children to be able to learn in order to function in the classroom. Emotional regulation allows children to handle events and situations that might cause emotional arousal. Children who develop emotional regulation are able to recognize that a situation is emotional—for example, a third grader experiences a best friend moving away. The child is able to express feelings and emotions about the loss of a best friend (sadness, anger, loneliness). And, finally, the child is able to manage their thoughts and feelings and 'regulate' the emotions they feel (e.g., the child expresses emotion while functioning in school or home/social settings). (Gupta & Gehlawat, 2020). Children with ACEs often struggle with emotional self-regulation and easily become dysregulated (e.g., unable to respond in typical or expected ways; unable to regulate impulses) (Brunzell et al., 2016; Thomason et al., 2015). In the classroom, dysregulated children may yell loudly or cover their ears when classroom noise level is too high for them; they may lash out at a classmate who accidently bumps into them; or they may erupt in tears for seemingly no reason. Trauma-sensitive classrooms provide structure and repetition which helps children who are easily dysregulated. Unpredictability is anxiety provoking for children who struggle with regulation. Teachers must understand how perceived "acting out" behavior is actually emotional dysregulation; creating predictability and structure is the first step in providing a trauma sensitive setting to support children who need support in developing emotional regulation skills. Research demonstrates "strategies and new skills must be consolidated, rehearsed, and practiced in a sequential manner" for dysregulated students to become more secure (Brunzell et al., 2016, p. 83).

Teachers create trauma-sensitive classrooms by practicing all forms of safety. While schools require regular fire drills, active shooter drills (unfortunately), and tornado drills, interpersonal and intrapersonal safety are often overlooked with regard to systematic instruction, modeling, and practice. For example, bullying, defined as "the use of force, coercion, or threat, to abuse, aggressively dominate or intimidate"—often occurs on a regular basis. Cunningham et al. (2019) reported almost one third of school aged children indicated having been the victim of bullying behavior, while over ten percent of school aged children admitted bullying classmates. The examples of Joshua, Jose, and Claire and their trauma responses unfortunately make them more vulnerable to bullying (Harris & Fallot, 2001). Research shows that children with post-traumatic stress disorder (PTSD) are more vulnerable to triggers that may re-traumatize them and they are more likely to be bullied (Cunningham et al., 2019).

To ensure classroom safety measures that encompass interpersonal safety, teachers explain how there are "non-negotiables" in the classroom: specifically, that each child has a learning experience free from bullying or harassment in any form. Trauma-sensitive teachers may then turn rule making into a collaborative effort, whereby students and the teacher discuss which rules they want for the classroom and why each rule is necessary. Verbiage for rules is positive, for example, "In Ms. Jones's classroom, we speak to each other kindly." Ms. Jones defines "kindly" and they collaboratively develop a working definition. Students would then have opportunities to write about and/or role play examples of "speaking to each other kindly." Just like any other skill, interpersonal communication is something that is learned (Jennings, 2019). Some children may have positive role models at home, while others may need more practice with this skill. Ms. Jones will also remark to the class and also (quietly) to individual students as she hears examples of speaking kindly in the classroom.

Dialogue circles (2014) are a quick and effective way for teachers to get a sense of which students need additional support and what kind of support. In addition, dialogue circles provide opportunities for teachers to listen to and observe situations occurring in the classroom where a student or students do not feel safe. Daily dialogue circles where students and teacher "take their temperature" help with student self-awareness as well as letting the teacher know of interpersonal or intrapersonal difficulties. Students meet in small groups (or a large class group); each student rates how he/she feels from one to five and tells why. In addition, allowing students who may have had trauma to *not* participate in group or whole class discussions reflects responsive pedagogy (Carello & Butler, 2015).

Mullett (2014) describes how traditional punishment practices (e.g., detention and suspension) typically result in students' protective mechanisms leading to an inward focus, instead of looking outward and reflecting on how their behavior impacted others. This is especially true among children who struggle with emotional regulation. Students impacted by trauma may be retriggered by harsh, seemingly capricious punishments and may simply give up on school altogether (Hemphill et al., 2017). Alternative discipline practices that focus on addressing the underlying causes of misbehavior, such as *restorative justice* (2016), provide a space where student behavior is calmly discussed. Restorative justice practices begin with discussing the event/student's behavior to help the student understand how his actions impacted others. Restorative justice practices also allow the student to understand the consequences of his actions and why they were harmful. The student may have used aggression as a trauma response or my live in an environment where impulsivity is a protective measure against harm. Helping students like this to understand why the classroom/school does not allow harmful behaviors provides a teachable moment where the student moves toward accountability, growth, and change (Mullett, 2014).

Applying the Principle of Safety in a Trauma-Sensitive Classroom

Peace circles and *concentric dialogue circles* are two ways pre-education students learn about focusing on creating a sense of safety in their class-room. *Peace circles* are empowering for students as they give students who are otherwise shy (e.g., English learners, students new to the class, students with anxiety) opportunities to share their ideas (Parker & Brickmore, 2020). Peace circles are used to achieve one or more of the following goals:

Responsive peacemaking (post-incident interventions that acknowledge the perspectives of all stakeholders, to recognize and repair conflict or aggression); proactive peace education (teaching how to communicate and make collective decisions constructively, building students' awareness of how constructive or destructive responses to conflict impact themselves, peers, and society); and engaging pedagogy (using students' perspectives on the conflicts embedded in curriculum subject matter as learning) (p. 82).

In EDUC 2130, small groups select one focus of peace circles and model a small group session for the class. Students write scripts for a vignette and then model the use of a peace circle. As students become more proficient in leading group discussions on issues related to conflict, they are given more challenging scenarios to process.

Concentric dialogue circles involve the whole class at once, with individuals having brief exchanges on a specific topic with half of their classmates (Kujawa-Holbrook, 2017). Half the class forms one circle and face outward toward a circle with the other half of the class. Questions are provided for each inner/outer circle pair of students. Each team of students (one from the inner circle and one from the outer circle) has three minutes to answer the question. At the end of three minutes, students in the inner circle move one seat to the right. The process of asking and answering a question happens again in three minutes. Students in the inner circle continue to move one space after each question is answered or by the three-minute timer. At the beginning of the semester, students are given a list of questions with low emotional intensity, for example, have you always lived in Georgia? How many siblings do you have? What grade level do you hope to teach? This provides opportunities to practice effectively communicating ideas and experiences. As the semester progresses and students develop respectful and productive communication habits, concentric dialogue circles are used to explore topics related to restorative justice within a trauma-sensitive classroom and ways teachers can help students of trauma by consistency and structure. Peace circles are practiced with class teams on topics related to social justice/classroom management, discussions related to equity and the impact of poverty, and ways teachers can respond in trauma-sensitive ways to specific situations.

Building Trust in a Trauma-Sensitive Classroom

The introduction to Fallot and Harris's (2009) self-assessment and planning protocol "Creating Cultures of Trauma Informed Care" described how the experience of trauma leads both adults and children to resist helping behaviors from school personnel. Specifically, children experiencing ACE or trauma may be hyper vigilant and suspicious in the classroom. While this behavior may be protective when dealing with ongoing trauma or was useful during past trauma, being distrustful and unwilling to ask for help are classroom behaviors that often perplex teachers who aren't trauma informed. In addition, exposure to trauma may result in difficulty "calming down and may lack impulse control and be prone to aggressive behavior" (Jennings, 2019, p. 12). Such trauma coping mechanisms are unique to the individual child and may range from hypervigilance and suspiciousness to dissociation (a clinical term for those children who respond to trauma by "tuning out" or withdrawing into the self) (American Psychological Association, 2015). In the classroom, such behaviors may be perceived by teachers as oppositional or lead to a psychological testing referral for attention deficit hyperactivity disorder (ADHD). Jennings (2019) suggests trauma responsive teachers need a "mind shift" (p. 50). Teachers who ask, "What happened to this child to make him act in this way" versus "What is wrong with that child?" are framing behavior as learned to serve a purpose which provides a starting point for the teacher to respond effectively to the child (Slavin, 2018).

A teacher creating a trauma-sensitive classroom is able to consider many different antecedents to behavior, including the effect of trauma. The teacher is not limited to judging the behavior as only a response to the situation at hand and understands the child may not even understand why he is behaving in a certain way because the behavior was learned and used in other—less safe—settings (Jennings, 2019). Trust begins in a trauma-sensitive classroom when a teacher recognizes there is a reason for challenging behaviors in the classroom and the teacher is willing to communicate with the student to understand how to meet the needs of the child. Training in recognizing and interpreting what is happening with the student during maladaptive behavioral moments is essential for teachers to create trauma-sensitive classrooms (Banks & Meyer, 2017; Hickey et al., 2020; Shalka, 2015).

Relationship building is key in any classroom and is especially important in building trust with children who have experienced trauma. Recent research revealed that preservice teachers' ideas of what building relationships with students would be like were very different from the reality of connecting with students, especially students from different backgrounds (Emdin, 2016; Salerno & Kibler, 2018). Salerno and Kibler's (2018) work with preservice teachers indicated, "one-on-one interactions, learning about individual students, using texts and writing to relate to students, having positive interactions with families, involvement in extracurricular activites, or watching mentors build relationships" greatly improved their success in building relationships with students during their student teaching experiences (p. 12). Nel Noddings (2013) explained how relationships are built around caring which "involves stepping out of one's own personal frame of reference into someone else's" (p. 16); this mirrors the types of experiences and activities Salerno and Kibler found to be beneficial in building positive relationships in the classroom.

Trauma-sensitive teachers model positive and respectful behavior toward students and set high expectations for all learners (Brunzell et al., 2016; Cole et al., 2013; Diaz et al., 2019; Keyes, 2002). These teachers are also mindful that some children do not observe respectful behavior modeled outside of school and need more examples and also opportunities to practice skills that will build trust and lead to academic success. Brené Brown (2017) explained how trauma-sensitive professionals suspend judgment and proceed by first letting the student know we want to understand and help them. Given the frenetic pace of teaching and the instructional day, teachers often see their role with students as a cheerleader. Providing bromides like, "Things will get better" or "It can't be that bad!" may actually prevent the building of trust as the child knows or believes things may not get better soon. Trauma-sensitive teachers approach students by asking, "May I sit with you for a bit" or "I know you're dealing with a lot and I'm here for you" (Brown, 2017). This show of empathy opens communication which leads to trust. Students who trust the teacher are less anxious in class and are able to focus more on academic tasks (Brunzell et al., 2016; Fallot & Harris, 2009).

Ways to help with self-regulation include learn to identify emotions and feelings within themselves and others (Brunzell et al, 2016; Cole et al., 2013; Gest et al., 2014). Children's literature is a great tool for teaching children about self-regulation. *Super George and the Invisible Shield* (Mendoza, 2017) is a great read aloud where the main character has a shield that helps him think about what behaviors are helpful and not helpful. Teachers who use the terms "helpful" and "not helpful" when talking with children about actions are framing behavior to assist the child in understanding their behavior without simply labeling the action as "good" or "bad." In addition, social scripts are very helpful when students come in each day and read over the 'script' of activities for the day. Movement breaks or brain breaks are essential for all children, and especially those who struggle with emotional regulation (Jennings, 2019). Finally, direct teaching and modeling of regulation is effective in the classroom (Pathway 2 Success, 2019).

Encouraging peer relationships when appropriate is another way to build trust among students in the classroom. Trauma-sensitive teachers who step back and observe students in formal and informal settings gain important information on the dynamics among students as well as insights on how to effectively group or partner children (Jennings, 2019). Researchers found that elementary teachers who actively monitored and participated in student interactions—including friendships and group assignments—correlated with students indicating a higher level of academic engagement and more satisfying peer relationships (Gest et al., 2014; Howard, 2019; Salerno & Kibler, 2018).

EDUC 2130 Relationship Building With Bags, Buddies, and Teams

Each semester, pre-education students participate in a *people bags* activity, with each class member bringing a 'bag' with artifacts representing who they are. This activity is a community building activity, as students learn which classmates share the same sport, religion, hometown, or even first grade teacher. Lively and sometimes exciting conversations ensue—one semester, two students discovered they were born in the same town in Mexico and knew the same people! One student immigrated to the United States in first grade while the other came to the States in third grade. In spring 2020, this activity became "virtual" as classes went fully online due to COVID, with students creating videos with their artifacts. The video option has been very well received by students who like being able to return to our course web page to the virtual people bag posts to learn names and to connect with classmates having shared interests.

Students participate in a class *buddy system*, where student pair up with each other with the responsibility of reaching out in supportive ways. This includes reaching out if sick to let a partner know to take notes or gather materials, share field information, or just to check in to see how the buddy is doing during a stressful week. In addition to relationship building, this level of communication can be reassuring to students who experience anxiety or depression. Having someone to reach out to can ease the stress of missing class, going through a stressful week, or needing assistance with an activity in the course. Partners communicate their preferred method of communication and discuss their desired level of contact as a way of respecting personal space.

Shared emotional response and perspective taking are two ways to build empathy in students (Noddings, 2013). In addition to having a class buddy/partner, students in my class are part of a small group, too. Small groups are formed by students selecting the same research presentation topic. An example of modeling trauma-sensitive practice of perspective taking uses children literature. Scieszka's (1996) children's book retells the story of the three little pigs (*The True Story of the Three Pigs*) from the wolf's perspective; the wolf explains it was his allergies that caused him to sneeze while trying to borrow a cup of sugar from the three little pigs and he accidently blew down the pigs' house. Each of the four groups/tables has a copy of the story; one student is the "teacher" who reads and discusses how perspective matters in communicating with and understanding each other.

Active listening is an important skill that trauma-sensitive teachers practice with students. In class, students practice the *HEAR* strategy in teams to develop listening skills:

Halt: Stop whatever else you are doing whether it's an activity or conversation or ideas you're thinking.

Engage: Let the speaker know you are ready to listen. You may lean in toward the speaker to show you're ready to listen.

Anticipate: Being positive about what the speaker will say puts the listener in the right frame of mind.

Replay: Think about what the speaker is saying after he finishes. Go over the information in your head before responding to be sure you understand (Wilson & Conyers, 2017).

Each class begins with a meditation or breathing activity. Students may volunteer to lead the class in five minutes of meditation, breathing, or simple yoga movements.

THE POWER OF CHOICE IN TRAUMA-SENSITIVE CLASSROOMS

A cornerstone in educational planning is the ability to differentiate academic content for the differing needs of children in the classroom (Tomlinson, 2014). In the case of children dealing with trauma, providing choices for assignments can relieve anxiety and prevent re-traumatization. Examples of differentiation with product vary based on the content and the grade level of the students. In elementary grades reading instruction, students have the option of reading a story aloud to the class, to their study buddy only, or to their stuffed animal at home. For students with social anxiety/phobia or who are dealing with trauma by withdrawing, the opportunity to read their story at home can lessen anxiety tremendously.

Differentiation also extends to seating and work arrangements in the classroom. Providing students with the choices during seatwork time of standing while working, sitting on the rug with a lap table, or sitting with classmates. In a trauma-sensitive classroom, students are allowed to move to another space if they are feeling anxious sitting in a group; they may take a quick break from small group work to practice breathing techniques; or they may ask to see the counselor or other mental health professional if they are struggling with images from a traumatic experience and need support. As many students who have experienced trauma may not show any outward signs in the classroom (e.g., acting out, extreme vigilance, somatic complaints), pre-education students develop 'greeting plans' for parents and students. This plan includes practicing the correct pronunciation of students' names; making a "script" of initial phone/email/in person communication with each parent (that occurs during the first two weeks of school); and providing information for all families on school and community services. Students "practice" conversations with class partners. One of the required questions for the script is "What is one thing about your child that will help me support the child's success this year?" That question opens the door for parents to share information they would not typically share. Establishing a positive rapport with parents/caregivers opens communication lines and provides teachers with insights into additional support the child may need.

EDUC 2130 Examples of Choice

Deciding whether to do a deeper research project or to do the "regular" research project along with completing written reading reflections each week. Pre-education students who select the deeper research project are required to interview someone working in the area of their research. For example, deeper research on the topic of the academic impact on children living in poverty would include interviewing a social worker or intervention specialist who serves families struggling in poverty. The deeper research would also include documenting area resources for families, like free medical services/clinics, foodbanks, mobile dental services. Students may also choose whether to write a summary midterm paper or create an original poem or song that includes their understanding of the particular topic.

EMPOWERMENT AND COLLABORATION WITHIN THE TRAUMA-SENSITIVE CLASSROOM

Restorative justice has been shown to be empowering for students and teachers. By using conversations to address undesirable behaviors and by allowing students opportunities to practice more "helpful" and prosocial behaviors, teachers reported lowered classroom conflicts. Hemphill et al. (2017) studied the use of restorative justice practices like peer mediation and found lower levels of repeat behavior than traditional discipline practices like detention or suspension. In fact, research by Hemphill et al. (2017) confirmed that traditional suspension increased negative behavior and resulted in lowered academic achievement among middle and secondary students.

Howard (2019) found teachers are more inclined to espouse trauma responsive discipline strategies when they have had training in TIP. Also, teachers reported greater job satisfaction and empowerment after receiving TIP training (Jennings, 2019).

EMPOWERMENT AND COLLABORATION ACTIVITIES WITH PRE-EDUCATION STUDENTS

An unintended consequence occurred as a result of pre-education students' fall 2019 experience with MHTT and field work mentoring students at The HUB as pre-education students shared with peers how the mental health toolkit training gave them a safe space to share their personal experiences with mental health issues and mental illness. Students described the impact increased self-awareness about mental health issues had in changing the way they see the role of a teacher as "first responder" for mental health issues in the classroom. Their personal stories encouraged classmates to share mental health issues as well. The number of students who openly shared struggles with mental health mirrored national statistics that indicate almost 75% of college students reported at least one ACE (adverse childhood event); approximately 25% of adolescents experienced mental health issues or diagnosed mental illnesses; and the majority of major mental illnesses are present by adolescence (Auerbach et al., 2018; Bentley, 2018; Dods, 2016). Participating in the mental health responsiveness workshop gave students the opportunity to learn about mental illnesses that typically begin by adolescence (anxiety, depression) and the space to reflect upon their efforts to compensate and 'push through' mental health challenges because they did not realize "it was a real thing." Research with college students experiencing anxiety and depression showed that the presence of help-seeking behaviors mitigated the social and academic impacts of the diseases (Gomez et al., 2016). Following the mental health training, these students had the opportunity to learn about university-based supports (e.g., counseling services) while also classroom opportunities to practice some of the self-care practices they would also use with K–12 students.

Three of the pre-education students who shared their experiences with mental health challenges with peers during class discussions later decided to do additional research on mental health/mental illness among minority populations (one student experienced poverty, one was gay, and one was Latinx). Two of the students began meeting with therapists at counseling services to develop strategies to manage their anxiety; both students shared this with classmates. Research shows when adolescents know someone personally who has sought mental health help, they are much more likely to seek help themselves (Bentley, 2018; Disabato et al., 2018). As most teacher candidates are still adolescents themselves, the significance of mental health toolkit training and discussions on trauma-sensitive classrooms are beneficial on multiple levels. Pedagogically, with mastery of skills and understandings needed to responsively approach K–12 students and to connect them with additional support in trauma-sensitive classrooms (Armstrong et al., 2015; Courtois & Gold; 2009; Jennings, 2019); and personally, in gaining awareness of their own mental health and opportunities for self-care (Bentley, 2018). Over 2020 spring and summer semesters (in the midst of COVID-19 lockdown and remote learning), students and faculty met virtually to read and discuss research on mental health issues among underserved populations. Currently, this volunteer research group has grown to 12 students, and they have established the "Mindfulness Space"; a room on campus where college of education students, faculty, or staff meet to discuss particular topics related to mental health, mental health literacy, and self-care. These pre-education students lead yoga classes and meditation; area mental health professionals give Zoom talks on wellness and all activities and speaking events are open to College of Education faculty, staff, and students. Recent guest speakers included: a child and adolescent psychiatrist specializing in emotional dysregulation, trauma, and brain development; a police sergeant whose staff has developed mental health responsiveness guidelines that include all officers receiving mental health training; and a first-grade teacher who uses home visits and Saturday morning storytelling with students as opportunities to understand learner needs and to provide emotional regulation skills. Starting with mental health toolkit training for teachers, engaging in practical classroom strategies of trauma-sensitive classrooms, and taking leadership roles in bringing more information and opportunities for self-care to peers has empowered these future teachers. Students who participated in at least one of the activities offered, indicated feeling more confident in approaching students who may be experiencing mental health issues as well as feeling more self-aware with regard to maintaining good mental health for themselves.

GROWING TRAUMA-SENSITIVE PEDAGOGY ACROSS TEACHER EDUCATION PROGRAMS

The professional development school (PDS) model for teacher education at my IHE requires deliberate and ongoing collaboration among the teacher candidate, university faculty, and mentor classroom teacher. Having strong communication and collaboration lines already in place through the PDS model makes the inclusion of mental health responsiveness training much easier. All pre-education students currently have the opportunity to complete mental health training. As the pre-education students who have had significant mental health training and mentoring experiences move into their respective programs, the hope is for them to bring their knowledge to peers and also for them to be ready to engage, observe, and reflect on the needs of students as they become teachers in trauma-sensitive classrooms. Student empowerment with taking leadership with scheduling for the *mindfulness spot* are enthusiastic in bringing both a social worker and adolescent psychiatrist to campus for discussions on how teachers can further support children who have experienced trauma. This work is very new, and these pre-education students are encouraged to meet twice a semester while they are in their respective programs to continue developing activities and support for mental health awareness among faculty and peers.

REFERENCES

Armstrong, D., Price, D., & Crowley, T. (2015). Thinking it through: A study of how pre-service teachers respond to children who present with possible mental health difficulties. *Emotional and Behavioural Difficulties, 20(4)*, 381–397. http://dx.doi.org/10.1080/13632752.2015.1019248

American Psychological Association. (2015). *Definition of trauma.* https://www.apa.org/topics.

Auerbach, R. P., Mortier, P., Bruffaerts, R., & Alonso, J. (2018). WHO world mental health surveys international college student project: Prevalance & distribution of mental disorders. *Journal of Psychopathology and Clinical Science. 127*(8), 818–829.

Ball, A., Iachini, A. L., Bohnenkamp, J. H., Togno, N. M., Brown, E. L., Hoffman, J. A., & George, M. W. (2016). School mental health content in state in-service K–12 teaching standards in the United States. *Teaching and Teacher Education, 60*, 312–320.

Banks, J. (2002). *An introduction to multicultural education*. Allyn & Bacon.

Banks, Y., & Meyer, J. (2017). Childhood trauma in today's urban classroom. *The Journal of Educational Foundations*, 63–75.

Becker-Blease, K. A. (2017). As the world becomes trauma informed, work to do. *Journal of Trauma and Dissociation, 18(2)*, 131–138.

Bentley, H. (2018). Understanding students of poverty in multicultural classrooms. *Multicultural Perspectives, 20*(3), 177–190.

Brown, B. (2017). *Daring greatly: How the courage to be vulnerable transforms the way we live, love, parent, and lead*. Avery.

Brown, E. L., Phillipo, K. L., Weston, K., & Rodger, S. (2019). United States and Canada pre-service teacher certification standards for student mental health: A comparative case study. *Teaching and Teacher Education, 80*, 71–82.

Brunzell, T., Stokes, H., & Waters, L. (2016). Trauma-informed positive education: Using positive psychology to strengthen vulnerable students. *Contemporary School Psychology, 20*, 63–83. https://doi.org/10.1007/s40688-015-0070-x.

Carello, J., & Butler, L. D. (2015). Practicing what we teach: Trauma informed educational practice. *Journal of Teaching in Social Work, 35*, 262–278. https://doi.org/10.1080/08841233.2015.1030059

Cavanaugh, B. (2016). Trauma-informed classrooms and schools. *Beyond Behavior, 25*(2), 41–46.

Cole, S. F., Eisner, A., Gregory, M., J. D., & Ristuccia, J. (2013). *Creating and advocating for Trauma Sensitive Schools*. https://traumasensitiveschools.org/wp-content/uploads/2013/11/HTCL-Vol-2-Creating-and-Advocating-for-TSS.pdf

Council for the Accreditation of Educator Preparation. (2013). *CAEP Standards*. http://www.caepnet.org/accreditation/caep-accreditation/accreditation-decisions/2020-spring

Courtois, C. A. (2002). Traumatic stress studies: The need for curricula inclusion. *Journal of Trauma Practice, 1*, 33–57. https://doi.org/10.1300/J189v01n01_03.

Courtois, C. A., & Gold, S. N. (2009). The need for inclusion of psychological trauma in the professional curriculum: A call to action. *Psychological Trauma: Theory, Research, Practice, and Policy, 1*, 3–23. https://doi.org/10.1037/a0015224.

Cunningham, C. E., Rimas, H., Vallancourt, T., Stewart, B., Deal, K., Cunningham, L., Vanniyasingam, T., Duku, E., Buchanan, D. H., & Thabane, L. (2019). What influences educators' design preference for bullying prevention programs? Multi-level latent class analysis of a discrete choice experiment. *School Mental Health, 12*, 22–37.

Dialogue Circles and Positive Classroom Culture. (2014, July 1). *Edutopia*. https://www.edutopia.org/practice/stw-glenview-practice-dialogue-circles-video

Diaz, C., Ju, P., Tillman, D. R., & Hof, D. D. (2019). Concepts influencing attitudes and beliefs toward mental health issues in a teacher education program. *International Journal of Psychology*, 11–38. https://doi.org/10.7220/2345-024x.23.1

Disabato, D. J., Short, J. L., Lameira, D. M., Bagley, K. D., & Wong, S. J. (2018). Predicting help-seeking behavior: The impact of knowing someone close who has sought help. *Journal of American College Health, 66(8)*, 731–738. https://doi.org/10.1080//0744848.2018.1440568

Dixon-DeSilva, L. E., Ponting, C., Ramos, G., Cornejo-Guevara, M. V., & Chavira, D. A. (2020). Urban Latinix parents' attitudes towards mental health; Mental health literacy and service use. *Children and Youth Services Review, 109*, 67–98.

Dods, J. (2016). Teacher candidate mental health and mental health literacy. *Exceptionality Education International, 26(2)*, 42–61.

Emdin, C. (2016). *For white folks who teach in the hood … and the rest of y'all too: Reality pedagogy and urban education*. Beacon Press.

Fallot, R. D., & Harris, M. (2009). *Creating cultures of trauma-informed care (CCTIC): A self-assessment and planning protocol*. Community Connections. https://www.theannainstitute.org/CCTICSELFASSPP.pdf

Georgia Department of Education. (2020). *Free and reduced lunch eligibility*. https://www.gadoe.org/Technology-Services/Data-Collections/Pages/FY2020-Free-and-Reduced-Price-Meal-Eligibility.aspx

Georgia Professional Standards Commission. (2016). *Teacher certification*. https://www.gapsc.com/Certification/Home.aspx

Gest, S. D., Madill, R. A., Zadora, K. M., & Rodkin, P. C. (2014). Teacher management of elementary classroom social dynamics. *Journal of Emotional and Behavioral Disorders, 22*, 107–118.

Glasper, B. (2020). Reports on the mental health of children during the pandemic. *British Journal of Nursing, 29(22)*, 15–30.

Gomez, J. M., Lewis, J. K., Noll, L. K., Smidt, A. M., & Birrell, P. J. (2016). Shifting the focus: Non-pathologizing approaches to healing from betrayal trauma through an emphasis on relational care. *Journal of Trauma and Dissociation, 17(2)*, 165–185.

Gupta, T. & Gehlawat, P. (2020). Emotional regulation in adolescents: A narrative review. *Journal of Indian Association on Child Adolescent Mental Health, 16*(3), 171–193.

Hanson, R. F., & Lang, J. (2016). A critical look at trauma-informed care among agencies and systems serving maltreated youth and their families. *Journal of Child Maltreatment, 21*(2). https://doi.org/10.1177/1077559516635274

Harris, M., & Fallot, R. (2001). *New directions for mental health services: Using trauma theory to design service systems*. Josey-Bass.

Hemphill, S. A., Broderick, D. J., & Heerde, J. A. (2017). Positive associations between school suspension and student problem behaviour: Recent Australian findings. *Trends & Issues in Crime and Criminal Justice, 531*, 1–13

Hickey, G., Smith, S., O'Sullivn, L., McGill, L., Kenny, M., MacIntyre, D., & Gordon, M. (2020). Adverse childhood experiences and trauma informed practices in second chance educational settings in the Republic of Ireland: An inquiry-based study. *Children and Youth Services Review, 118*, 1–17.

Howard, J. A. (2019). A systematic framework for trauma informed schooling: Complex but necessary. *Journal of Aggression, Maltreatment, and Trauma, 28*(5), 545–565. https://doi.org/10.1080/10926771.2018.1479323

Jennings, P. A. (2019). *The trauma-sensitive classroom: Building resilience with compassionate teaching.* Norton.

Jorm, A. F., Kitchner, B. A., Sawyer, M. G., Scales, H., & Cvetkovski, S. (2010). Mental health first aid training for high school teachers: A cluster randomized trial. *BMC Psychiatry, 10*(51), 1–21. http://biomedcentral.com/1471-244x/10/51

Kujawa-Holbrook, S. A. (2017). Concentric circles dialogue exercise. *Teaching Theology and Religion,* 1–2.

Keyes, C. (2002). The mental health continuum: From languishing to flourishing in life. *Journal of Health and Social Behavior, 43*(2), 207–222.

Mendoza, L. P. (2017). *Super George and the invisible shield.* SCF Press.

Mental Health First Aid. (2018). https://www.mentalhealthfirstaid.org

Mullett, J. (2014). Restorative discipline: From getting even to getting well. *Children and Schools, 36*(3), 157–164. https://doi.org/10.1093/cs/cdu011

Noddings, N. (2013). *Caring: A relational approach to ethics and moral education* (2nd ed.). University of California Press.

Osayande, O., Costa, S., Spaulding, A., Rose, J., Allen, K. M., Rose, M., & Apatu, E. (2018). Teachers' perceptions of student mental health: The role of school-based mental health services delivery model. *National Association of Social Workers, 40*(4), 240–248. https://doi.org/10.1093/cs/cdy020

Parker, C., & Bickmore, K. (2020). Classroom peace circles: Teachers' professional learning and implementation of restorative dialogue. *Teaching and Teacher Education, 95,* 1–10. https://doi.org/10.1016/j.tate.2020.103129

Pathway2Success. (2019). Retrieved August 9, 2021. http://thepathway2success.com

Reece, L., & Nodine, P. (2014). When immigrant is synonymous with terrorist: Culturally responsive teaching with English learners. *The Social Studies,* 1–7.

Reece, L., Roberts, A., & Smith, K. (2016). Is it possible to sustain innovation, community, and responsiveness in teacher education when a unique pilot PDS becomes a program-wide model? *School-University Partnerships: The Journal of the National Association for Professional Development Schools (Special Issue), 9*(3).

Restorative justice: What it is and is not. (2016). https://rethinkingschools.org/articles/restorative-justice/

Salerno, A. S., & Kibler, A. K. (2018). Relational challenges and breakthroughs: How preservice English teachers' figured worlds impact their relationships with students. *Teachers College Record, 120,* 1–36.

Scieszka, J. (1996). *The true story of the three little pigs.* Norton.

Shalka, T. R. (2015). Toward a trauma-informed practice: What educators need to know. *About Campus,* 21–27. https://doi.org/10.1002/abc.21217

Slavin, R. E. (2018). *Educational psychology: Theory and practice.* Pearson.

Sparks, S. D. (2020, November 12). Children's mental health emergencies skyrocketed after COVID-19 hit. What schools can do. *Education Week,* 1–13.

Spera, S., & Monnat, S. (2020). Adolescent and young adult mental health is better in states that mandate more school mental health policies. *Learning Center for Public Health Promotion, 15,* 1–10.

Stratford, B., Cook, E., Hanneke, R., Katz, E., Seak, D., Steed, H., Fulks, E., Lessans, A., & Temkin, D. (2020). A scoping review of school-based efforts to support students who have experienced trauma. *School Mental Health*, 1–20. https://doi.org/10.1007/s12310-020-09368-9.

Thomason, M. E., Marusak, H. A., Tocco, M. A., Vila, A. M., McGarragle, O., & Rosenberg, D. R. (2015). Altered amygdala connectivity in urban youth exposed to trauma. *Social Cognitive & Affective Neuroscience*, 1460–147.

Tomlinson, C. (2014). *The differentiated classroom: Responding to the needs of all learners.* ASCD.

U.S. Centers for Disease Control and Prevention. (2019). *Data and statistics on children's mental health.* https://www.cdc.gov/childrensmentalhealth/data.html

Venta, A., Bailey, C., Munoz, C., Godinez, E., Colin, Y., Arreola, Al, Abate, A., & Camins, J. (2019). Contribution of schools to mental health and resilience in recently immigrated youth. *School Psychology, 34*(2), 138–147.

Werner-Seidler, A., Perry, Y., Calear, A. L., Newby, J. M., & Christensen, H. (2017). School-based depression and anxiety prevention programs for young people: A systematic review and meta-analysis. *Clinical Psychology Review, 51*, 30–47.

Wilson, D., & Conyers, M. (2017). *Four proven strategies for teaching empathy.* Edutopia https://www.edutopia.orgc/article/4-proven-strategies-teaching-empathy-donna-wilson-marcus-conyers

CHAPTER 10

AUTOBIOGRAPHY AND SELF-PORTRAITURE

A Strengths Based Framework for Trauma-Informed Pedagogy and Identity and Resiliency Transformation

Ellen J. Spitler
Metropolitan State University of Denver

Carly Laukaieie Setsumi Ibara
Mid-Pacific Institute, Honolulu, Hawaii

Marisa Jucutan Mendoza-Maurer
Henry J. Kaiser High School, Honolulu, Hawaii

ABSTRACT

Whether we are teaching in K–12 or university teacher education class-rooms, the invention and re-invention of *self* must invite and include the challenges and struggles human beings experience throughout their lives, so our instructional design and facilitation of learning must include, very purposefully, a conscious inclusion of students' realities. Our ongoing work is grounded in and informed by trauma-informed pedagogy where we strive to consciously construct a safe space alongside students, open space for student choice, collaboration and creativity that is enveloped in the language, and a focus on personal beliefs and personal actions of resiliency and empower-

Developing Trauma-Informed Teachers: Creating Classrooms That Foster Equity, Resiliency, and Asset-Based Approaches: Research Findings From the Field, pp. 169–193

ment. This chapter describes a strengths-based framework for autobiography and self-portrait instructional engagements, illustrating how they embody trauma-informed pedagogy, and offering specific practical examples for secondary and higher education classrooms. In our classrooms, autobiography, and self-portraiture (representations of self in visual art) provide opportunities for students' lives to direct, enhance, and extend the curriculum, as well as present authentic openings for teachers and students to rebuild, reinvent, and transform resiliency and personal agency/empowerment.

The autobiography and self-portrait work was the first time I was asked to focus on the melding of my personal and teaching identity. I was able to effectively make those decisions through in-depth explorations into my successes and failures. The sharing of our self-portraits opened my mind to the realization that trauma was beyond my limited definition. Sharing our stories helped us be open and vulnerable, to empathize with each other on a basic and human level. It helped us build a safe community. (Carly, coauthor)

The autobiography and self-portrait project was the wake-up call that started my self-actualization process. It helped me awaken to two transformed understandings: (1) I was coming from the perspective of one with a learner's privilege that needed to radically change, and (2) that instructional frameworks didn't matter if you didn't get to intimately know your students first. As a future teacher, this was revolutionary, as I shifted from planning my curriculum for the ideal academic to designing specific strategies to get students to open up about trauma as a means for purposeful emotional, social and academic learning and empowerment. (Marisa, coauthor)

As preservice teachers, both Carly and Marisa experienced autobiography and self-portrait instructional engagements in Ellen's (coauthor) university teacher education course, and later took up the work in their classrooms as in-service teachers. Our ongoing collaboration during the design and implementation of these identity engagements focuses on self-exploration in support of content knowledge and resiliency transformation. Our work is grounded in and informed by trauma-informed pedagogy where we strive to consciously construct a safe space alongside students, open space for student choice, collaboration and creativity that is enveloped in the language, and focus on personal beliefs and actions of resiliency and empowerment (Davidson, 2017). Our chapter describes a strengths-based framework (Hopper et al., 2010) for the autobiography and self-portrait instructional engagements, illustrating how they embody trauma-informed pedagogy, and offering specific practical examples for secondary and higher education classrooms. As educators, we embrace Freire's (2003) assertion that knowledge "emerges only through invention and reinvention, through the restless, impatient, continuing, hopeful inquiry human beings pursue in the world, with the world, and with each other" (p. 72). Whether we are teaching in K–12 or university classrooms, the invention and reinvention of *self* must invite and include the challenges and struggles human beings experience throughout their lives, so our instructional design and facilitation of learning must include, very purposefully, a conscious inclusion of students' realities. This means that traumatic experiences will, very likely, emerge in that process, which we believe provide a potent opportunity for students to explore their personal experiences through the lenses of both strength and struggle so as to reposition themselves (Bathina, 2014) and recognize that they have powerful understandings about and control of their journey. In essence, we believe that,

> Trauma-informed care is a strengths-based framework that is grounded in an understanding of a responsiveness to the impact of trauma that emphasizes physical, psychological, and emotional safety for both providers and survivors, and that creates opportunities for survivors to rebuild a sense of control and empowerment. (Hopper et al., 2010, p. 82)

Autobiography and self-portraiture (re-presentations of self in visual art) provide teachers and students with authentic openings to rebuild, reinvent, and transform resiliency and personal agency/empowerment, and illustrate trauma-informed pedagogy which open opportunities for students' lives to direct, enhance, and extend the curriculum.

TEACHER IDENTITY PEDAGOGY

Opportunities and Challenges in Teacher Preparation

If future teachers are going to confidently design and facilitate instruction to support personal agency/empowerment, resiliency, and community membership in their future classrooms, they should experience and reflect on that kind of instruction firsthand in their own preparation learning journey. In essence, teacher preparation must focus on the identities of future teachers, explicitly, when designing and facilitating that pedagogy. Danielewicz (2001) describes a pedagogy that she asserts transforms preservice teacher identity. She states, "By pedagogy, I mean the process of structuring of activities, interactions, events, and assignments in teaching according to ideas that are congruent with or grow out of theories of identity development" (p. 133). Alsup (2006) argues, most often teacher education,

> Is usually focused on the future students of the preservice teacher, not on the development of the teacher her- or himself. [T]his externally focused approach tends to assume that the teacher is already self-actualized, already emotionally and affectively prepared to assume the teacher identity, with few personal challenges left to face. This assumption is rarely accurate. (pp. xiv–xv)

Additionally, Bean (1997) maintains that preservice education and university courses "create an idealized (and) decontextualized setting where (teaching) appears easier than it really is" (p. 155). These educators, and many others, have investigated the significance of identity as teachers develop (Cox & Lyddon, 1997; Freeman, 2001; Sumara & Luce-Kapler, 1996); however, few have researched ways to overtly bring the critical aspect of identity into teacher education pedagogy. Risko et al. (2008) state that, "Two important issues to carry forward for additional study are the suggestions that beliefs are affected by situated events and that it is important to help prospective teachers make explicit their beliefs and events as objects of study" (p. 263). The authors also noted that, "limited research is available to guide teacher education programmatic design or specific course development" (p. 253). Alsup (2006) asserts,

> One reason I think identity concerns are rarely addressed in teacher education courses is that they are difficult to tackle and are often uncomfortable for the instructor or mentor to talk about ... the process of identity development is difficult, messy, and complex, and (it) must be exactly this way to be successful. (pp. 4– 5)

Moreover, in teacher education programs, we focus intensely on the crucial pedagogical elements of pre-assessment and the role of prior knowledge, guiding future educators to embrace the reality that unless we start where students are, and know where the students are at the beginning of a learning journey, we are not authentically teaching content and opening space for content learning. If this is our truth as teacher educators, it must be true when teaching future teachers, as well. We must know where students in our programs are in relation to the outcomes interwoven with social emotional learning and accept the reality of traumatic experiences in their lives. We must know the challenges students in our education courses have faced, and are facing, especially connected to the content we are teaching in our courses.

In our classrooms, autobiography and self-portraiture (representations of self in visual art) provide opportunities for students' lives to direct, enhance, and extend the curriculum, as well as create an opportunity to support the transformation of agency, confidence in the learning process, and critical thinking consciousness and development (Eisner, 2002; Freire & Macedo, 1987; Moje, 2000). When used in learning spaces organized and orchestrated to support identity and resiliency transformation, this power of creation can guide an analytical deconstruction of, and critical insight into a view of self, developing and supporting complex thinking, resiliency development, and a rich analysis of academic content that would not exist in the absence of such opportunities. "To cultivate a growth mindset, trauma-affected students must be taught to explore and learn in the context of their own life experiences so they can begin to repair relationships, engage with caring individuals, and become empowered" (Cole et al., 2013, p. 7). Autobiography and art are compelling opportunities for equitable access, resiliency awareness and transformation (Kress, 2003, 2006; Moje, 2000; Vygotsky, 1978) that can powerfully support the ways students authentically experience the core values of trauma-informed practice: safety, trustworthiness, choice and control, collaboration, and empowerment (Davidson, 2017). In essence, students are invited to tri-dimensionalize (Freire, 2003) their lives in order to create as they look back on their past, contemplate their present, and predict their future. Students are immersed in their own lived experiences, providing a crucial framework for agency and empowerment to consciously emerge and transform. Eisner (2002) asserts, "Work in the arts ... is a way of creating our lives by expanding our consciousness, shaping our dispositions, satisfying our quest for meaning, establishing contact with others, and sharing a culture" (p. 3). Likewise, Vygotsky explained, "Art is the social technique of emotion, a tool of society which brings the most intimate and personal aspects of our being into the circle of social life" (as cited in Moran & John-Steiner, 2003, p. 62).

UNIVERSITY TEACHER EDUCATION CLASSROOM

Ellen's research focus on teacher identity drove the design of her teacher education coursework after several years of teaching high school and facilitating autobiography and multimodal (artistic) learning engagements that fostered adolescents in her classroom to explore their life experiences as influential personal history that fed and impacted their confidence and transformed ownership of content knowledge, alongside knowledge of themselves and their world (Spitler, 2009). These same pursuits frame the instructional opportunities for future teachers in Ellen's university courses where they (a) write an autobiography, focusing on aspects of their lived experiences and framed by content of the course; (b) represent those ideas in a multimodal (artistic) self-portrait; (c) orally present their autobiography and self-portrait in our classroom community; and finally, (d) metacognitively reflect on the writing, creating, and sharing process.

Autobiography

The autobiography is designed to connect to and support the specific content under study in the university course. For example, in the disciplinary literacy course, future teachers are guided to explore their lived and transformative literacy experiences and literate practices; in essence, all the ways they read, write, speak, and think about, as well as visualize and represent the world. Students contemplate their previously lived experiences of learning to read, write, speak, and represent, that have influenced and transformed who they are as people. In the English methods course, in which Carly and Marisa were university students, future teachers are guided to explore the ways they *author* their world, again focusing on reading, writing, speaking, visualizing, and representing experiences from their lives that have changed them in important ways with more of a literary framework. To support and guide the prewriting of the autobiography, students complete a modified Reading Interest Inventory (Goodman et al., 1987) that presents a variety of questions framed in meaning-making and reading the world and the word (Freire & Macedo, 1987). Additionally, students read sources that discuss and describe ways we make sense of the world (Freire & Macedo, 1987; Gee, 1987) and the critical role autobiography plays in supporting students' repositioning of self when striving to regain control and transform their own resiliency and empowerment (Bathina, 2014). The focus is on strength-based experiences where students articulate their own lives by exploring, naming, and sharing their own strengths and struggles (Davidson, 2017; Hopper et al., 2010), purposely moving away from deficit thinking and believing.

Notably, students are invited to choose a genre of writing to compose their autobiographies, which can include essay format, poetry, script, story narrative, and other genres we brainstorm as a class, making sure to include 21st century narrative options (e.g., blogs, podcasts). The choice of genre, alongside the choice of their own lived events to include in their autobiography, presents the authentic opportunity for students to feel that foundational ownership of the composition and autonomy in the process, a crucial component of trauma-informed pedagogy (Substance Abuse and Mental Health Services Administration [SAMHSA], 2014).

Multimodal Self-Portrait

Once students compose their autobiography, they are guided to visually represent six of those lived experiences written about in the autobiography into an artistic, multimodal self-portrait; in essence, "breathing life experiences into abstract language (Buehl, 2014, p. 5). Again, choice is key in the representation artifact where students can draw, paint, dance, use photographs or computer generate their self-portrait based on their own interests and strengths, as well as choose a format that makes them feel safe and/or comfortable but still challenges them to think about their lived experiences in new ways and from new perspectives. Ellen introduces a Picasso style collage as an option to start the artistic process and then invites students to brainstorm other artistic pathways they might take.

Oral Presentation

Several days are dedicated to the oral presentation of the autobiographies and self-portraits in class. Students decide when they want to present, volunteering when they feel ready. Before the oral sharing begins, Ellen guides the class to write about and discuss the acceptable parameters of audience behavior, as well as being reminded that sharing what they each feel comfortable sharing is the goal and accepted option. No student is forced to share more than they decide they want to share, which is the case with the writing of the autobiography and the creation of the self-portrait. This ownership is introduced from the start and reinforced throughout the steps of the creation process to consciously invite personal choice and empowerment. Ellen also encourages students to use their written autobiographies as "scripts" from which they can read or refer during the oral presentation as they see fit, recognizing that students are learning to trust the community and even their own voices.

As presenters orally share, and show their self-portraits, Ellen provides students with a comprehension note-taking strategy, called a dialectic journal or double-entry diary (Buehl, 2014), to note each presenter's name and important ideas they hear [and see] during each presentation. The notetaking represents a critical thinking opportunity as students must determine the importance of the ideas, make inferences in the determining process, and make connections between the shared ideas and their own authoring (literate) practices. This supports the content learning of the course, but overtly guides and models the construction of a learning community based on trust, mutual respect and collective efficacy, which is foundational to trauma-informed pedagogy and social emotional learning. "Communities of adults who know and trust one another and who are skilled at working together toward shared goals are more successful in implementing, improving, and sustaining SEL [social, emotional learning]" (Collaborative for Academic, Social, and Emotional Learning [CASEL], 2019, p. 1). Moreover, future teachers are exploring their own understandings of social, emotional, and cultural competence in the process of noting and engaging in the sharing of their lives.

> (Students) not only need opportunities to learn about the research and practices behind SEL, but also to critically reflect on and deepen their own social, emotional, and cultural competencies. This may include examining their own sociocultural identities and biases, strengthening their ability to empathize and take on perspectives of those who are different than them, practicing skills to help build their relationships with students, and assessing how their actions impact equitable outcomes. (CASEL, 2019, p. 1)

The speaking experience provides each student who is sharing, and the students who are listening, a newfound consciousness into realizing and recognizing the significance of those lived experiences in nuanced ways, made possible by articulating aloud to others in a community. This often begins a potent response process where the transformation of self takes hold and can propel students' empowerment over their traumatic pasts and into their strength-based perspectives of the path forward for themselves and others.

Metacognitive Reflection

The process of reflection and its inclusion in teacher education is widely discussed, but Risko et al. (2002) make significant statements about how reflection should be utilized when supporting teacher development. "It is most probable that as instructors we need to mediate prospective teachers' development by encouraging reflection as a process that is like 'turning a glove inside out,' the making of the familiar unfamiliar and the unfamiliar understandable" (p. 166). Furthermore, the authors posit that, "reflection that serves to 'reify' personal beliefs has little chance for developing a deep thinking" (p. 166). Reflection should be a vehicle to deconstruct and re-present, in conscious and sophisticated ways, the lived experiences of preservice teachers so they can begin to see the complexities of teaching and learning and their participation in those spaces (Spitler, 2009, pp. 21–22). To support this process, future teachers in Ellen's university classes write reflections of the creation and presentation of the autobiography and self-portrait, along with the oral presentation. Several prompts guide the written reflection and the exploration of their transforming understandings and perspectives of self and others:

What was most surprising about the writing process steps, including the provided scaffolding support, and what was *most* surprising about actually composing your autobiography?

1. What memories unexpectedly emerged as powerful in some way?
2. How did the writing process steps/scaffolding support the emergence of those memories?
3. What moments in the creation process of your multimodal self-portrait were unexpected and brought new understandings, insights, and perspectives of your own life? In other words, how has your thinking about your life transformed as a result?
4. How did the writing of this autobiography, and the creation of this multimodal artifact further develop your understanding of your life and the world?

5. As you were orally presenting your autobiography and self-portrait, what surprising moments occurred in your thinking and understanding of your authoring (literate) practices and experiences?

6. How could this type of work, the autobiography and the multimodal artifact be powerful in your own future classroom? How could you utilize the project and the writing?

CARLY'S PRESERVICE EXPERIENCE OF AUTOBIOGRAPHY AND SELF-PORTRAITURE

Like many aspiring teachers, I entered the College of Education filled with good intentions and a desire to make a difference. I knew that I wanted to work with students who had similarly challenging childhoods like my own. It was my aim to provide them with empathy and understanding for what they were experiencing. However, at the start of my College of Education experience, I was met with pure academia; loads of lectures, the memorization of educational theories, and essays that compared one pedagogy to another. While all these courses were important and helpful, they did not allow me to explore and build my unique teacher identity. It was as if my individuality was stripped away to make room for theory and standards. In that first year, I was often left frustrated and disconnected.

Upon entering my second year in the preservice program, the biggest opportunity was exploring and applying theories that had been covered in lecture education courses. I was able to take the theories that I felt worked with my area of study, with the culture of my school community, and with my personality.

My late start into university education and teaching allowed me to be more emotionally prepared to take on my teacher identity. I never fully realized the numerous traumatic events of my childhood and early adulthood until I had my own children. I grew up in a household in which alcoholism, drug addiction, domestic violence, and poverty were part of the normal day to day events. Those are the levels of trauma that come to mind.

Looking back at this experience through the 4 R's of SAMHSA's (2014) model, I can see that the autobiography and self-portraiture pushed me to:

- Realize: The university teacher education course was the first time I was asked to focus on the melding of my personal and teacher identity.

- Recognize: It allowed me the time and space to revisit and connect those formative childhood experiences with my emerging teacher identity as a safe place for students.
- Respond: I was able to effectively make those decisions through in-depth explorations into my successes and challenges.
- Resist re-traumatization: This process was profound because it gave me the safe space to both explore my personal and teacher identity during a highly stressful time. I was attending school full-time while taking care of my 5-year-old daughter and 1 year old son. To balance my home life and schoolwork, I would do my schoolwork after my children went to sleep. This often left me with five hours of sleep every day. I believe I was able to handle the stress because I felt safe both at home and at school.

Through this new perspective of myself, I was able to apply this new lens about the trauma that walks in with each student. "A trauma informed environment ... realizes the widespread impact of trauma and understands potential paths for recovery. People's experience and behavior are understood in the context of coping strategies designed to survive adversity and overwhelming circumstances" (SAMHSA, 2014, p. 9). If a teacher is to realize the widespread impact and existence of trauma, they must be exposed to and educated about these impacts. While some may think that the only way to be exposed is to experience trauma firsthand, I believe that is not the case. It wasn't until the sharing of our self-portraits that I was able to open my mind to the realization that trauma is more widespread and beyond my limited definition. I recognized and embraced that trauma can be the loss of a loved one, the divorce of one's parents, or the difficulties in finding one's identity. Sharing our stories helped us be open and vulnerable. It helped us empathize with each other on a basic and human level. It helped us build a safe community.

With all of these important factors taken into consideration, the university teacher education course allowed me to develop a teaching style and classroom community that is my own and supportive to the needs of my students. These experiences gave me the chance to balance those trauma-informed goals with a meaningful curriculum. I learned how to build lessons that supported the standards of secondary English Language Arts and to teach students the power in their experiences.

MARISA'S PRESERVICE EXPERIENCE OF AUTOBIOGRAPHY AND SELF-PORTRAITURE

There were two keyways in which Ellen's university teacher education course helped me self-actualize. The first was that it awakened me to the realization that I grew up with learner's privilege. Similar to White privilege, I consider it to be the exposure to a very rich, supportive environment that fosters many learning opportunities. Second, the autobiography and self-portrait guided my analytical deconstruction of, and critical insight into, a view of myself alongside a complex investigation of academic content that would not have occurred without the pedagogical invitations.

The focus of Ellen's autobiographical assignment was to inspire preservice teachers to reflect on and construct our identity in terms of how we learned to read and write. As I constructed my authorship identity, it was evident how I grew up in an educationally supportive, loving and learning rich environment. I was read to every night, went to the library with my parents on a weekly basis, and had active educational mentors. I am almost ashamed to say that as I prepared to become a certified teacher, I assumed that the students I would be teaching would be coming from the same place. As a veteran teacher now, I cringe at that naivety! What a horrible setback and detriment that would've been if I had approached my curriculum design from that extremely limited and discriminatory perspective!

I can also see the challenge that Ellen, as my teacher education professor, faced. How can preservice teachers become aware of and address their *own* biases prior to teaching? How can they then prepare themselves to address the social, emotional, and academic biases of their students, especially those who have gone through trauma?

From my growing teacher perspective, the key lay in the oral presentations. It sounds simple and nonrevolutionary, but it was a crucial aspect in my personal self-actualization process. As I listened to classmate after classmate present, and compared their experiences to my own, I realized that every learner/teacher identity was heavily influenced by some form of trauma—a disease that prevented them from comprehending and constructing language, the abuse of parents, the influence of drugs. It was at that moment where I realized that my learning experience was not the norm, and that it was vital not to assume everyone learned the way I did.

Most importantly, however, it helped me realize that if trauma was the norm for my classmates, it must also be the same for my students. Furthermore, if many of them are living with trauma, I need to design a thoughtful and purposeful curriculum that comes from a place of understanding its effects and how it hinders one's ability to process and construct meaning of not just the academic content, but also their understanding of themselves as learners.

By going through that metacognitive reflection process, I was able to design similar instructional strategies for my students so that they could go through a comparable transformation. An element of English/Language Arts (ELA) instruction that I previously understood on a superficial level was also further clarified. Beach et al. (2011) state that "without understanding their purpose, tools are meaningless" (p. 16). I realized that in order to meld content, curriculum and pedagogy, I could not utilize random instructional strategies. Rather, they need to be extremely purposeful, personal, and social in their intentions.

My previous viewpoint, in contrast, was insufficiently two dimensional. I knew that ELA instruction had to be relevant to the learner in order to increase connection and application. However, I thought that the relevance of the learner need only be on an individual basis in regard to how the text connected to them. It was by engaging in the self-reflective authorship process that I was forced to analyze how learning was not an individually based act at all. In contrast, learning is extremely and necessarily social. In aligning with Vygotsky's sociocultural theory, Beach et al. (2011) state that "people learn to use tools as serving various social issues ... we learn first through purposefully navigating through social interactions and collaboration, which is then internalized as inner dialogue" (p. 16). After analyzing the way in which I learned how to read, I began to uncover how the act of reading served as a way to grow myself socially and strengthen the relationships to which I was continually exposed.

Knowing this, in order to create effective strengths-based curriculum, it is necessary to develop lessons that "create a social community that supports learning literature" (Beach et al., 2011, p. 8). Students need a safe environment that allows them to use literary tools purposefully and meaningfully with others. Furthermore, the goal is to "socialize them into membership" by allowing students to "assume the identities of careful readers who acquire various practices included in interpreting and producing literature" (Beach et al., 2011, p. 8). Creating safe, supportive, social environments that are collaborative and allow students to support one another and grow together is a must. It is through these safe learning environments that they can make the connections themselves and see how working together affects not only how individuals learn, but also the learning of the community as a whole.

The development of the author autobiography and the multimodal self-portrait artifact also helped me understand the importance of incorporating reflection in ELA instruction. As Smagorinsky (2008) asserts, "Often we learn the most from our rough drafts, our frustrated efforts, and other experiences that do not yield our best products" (p. 56). In that way, assessment may not necessarily be graded on the perceived quality of work but on "how carefully you reflect on what you learned from producing them" (p. 56). By going through this experience as a learner, I realized how powerful self-reflection can be as a teaching tool. My preservice teacher self would not have been able to realize the significance and functionality of socialized learning if I was not forced to reflect on the nature and circumstances of my upbringing. Nor would I have been able to make the connection between literacy and my life practices if I was not tasked to reflect on those concepts through specific author lenses.

Finally, reflection is key, but a crucial element in that process is doing it purposefully. It is essential that when a "teacher introduces a skill, strategy or procedure to the whole class" it should "include a clear explanation of the nature of the task" and "explicit information about the expectations for what students will do" (Smagorinsky, 2008, p. 24). Making a clear connection to the primary objectives in mind is crucial when applying and integrating metacognitive reflection. The purpose of the project isn't to unveil deep, dark secrets, but to reflect on how past events shaped our literacy practices. My past has a direct effect on me, but there are a myriad of things that affect me in different ways. The genius behind Ellen's university course was the authentic way in which she inspired us not only to think about our past, but within the purposeful framework of her teacher education content. Thereby not only teaching us authentic strengths-based pedagogy, but also modeling how to do it ourselves. There needs to be a purpose to the madness of teaching. Otherwise, instruction becomes meaningless.

I am forever grateful for the transformative experience I had as it was the only coursework that adequately prepared me—emotionally, mentally, academically—to embrace the types of trauma that my students would have, and to be the authentic teacher I needed to be for them. When I began teaching my own autobiography and self-portrait units, the self-portrait sharing and metacognitive reflection were the two instructional strategies that were modified the most because of the fact that it provided such a high impact effect of both changing my perspective, as well as deepening my understanding of the content and concepts being taught.

CARLY'S INSERVICE EXPERIENCE WITH AUTOBIOGRAPHY AND SELF-PORTRAITURE

Through my experiences with the autobiography and self-portrait instructional engagements in Ellen's university teacher education course, I developed the theme that educational experiences are strongly tethered to the theory that relationship building and the sharing of experiences are instrumental in individualized learning and trauma support. If all trauma or Adverse Childhood Experiences (ACEs) are individualized, then all learning must be individualized in order to allow every student to feel supported and engaged.

At my school, Mid-Pacific Institute, we pride ourselves on educating the holistic needs of the learner. While academics are very important, we have many supports in place for the social and emotional needs of the students.

From grade level deans who serve as counselors to the students to Hawaii Center for Children and Families (HCCF) to provide additional psychological support for those that need more assistance academically, socially, and emotionally.

In the past two years, our middle school program has begun exploring options to provide Social Emotional Learning (SEL) opportunities. While some thought it would be best to carve out time from our advisory hours and create SEL lessons, our eighth-grade team posited that effective SEL opportunities happen within the regular classroom and are woven into the curriculum. To support our idea, I cited the autobiography and self-portrait project that we have in the eighth-grade Language Arts course. The design of the identity autobiography and self-portrait project allows students to explore their own stories (both positive and negative), builds empathy, and creates the foundation of a safe classroom community. Below are some of the included sample projects.

Exploring and Sharing Stories

1. Mo'olelo journal: The mo'olelo journal is a constant in our learning community. Mo'olelo is Hawaiian for storytelling or *talk story*. I decided to embrace this idea of talk story to explore how personal narrative writing can fuel informational writing. The 10 or 20 minutes that students spend writing their mo'olelo is a beneficial way to start the learning process early in the morning or late in the afternoon. It helps students to get focused and engaged in the writing process. It helps to quiet their minds from life's pressures, and it helps them open up their minds to the creation of writing. Much like bell work, it is a great way to have students focus on a concept and/or learning objective.

2. We Are Poetry: Using inspiration from Hawai'i poet Lisa Linn Kanae's (2012) poem "Bike Rides to the Ocean," we start every school year getting to know each other by creating We Are poems. Students are placed in small groups and asked to build a cohesive poem that includes personal details about their environment, their familiar foods and dishes, the typical expressions heard around them, and the important people in their lives. This assignment always brings students together as they learn about their similarities and differences. Surprisingly, those differences are the aspects that allow students to learn more about the challenges that their fellow students may face daily. This exploration is how we build a solid foundation for our learning community.

Building Empathy

3. Skin Stories Project: In the Skin Stories Narrative unit, high school students explore the art and culture of Polynesian tattoo. Students analyze an information website through a scavenger hunt, by watching a documentary, and through class discussion. This unit ends with students reflecting these important experiences into their own skin story artifact and a personal narrative about their skin story. When asked to reflect on what was learned from the unit, one student answered: "I can use the information I learned because [in] outside life you need to make better decisions and respect others to have yourself be respected and to have good things happen in your life."

Creating a Safe Classroom Community

4. Mo'olelo circle: After students practice trusting the process of the Mo'olelo Journal, we begin sharing our ideas. We form a Mo'olelo Circle and I give the following instructions: *Mo'olelo means storytelling. We will be telling some of our stories to each other. By sharing our stories, we can improve our writing. You can share as much or as little as you want. It is purely voluntary.*

As the teacher, my only job is to wait for volunteers and monitor the time. As a participant of our learning community, I usually share first on the very first day. While there are often long moments of silence, I do not force students. The mo'olelo circle again builds trust, empathy, and continues to create a safe space for everyone.

According to Herrenkohl and Prince (2021), "if you shape the environment so that all kids regardless of level of risk are treated in a way conducive to mental health, healing, resilience, and well-being, you can do a better job at addressing trauma for all students" (p. 38). The early integration of the autobiography and self-portrait assists educators to meet the needs of those that do and do not fit the so-called *image* of trauma. Through the experience of writing the autobiography, creating the self-portraiture, and sharing their experiences, the teacher and students build a strong, trusting, and safe learning community. The implication is that the teacher transforms into a protective factor for students and helps to mitigate the risk factors they encounter every day. When recognized as a supportive adult, I show all students that I will be stable, I will always be there, I will be sensitive to their needs, and I will love them unconditionally. Such relational factors are highlighted by Doom (2021), as helping to prevent the negative effects of trauma. A powerful example that illustrates the significance of relational factors is clear in a recent message sent to me by one of my former students:

> I don't think I ever told you but you were one of the teachers that actually made me want to come to school. You actually understood the mind of a high schooler lol. But I mean there was that one time you wouldn't let me attend senior ditch day cause I was on the borderline of failing. Still you saved my butt on that one.

He graduated back in 2012 and his message made me realize that we leave a lasting impression for these students (who have and will shortly become adults) to reflect upon. As I always share with students in my classroom, my first goal is to make them feel loved, seen, and important. And we will also learn how to build up our reading, writing, and speaking skills.

Those moments are key because every human needs those memories to help them face the rest of the world, just as they are described in the 4 Rs of trauma informed practices: we realize, we recognize, we respond, and we resist re-traumatization (SAMHSA, 2014, pp. 9–10). Like I tell my students, they cannot carry me around in their pocket, but I have to hope that the lessons and experiences they had in our classroom will carry them forward in the future.

MARISA'S INSERVICE EXPERIENCE WITH AUTOBIOGRAPHY AND SELF-PORTRAITURE

A vivid memory I have as a new student teacher was being confused on how to design curriculum. I was eager to introduce the autobiography and self-portrait project but was utterly unsure how to do it. I thought I had to recreate the content Ellen utilized in the teacher education course, and it was like trying to fit a square peg in a round hole. From a preservice teacher's perspective, I yearned for a Part 2 of the course: "How to Incorporate Your Own Teaching Standards within the Basic Framework." It was only through one-on-one coaching by Ellen that I was able to design a version of the project that allowed me to take out the authorship piece and bring in the specific literature and the concepts that I needed to teach in my class. Back then I still didn't understand how to draw out a student's personal life in order to learn content.

One example is framed in a literary analysis of *The Alchemist* (Coelho, 1988). Students analyze the story's theme of personal legend as they track the main character taking a journey through the soul of the world. In their literary exploration, they are guided to define and unpack the essential attributes of a personal legend and the soul of the world journey and pull textual examples from the novel to support their constructions. Students are then provided with structure and parameters to (a) write their own personal legend autobiographies that describe their six soul of the world moments, and (b) create a personal legend self-portrait to represent each. The result is an exploration of the ways in which students can represent and reconstruct their lives in that multigenre and multimodal work within the content framework to help them better understand those content concepts on a much more authentic and deeper level.

I realized through repeated teaching of the unit, however, that it is not enough for the students to construct their own autobiography and self-portrait. The real juice that drives the crucial step of adopting a different perspective, developing empathy for others, and ultimately reconstructing their identity in a more positive, healthy, and self-healing manner happens when they do the following:

- thoughtfully listen to other perspectives within a safe, coconstructed environment;
- practice purposeful metacognition and analysis;
- practice safe community building rituals as a class in order to construct new understandings and relationships.

I strongly feel that relationship building and the sharing of experiences, purposefully coupled with reflective metacognitive analysis, are instrumental in individualized learning and trauma support.

Oral Presentation: Safe Rituals and Environment Set-Up

Most secondary students are extremely reluctant to share their stories, especially if they have experienced personal trauma. The following are practices that have been adopted and modified in order to create a safe space for secondary students to share, connect, become aware of and adopt different perspectives, and ultimately build a safe classroom community:

1. Cocreate the oral presentation order with the students days in advance. Students determine the order and manner in which they want to present, as well as share the modality of their self-portrait. This serves to both provide a safety zone, as well as set high expectations through the sharing of intended products.
2. Change the normal class setting environment to promote community and signal a designation of a new safe space that is conducive to the sharing of stories. Examples include:

- In classroom: Take away desks and install a big carpet for students to sit in a big circle.
- Out of classroom: Go on a field trip to a natural and shady environment, such as a garden or beach. Create a circle with picnic blankets, lounge chairs or one big mat.

In each scenario, students have permission to make themselves comfortable, as long as they can write in their Listening Dialectic Journal (DJ) strategy, look at the presenter, and show respect.

3. Positive Affirmations and Note Sharing: In the center of the circle, as well as inter-spaced throughout the borders of the circle, provide buckets with post-its or small sheets of paper, and colorful writing materials such as markers and colored pencils. After each presentation, students are encouraged and given time to write and pass notes to each presenter. They also have the option to give anonymous notes to the teacher, who will later deliver the note to the designated student.

It is important to note that the teacher presents first to ensure that (a) students have a model of how to present their autobiography and self-portrait, and (b) the sharing of the teacher's own personal emotional trauma (Bathina, 2014) opens up the space for students to do the same.

4. Set the tone. An individual student who is emotionally ready and has a particularly powerful or traumatic story (based on prior teacher vetting) is discreetly approached and extended an invitation to be the first student presenter.

I have found that if the presentations open up with a student who is very open and honest about their trauma, it sets the tone for authentic sharing and the rest of the students are more willing to open up and be comfortable with sharing their own trauma. For example, a student in one class shared how she was date raped. As a result, many more students approached me asking if they could change their project to include their stories of sexual abuse. About one third of the class had experienced a form of sexual abuse and many of them expressed how they would not have shared if it were not for the bravery of that first student presenter.

5. Closing Procedures: At the end of all of the presentations, each student composes a formal letter to one person in the class, and there is a share out of who they composed their letter to and why. However, I have also incorporated new closing rituals as well:

- Students are asked to mingle in the center of the circle, giving each classmate a high five.
- Create a Toast for Change where each student shares one word or wish (related to the content being taught) and is toasted.

Metacognitive Reflection

In order to complete the circle and provide opportunities for students to experience authentic identity and community transformations, the oral presentations must be followed by thoughtfully designed metacognitive reflections. One without the other would interrupt the process of transformed empowerment and resiliency.

The clarifying moment for me, when I realized how key the metacognitive reflection was in terms of drawing out and assessing the effectiveness of unit goals and objectives, happened during a thematic unit professional development workshop. One question frequently asked was, "How will we know that the students understand, comprehend and can apply the key concepts that we are looking for?" This forced me to ask myself, "What is the one thing that I want the students to be able to do?" From an academic standpoint, it was a critical thinking application. I did not want students to mechanically go through the steps of the writing process, for example, and complete a particular prewriting activity because I assigned it. It was important that they do it *purposefully*. A win would be to assign a writing activity and based on the students' unique thinking process and the desired content, see them develop the confidence to decide which specific prewriting activity would be most conducive to accomplish their goal. In other words, I don't want to give them the metaphorical fish. I always tell them; this is so you can fish on your own. Therefore, as part of the final summative, whatever skill that needed to be assessed was the skill they had to apply. For example, if it was the writing process, each step was broken down and metacognitively assessed. Students used their metacognitive reflections to explain specific strategies they used while completing the writing process and how it was effective for them to construct meaning as authors.

This was an amazing learning moment as a teacher because I was able to see the student move from memorization to application of the concepts behind each step. They were able to verbalize which prewriting strategy was more effective and why, so that when presented with another writing activity, they could then put their critical thinking skills to use. That subtle but purposeful switch was key and, moving forward, I learned that I needed to be more purposeful in designing instructional strategies that move students to internalizing critical thinking application skills they can practice and refine. It is important to note that while designing trauma-informed pedagogical practices, this also stands true for meeting social and emotional learning objectives, guiding students to gain new, more positive and healthy perspectives of both themselves and others.

Following the same framework in which the critical thinking application skills were designed for academic standards, I created metacognitive reflections that asked students to analyze their emotions, perspectives of others, relationships, and so forth. These were all seemingly intangible human actions that I felt previously could not be measured. Sample metacognitive reflection questions are provided below to illustrate how both academic and social emotional learning standards were elicited from students through assessment.

ACADEMIC STANDARDS: WRITING PROCESS

Compare and contrast two different prewriting strategies you used while writing your Autobiography, explaining why one was more effective than the other in helping develop your final draft.

Using your rough draft, write down one to three sentences that were a part of your original rough draft. Please write down that sentence in blue or black ink. In another color, show how you used ARMS (Add, Remove, Move, Substitute: sentences, words, or phrases) to revise that sentence(s). Next, show and explain the thinking behind why you used one or more revision strategies to further develop your work.

ACADEMIC STANDARDS: PERSONAL NARRATIVE AND SOCIAL EMOTIONAL LEARNING

1. Look over the list of presenters and circle the presenter that provided a sequence of events that built on one another to provide a coherent whole. Next, describe why you chose that person. What did that storyteller do in order to provide a smooth progression of experiences that ultimately helped you understand a big picture?
2. What makes a story a good story? What critical attributes do you think a story must have in order for it to be an engaging and effective personal narrative?

ACADEMIC STANDARDS: CONCEPTS

1. Define resilience. Describe how you will apply resilience the next time you need to write a paper and go through the writing process.

2.   How did the writing of your powerful and powerless moments and the creation of the self-portrait further develop your understanding of what power means? How would you define power?

SOCIAL EMOTIONAL LEARNING

1.   Define metacognition. Describe how metacognition and the reflection process helped you better understand and/or learn something about yourself. In other words, how did looking back in the past, or going through the writing and creation process, help you realize something about yourself that you have not previously thought of?

2.   Using your Listening DJ, provide a personal example of how listening to the Self-Portrait presentations helped you better understand someone else in your class. Describe what they said or did and explain how that helped you better understand or relate to them.

3.   Using your Listening DJ, describe at least two key learnings or strategies that several of your classmates used in order to be resilient and overcome their obstacles. Next, describe how listening about how they were able to overcome their challenges helped give you insight into how the world works for the better.

This purposeful construction of metacognitive analysis fuels the critical thinking necessary to use the academic content to deconstruct and reconstruct their identities, consequently not only deepening their academic comprehension, but simultaneously deepening their understanding of themselves, others, and the world. In sum, I learned that for true perspective taking and identity reconstruction to happen, especially when incorporating trauma pedagogy, a safe environment and community building rituals for authentic sharing, as well as metacognitive reflection and analysis, need to be purposefully designed and implemented.

REFLECTIONS AND IMPLICATIONS

Insights from all three of our experiences with this work continue to drive the lessons we have learned and support our goals moving forward, based on those implications. Regularly in our classes, students reflect on how surprised they are when they realize just how much they have achieved in their past *because* of trauma, and how it helped them get to know themselves on a deeper level. For example, one student in Marisa's classroom realized "that no matter what little insignificant thing I did, it all still impacted and contributed to making me into the person I am today. The autobiography and self-portrait project made me actually think and get to know myself." Through that process of getting to know herself within the trauma-informed framework, she was surprised to learn "how much more accepting I now am of myself and what I have accomplished ... even if I was writing about a negative period in my life, it made me stop and think, 'hey look where I am now. Wow.'" This is a powerful learning moment for both the student and teacher, as it helps students clearly see their personal *chain of events* and how the choices they do or do not make have a powerful impact on them. It is also heartwarming and significant because, from a trauma pedagogical standpoint, this metacognitive developmental process helped the student move toward self-acceptance. For a teenager going through so much anger and self-esteem issues, the act of accepting herself and growing more confident in who she is and who she wants to be is powerful. This is why we went into teaching. Hence, purposefully guiding students who have been through trauma through highly metacognitive practices has very powerful implications in terms of guiding students to "expanding our consciousness, shaping our dispositions, satisfying our quest for meaning" (Eisner, 2002, p. 3).

Autobiography and self-portraiture also have powerful and transformative implications in the ability to inspire students to establish contact with others and coconstruct a more understanding, empathetic, and supportive culture. The most difficult hurdle, and therefore powerful transformation, is guiding students toward empathy; specifically, inviting them to step into the shoes of their classmates and begin to understand and accept each other on a deeper level. By listening to each presentation and later metacognitively reflecting and analyzing that experience, one student in Marisa's class shared that she was able to learn that,

> I shouldn't be so quick to judge or put people in categories or label them. Petty names like loser, blockhead, pimple face, gay, lesbian, fag, dork. None of these are nice and you can't judge someone by what they wear, how they talk, what grade they get, anything until you actually hear what they went through, their influences, etc.

For her to understand the concept of being non-judgmental and empathetic, and to honestly internalize it, was incredible. If educators and teacher educators are to guide students to move past the pain inflicting models that have been taught to them as a result of trauma, it is necessary to help them construct new ways of thinking and acting that not only break that cycle on an individual level, but from a sociocultural level, as well.

To conclude her reflection, the same student wrote that "listening to my classmates share their beautiful stories really made me acknowledge them and helped me understand a little bit more about that person and helped me be more compassionate to my fellow classmates." It is through transformative experiences like these that we have the power to help students renew confidence in the way they view themselves, connect with others and reconstruct their world.

REFERENCES

Alsup, J. (2006). *Teacher identity discourses: Negotiating personal and professional spaces.* Lawrence Erlbaum Associates.

Bathina, J. (2014). When the subaltern finally speaks: Personal narrative as a means to identity and voice. *Journal of Adolescent & Adult Literacy, 58*(1), 27–35. https://doi.org/10.1002/jaal.317

Bean, T. (1997). Preservice teachers' selection and use of content area literacy strategies. *The Journal of Educational Research, 90*(3), 154–163. https://doi.org/10.1080/00220671.1997.10543771

Beach, R., Appleman, D., Hynds, S., & Wilhelm, J. (2011). *Teaching literature to adolescents* (2nd ed.). Routledge Taylor & Francis Group.

Buehl, D. (2014). *Classroom strategies for interactive learning* (4th ed.). International Reading Association.

Coelho, P. (1988). *The Alchemist.* HarperCollins.

Collaborative for Academic, Social, and Emotional Learning. (2019). *CASEL SEL Trends: Strengthening Adult SEL.* Retrieved from CASEL website: https://casel.org/wp-content/uploads/2019/11/SEL-Trends-7-11182019.pdf

Cole, S., Eisner, A., Gregory, M., & Ristuccia, J. (2013). *Helping traumatized children learn: Vol. 2. Creating and advocating for trauma-sensitive schools.* Massachusetts Advocates for Children, Trauma and Learning Policy Initiative website: https://traumasensitiveschools.org/tlpi-publications/download-a- free-copy-of-a-guide-to-creating-trauma-sensitive-schools/

Cox, L. M., & Lyddon, W. J. (1997). Constructivist conceptions of self: A discussion of emerging identity constructs. *Journal of Constructivist Psychology, 10,* 201–219. https://doi.org/10.1080/10720539708404623

Danielewicz, J. (2001). *Teaching selves: Identity, pedagogy, and teacher education.* State University of New York Press.

Davidson, S. (2017). *Trauma-informed practices for post-secondary education: A guide.* Retrieved from Education Northwest website: https://educationnorthwest.org/resources/trauma-informed-practices-postsecondary-education-guide#:~:text=This%20guide%20is%20intended%20to,have%20been%20exposed%20to%20trauma.

Doom, J. (2021, January 5) *How can pandemic trauma impact students in the long run? What does it mean to be trauma-informed? A 4-Part Video Explainer* [Video]. Education Week. https://www.edweek.org/leadership/what-does-it-mean-to-be-trauma-informed-a-4-part-video-explainer?utm_source=nl&utm_medium=eml&utm_campaign=vid&M=59832286&U=2 666796&UUID=dd613e3f87eadea3132fe3aed513ba98

Eisner, E. (2002). *The arts and the creation of mind*. Yale University Press.

Freeman, M. (2001). From substance to story: Narrative, identity, and the reconstruction of self. In J. Brockmeier & D. Carbaugh (Eds.), *Narrative and identity: Studies in autobiography, self, and culture* (pp. 284–298). John Benjamins.

Freire, P. (2003). *Pedagogy of the oppressed*. Herder and Herder.

Freire, P., & Macedo, D. (1987). *Literacy: Reading the word and the world*. Bergin & Garvey.

Gcc, J. P. (1987). What is literacy? In C. Mitchell & K. Weile (Eds.), *Rewriting literacy: Culture and the discourse of the other*. Bergin & Garvey.

Goodman, Y., Watson, D., & Burke, C. (1987). *Reading miscue inventory*. Richard C. Owen.

Herrenkohl, T., & Prince, R. (2021, January 5) *Tips for building trauma informed programs. What does it mean to be trauma-informed? A 4-Part Video Explainer* [Video]. Education Week. https://www.edweek.org/leadership/what-does-it-mean-to-be-trauma-informed-a-4-part-video-explainer?utm_source=nl&utm_medium=eml&utm_campaign=vid&M=59832286&U=2666796&UUID=dd613e3f87eadea3132fe3aed513ba98

Hopper, E. K., Bassuk, E. L., & Olivet, J. (2010). Shelter from the storm: Trauma-informed care in homelessness services settings. *The Open Health Services and Policy Journal, 2*, 131–151. https://doi.org/10.2174/1874924001003010080

Kanae, L. L. (2012, May 3). *Ka'Umeke*. Kapi'olani Community College. https://kaumekekcc.wordpress.com/2012/05/03/i-am-from-poem/

Kress, G. (2003). *Literacy in the new media age*. Routledge.

Kress, G. (2006). *Before writing: Rethinking the paths to literacy*. Routledge.

Moje, E. (2000). *All the stories that we have: Adolescents' insights about literacy and learning in secondary schools*. International Literacy Association.

Moran, S., & John-Steiner, V. (2003). Creativity in the making: Vygotsky's contemporary contribution to the dialectic of development and creativity. In R. K. Sawyer, V. John-Steiner, S. Moran, R. J. Sternberg, D. H. Feldman, J. Nakamura, & M. Csikszentmihalyi (Eds.), *Creativity and development* (pp. 61–90). Oxford University Press.

Risko, V. J., Roskos, K., & Vukelich, C. (2002). Prospective teachers' reflection: Strategies, qualities, and perceptions in learning to teach reading. *Reading Research and Instruction, 41*(2), 149–176. https://doi.org/10.1080/19388070209558363

Risko, V. J., Roller, C., Cummins, C., Bean, R., Collins Block, C., Anders, P.L., & Flood, J. (2008). A critical analysis of research on reading teacher education. *Reading Research Quarterly, 43*(3), 252–288. https://doi.org/10.1598/RRQ.43.3.3

Smagorinsky, P. (2008). *Teaching English by design: How to create and carry out instructional units*. Heinemann

Spitler, E. (2009). *Transformation of preservice and new teacher literacy identity: Three transactional dimensions*. https://repository.arizona.edu/handle/10150/194822

Substance Abuse and Mental Health Services Administration. (2014). SAMHSA's *Concept of Trauma and Guidance for a Trauma-Informed Approach*. Retrieved from Substance Abuse and Mental Health Services Administration website: https://ncsacw.samhsa.gov/userfiles/files/SAMHSA_Trauma.pdf

Sumara, D., & Luce-Kapler, R. (1996). (Un)becoming a teacher: Negotiating identities while learning to teach. *Canadian Journal of Education*, *21*(1), 65–83. https://doi.org/10.2307/1495065

Vygotsky, L. (1978). *Mind in society*. Harvard University Press.

CHAPTER 11

TEACHER CANDIDATE PERCEPTIONS AND KNOWLEDGE OF TRAUMA-INFORMED PRACTICES IN SCHOOLS

Tommy Wells
Bellarmine University

Vanessa Gee
Indiana University-Purdue University

Madeline Chimka
HighScope Educational Research Foundation

ABSTRACT

Teachers are well-positioned to identify and respond to students who have experienced trauma, yet teacher preparedness in trauma-informed practices can vary significantly. This study explores teacher candidates' perceptions and knowledge of trauma-informed practices at two teacher preparation programs located in urban cities. Specifically, we examined teacher candidates' values and beliefs regarding their role in supporting students experiencing trauma, ways in which their identity influences their understanding of trauma, and the extent to which they perceived their teacher preparation programs

Developing Trauma-Informed Teachers: Creating Classrooms That Foster Equity, Resiliency, and Asset-Based Approaches: Research Findings From the Field, pp. 195–215
Copyright © 2023 by Information Age Publishing
www.infoagepub.com

provided the skills and knowledge necessary to address future students' needs. Findings indicate that many teacher candidates receive little to no training in trauma-informed practices, and their experiences differ both within and between universities. Future directions for teacher preparation programs are explored, including a framework for culturally responsive, trauma-informed educator identity.

Because of the ongoing effects of the COVID-19 pandemic, many students, educators, and school leaders may return to school with a shared traumatic experience. While COVID-19 is a unique, shared traumatic experience, trauma is not uncommon. The first understanding of the prevalence of trauma was identified in Felitti et al.'s (1998) study on adverse childhood experiences (ACEs). Anda et al. (2006) found that almost two-thirds of adults had experienced ACEs, which is similar to Copeland et al.'s (2007) findings that by the age of 16, 30.8% had experienced one ACE and 37% had experienced two or more. According to the National Child Traumatic Stress Network (NCTSN, 2017), trauma can also manifest from oppression and racialized experiences. Racial trauma can occur after witnessing or experiencing racism, discrimination, or structural prejudice (National Child Traumatic Stress Network [NCTSN], 2017). To help address the effects of trauma, organizations, such as the Substance Abuse and Mental Health Services Administration (SAMHSA, 2014), developed trauma-informed frameworks designed to inform and promote systems of care.

The relationship between trauma and its impacts on learning is well-documented. A trauma-informed system, where all stakeholders recognize and respond to the impact of trauma, can include schools and school districts (Chafouleas et al., 2016; Thomas et al., 2019). Exposure to trauma is associated with barriers to school achievement, given that trauma can disrupt social, emotional, cognitive, and brain development (Cole et al., 2005; Raby et al., 2019; Thomas et al., 2019). Specifically, trauma can adversely impact one's self-regulation and executive functioning (e.g., organization, comprehension, and memorization), negatively impacting learning (Blaustein & Kinniburgh, 2019; Thomas et al., 2019). Metzler et al. (2017) described how adults who have more ACEs were less likely to graduate from high school, more likely to be unemployed, and more likely to live below the federal poverty line. Moreover, people may experience racial trauma from the impacts of experiencing racism or discrimination (Carter, 2007). Schools can thus re-traumatize students of color who already may be more likely to experience trauma compared to White children when educators hold biases against students from historically marginalized backgrounds and enact policies and practices that uphold systems of oppression (e.g., exclusionary discipline practices) (Iruka et al., 2020; NCTSN, 2019; Thomas et al., 2019; Williams et al., 2018).

Through use of trauma-informed practices, educators can help support students who have experienced trauma (Baum et al., 2009) both in and outside the classroom (Wiest-Stevenson & Lee, 2016). For example, teachers can express that they care and expand opportunities for their students (Sethi & Scales, 2020), as well as connect students and their families to mental health resources (Farmer et al., 2003). However, many teachers lack training in trauma-informed practices (Alisic et al., 2012; Baweja et al., 2016). Consequently, in the wake of the COVID-19 pandemic, students may have traumatic experiences that educators might not be prepared to address.

A standardized framework for trauma-informed practices in education does not exist (Thomas et al., 2019), which presents challenges for teacher preparation programs in determining the extent of training in trauma-informed practices they should provide. For example, Alisic et al. (2012) found that only 9% of teachers had training in trauma-informed practices, but little is known about the extent of this training in teacher preparation programs. While organizations have developed system frameworks for trauma-informed schools (see NCTSN, 2021), we hope to address the gap in the literature by outlining a trauma-informed framework for building capacity in educators, including specific knowledge and skills. We posit that a primary component of this framework is social emotional learning (SEL). SEL helps students develop healthy identities, regulate their emotions, and build supportive relationships (Collaborative for Academic, Social, and Emotional Learning [CASEL], 2020). In the classroom, Wiest-Stevenson and Lee (2016) described how teachers embed social-emotional learning into their curriculum to teach empathy, emotional regulation, and interpersonal skills, which would be particularly beneficial for students who have experienced trauma, as they often struggle with self-regulation (Blaustein & Kinniburgh, 2019). However, similar to the lack of research on the impact of training in trauma-informed practices in teacher preparation programs (Thomas et al., 2019), the extant research focused on training in SEL in teacher preparation programs is also limited. According to Schonert-Reichl et al. (2017), "the promotion of students' SEL is given little attention in required courses in teacher preparation programs in colleges of education in the U.S." (p. 11) despite the research that highlights the need for students to develop these skills to promote school success. The SEL component also includes strategies for adult SEL, which Woolf (n.d.) defines as the "process of helping educators build their expertise and skills to lead social and emotional learning initiatives. It also involves cultivating adults' own social and emotional competencies" (para. 5). Adult SEL is critical, as Reyes et al. (2012) found that teachers who were required to teach SEL but did not develop their own practice worsened their students' SEL skills. A part of adult SEL also includes self-care (Woolf, n.d.), as educators are indirectly exposed to hearing about the trauma of students, families, and colleagues, placing them at risk for secondary traumatic stress or vicarious trauma (Hydon et al., 2015; Lawson et al., 2019). Engaging in self-care practices helps promote the health and well-being of educators (Thomas et al., 2019), and both adult SEL and self-care are essential in promoting educator resilience.

As educators, an essential part of working with students exposed to trauma is reflecting on one's practice (NCTSN, 2017). Reflection promotes an introspective look into our own identity, worldview, and beliefs, which may inform our experiences, biases, and responses to students and colleagues (NCTSN, 2017), Therefore, the final component of trauma-informed practices is the ability of educators to practice reflexivity. D'Cruz et al. (2007) described key aspects of reflexivity, including a critical self-awareness in how one engages with social issues, a recognition that assumptions of social issues have ethical and practical consequences, and ongoing reflection on personal practice, knowledge, and assumptions. Engaging in reflexivity supports educators in two important facets. First, it supports educators in developing their resilience through the process of reflecting on their position, values, and areas of personal and professional growth. Second, it helps educators to mitigate their assumptions and biases and to dismantle systems of oppression.

Culturally Responsive, Trauma-informed Educator Identity Framework

We posit a framework titled the *culturally responsive, trauma-informed educator identity* framework. This framework was developed from a scoping review of the literature on trauma-informed practices in the school setting that included peer-reviewed literature as well as guidance documents and other publications on trauma. The scoping review process followed steps outlined in Newman and Gough (2020), including 1. specifying a research question (i.e., what trauma-informed practices do individual educators need to know for implementation?), 2. designing a conceptual framework, 3. constructing selection criteria (i.e., resources published within the last 10 years, described trauma-informed strategies in the school setting, guidance for educators), 4. developing a search strategy, 5. selecting and coding studies, 6. assessing and synthesizing studies, and 7. reporting findings. In this instance, the conceptual framework that was "developed, refined [and] confirmed during the course of the research" (p. 7) was also our reported finding, in that our framework is to be used as "research tool" for understanding trauma-informed practices in the school setting (Newman & Gough, 2020). We also engaged in document analysis of the existing systems of care frameworks from SAMHSA (2014) and NCTSN (2021). Our framework promotes SAMHSA's four aspects of a trauma-informed approach in the context of care: realize the widespread impact of trauma; recognize the signs and symptoms of trauma; respond by fully integrating knowledge about trauma into policies, procedures, and practices; seek to actively resist re-traumatization), as well as its six principles of "1. Safety, 2. Trustworthiness and Transparency, 3. Peer support, 4. Collaboration and Mutuality, 5. Empowerment, Voice and Choice, 6. Cultural, Historical, and Gender Issues" (p. 10). The culturally responsive, trauma-informed educator identity framework places emphasis on "cultural, historical, and gender issues" and the need to "resist re-traumatization." Additionally, the framework incorporates aspects of teacher identity, defined as a "concept or analytical tool [that] examines how individuals, inside social contexts, construct and continually reconstruct understandings of and for themselves as teachers" (Olsen, 2012, p. 1122). Identity is developed through lived experiences and social context. Olsen (2012) argues teachers must always identify how their experiences and milieu interact with their teacher identity, including

> vestiges of racism, deficit thinking, gender biases, heteronormativity, and other preconceptions that can penalize or damage children's learning. Teacher identity holds that every teacher [including their students] will benefit from engaging in critical self-examination and managing the various ways [they allow] personal biographical, cultural, and political perspectives to enter into [their] teaching self. (p. 1124)

The posited culturally responsive, trauma-informed educator identity framework relies on knowledge and skills (see Figure 11.1) of culturally responsive (Ladson-Billings, 2014), trauma-informed practices that also incorporate the work of educator identity development. This framework aligns with Brown et al. (2020), who stated how "educators practicing culturally responsive, trauma-informed practices understand the intersection of systemic oppression and trauma and use this framework to effect change" (p. 5). This framework requires that educators explore identity in the context of the education system (see NCTSN, 2017), including an examination of historical, educational practices, policies, and systems that enshrined inequities based on student characteristics, such as race/ethnicity, gender, sexual orientation, and disability, as well as intersectional identities (Crenshaw, 1991). This exploration must occur before educators can have a thorough understanding of and appropriate intentionality in implementing trauma-informed practices that are culturally responsive and promote equity.

Figure 11.1

Knowledge and Skills of the Culturally Responsive, Trauma-Informed Educator Identity Framework

1. Social, emotional, cognitive, and physical impacts of trauma
2. Trauma-informed classroom and school-wide practices
3. Culturally responsive practices
4. Social-emotional learning practices
5. Practicing of self-care
6. Understanding of one's own cultural identity and values
7. Engaging in reflexivity

Educator identity development and learning of culturally responsive, trauma-informed practices are particularly significant in educators' efforts to resist the re-traumatization of their students. To ensure that trauma-informed practices minimize re-traumatization, educators must consider how their identity, including their position of influence, may interact with students' prior trauma because of the historical practices and policies of schools that promote and uphold systemic oppression: "Staff who work within a trauma-informed environment are taught to recognize how organizational practices may trigger painful memories and re-traumatize clients with trauma histories" (SAMHSA, 2014, p. 10). The attention to one's own cultural identity and values in relation to those of their students is critical, as the demographics of the teaching force are primarily women who identify as White (National Center for Education Statistics, 2020). The culturally responsive, trauma-informed educator identity framework includes all staff, regardless of their role in the school, district, or educational organization (Thomas et al., 2019). Therefore, we employed our culturally responsive, trauma-informed educator identity framework as the lens through which analysis occurred as we explored teacher candidates' perceptions and knowledge of trauma-informed practices.

CURRENT STUDY

This study examined teacher candidates' perceptions and knowledge of culturally responsive, trauma-informed practices at two universities—one public university in the Midwest and one private university in the South, both located in urban cities. The public university promotes how it prepares its candidates to create social change in urban settings with an emphasis on anti-racist stances. The private university offers graduate-level coursework in trauma-informed practices but does not offer them in initial teacher certification programs. We sought to uncover how each university may have integrated trauma-informed practices at the undergraduate or initial teacher certification level to better understand teacher candidate preparedness. This study addressed two research questions: (1) What are teacher candidates' perceptions of (a) the needs of students experiencing trauma, (b) their role in supporting students experiencing trauma, and (c) their self-efficacy in supporting these students? and (2) Do differences exist in teacher candidates' perceptions of these three facets based on content, curriculum, and pedagogies addressing trauma-informed practices provided by their teacher preparation programs?

This study employed a convergent mixed methods design (Creswell & Guetterman, 2019) for data collection. Quantitative and qualitative data were collected simultaneously and merged to develop a more complete understanding of participants' perceptions and knowledge. We used a cross-sectional survey design (Creswell & Guetterman, 2019) to administer a questionnaire that included rating scales, open-ended response items, and demographic questions. In addition, document analysis occurred to review relevant sources that described the goals of both teacher preparation programs.

METHOD

Participants

The questionnaire was distributed to 154 teacher candidates at the private university and 396 teacher candidates at the public university. The final sample resulted in 134 responses out of 550, 47 participants from the private university and 87 from the public university, for a response rate of 24.4%. See Table 11.1 for sociodemographic characteristics.

Table 11.1

Sociodemographic Characteristics of Participants

Characteristic	n	%
Year in School		
Freshmen	5	4
Sophomore	10	7
Junior	35	26
Senior	71	53
Graduate student	9	7
Prefer not to disclose	4	3

(Table continued on next page)

Table 11.1 (Continued)

Sociodemographic Characteristics of Participants

Characteristic	n	%
Certification Track		
Early Childhood	9	7
Elementary School	81	60
Middle School/Junior High	9	7
High School	22	16
K-12/All Grades	9	7
Prefer not to disclose	4	3
Gender Identity		
Woman	115	86
Man	11	8
Nonbinary/third gender	3	2
Prefer not to disclose	5	4
Race		
Asian American/Pacific Islander	5	4
Black/African American	5	4
Caucasian/White	109	1
Native American/American Indian	2	1
Two or more races	6	4
Prefer not to disclose	7	5
Ethnicity		
Hispanic/Latino	9	7
Not Hispanic/Latino	117	87
Prefer not to say	8	6
Experienced a Traumatic Event	36	27

Recruitment

This study received approval from the Institutional Review Boards at both the private and public universities. We used purposive sampling to collect responses from two specific universities to create a comparison group. All students enrolled in the teacher preparation program at both these universities were emailed a Qualtrics link describing the questionnaire and informed consent.

Measures

Participants completed the *Teacher Candidate Perceptions and Knowledge of Trauma-informed Practices* questionnaire designed for this study. We followed processes outlined by Fowler (2014) to develop the questionnaire. First, we conducted a review of the extant literature and developed the culturally responsive, trauma-informed educator identity framework. Next, we held a small focus group with teacher candidates to gain their understanding of concepts from the literature. After, we drafted an initial set of questions that underwent a critical systematic review by a team of five educators with expertise in trauma-informed practices and/or teacher preparation to establish face and content validity. Lastly, we conducted a field pretest with five teacher candidates to test questionnaire items. Based on reviews, some items were edited for clarity and improved sequencing.

The questionnaire included rating scales, open-ended response items, and demographic questions. For reliability statistics, rating scale variables showed strong internal consistency: Program Quality ($\alpha = .901$), Teacher Beliefs ($\alpha = .744$), and Self-efficacy ($\alpha = .883$). Questions within Program Quality asked about the level of training teacher candidates received in how to support students experiencing child traumatic stress, how much the training was embedded in the curriculum or instructor pedagogy, and how satisfied respondents were with the level of training received. Questions within Teacher Beliefs asked about the areas in which respondents believe they should be required to offer additional academic, behavioral, or emotional support to students experiencing child traumatic stress. Lastly, Self-efficacy questions asked respondents' perceived confidence levels (see Bandura, 1977) of knowledge and skills to support future students experiencing child traumatic stress and how their own identity influenced their understanding and abilities.

Procedure

Data were collected online from October 2020 until November 2020. Participants were not compensated and were able to withdraw from the questionnaire at any time without penalty. Data were entered and analyzed in IBM 2019 SPSS Statistics 25 software. Correlations, *t*-tests, and an analysis of variance (ANOVA) were conducted to interpret the relationships between variables. Content analysis (Krippendorff, 2018) was employed to code and analyze qualitative data acquired from the open-ended response items and document analysis to describe emerging themes.

RESULTS

Quantitative Results

Out of 134 responses, 21.6% of teacher candidates ($n = 29$) indicated that they received no training in how to support students experiencing child traumatic stress. Additionally, only 37.3% of teacher candidates ($n = 50$) were somewhat or extremely satisfied with their teacher preparation program's level of training on supporting students experiencing child traumatic stress, whereas 46.2% were somewhat or extremely dissatisfied ($n = 62$). Teacher candidates also rated their beliefs regarding how much teachers should be responsible for providing additional support to students experiencing child traumatic stress. 89.6% ($n = 120$) believed teachers should provide additional academic support, 92.5% ($n = 124$) believed teachers should provide additional behavior support, and 92.5% ($n = 123$) believed teachers should provide additional emotional support. For self-efficacy, 47.8% ($n = 64$) of teacher candidates somewhat or strongly agreed that they had the knowledge and skills necessary to support students experiencing child traumatic stress, whereas 37.3% ($n = 50$) somewhat or strongly disagreed.

Results of Pearson correlations indicated that there was a significant positive association between perceived Program Quality and university type (i.e., public or private), $r (132) = .34$, $p < .001$, but there was not a significant association between Teacher Beliefs and university type, $r (132) = .07$, $p = .44$, or between Self-efficacy and university type, $r (132) = .11$, $p = .20$. Also, results of the Pearson correlation indicated that there was not a significant association between Program Quality and Teacher Beliefs, $r (132) = .13$, $p = .123$. However, results of the Pearson correlation indicated that there was a significant positive association between Program Quality and Self-efficacy, $r (132) = .60$, $p < .001$.

In Table 11.2, results of t-tests on all four questions within the Program Quality variable indicate a statistically significant difference between those attending the private university compared to those attending the public university. In all cases, participants attending the private university report a perceived higher level of training to support students experiencing child traumatic stress, amount of this training embedded in course curriculum and embedded in the instructor's pedagogy, and level of satisfaction of training received.

Three one-way between subjects ANOVA were conducted to compare the effect of certification level (i.e., early childhood, elementary school, middle school/junior high, high school, K–12/all grades) on Program Quality, Teacher Beliefs, and Self-efficacy. There was a significant effect of certification level on Program Quality at the $p < .001$ level for the three conditions

Table 11.2

Results of t-Test and Descriptive Statistics for Questions Compromising Program Quality

	University Type						95% CI for mean Difference		t	df
	Private			Public						
	M	SD	n	M	SD	n				
Level of training overall	2.77	.85	47	2.15	.98	87	0.28,	0.95	3.19*	108
Level embedded in curriculum	2.96	1.13	46	2.24	1.09	87	0.32,	1.11	3.51*	89
Level embedded in instructor pedagogy	3.17	.99	47	2.47	1.24	87	0.29,	1.11	3.57*	114
Level of training satisfaction	3.34	1.17	47	2.40	1.33	87	0.48,	1.39	4.23*	105

*$p < .01$

[F(4, 125) = 7.78, $p < .001$] and Self-efficacy at the $p < .001$ level for the three conditions [F(4, 125) = 5.67, $p < .001$]. However, there was not a significant effect of certification level on Teacher Beliefs at the $p < .05$ level for the three conditions [F(4, 125) = .73, $p = .576$]. Post hoc comparisons using the Tukey HSD test indicated that the mean score for the Elementary School ($M = 8.88$, $SD = 4.04$) was only significantly different for Early Childhood ($M = 13.44$, $SD = 2.83$), High School ($M = 12.41$, $SD = 3.46$), and K–12/all grades ($M = 13.44$, $SD = 2.79$) in terms of Program Quality. Additionally, post hoc comparisons using the Tukey HSD test indicated that the mean score for the elementary school ($M = 11.23$, $SD = 4.31$) was only significantly different for early childhood ($M = 15.22$, $SD = 2.99$), high school ($M = 14.36$, $SD = 3.70$), and K–12/all grades ($M = 15.33$, $SD = 2.45$) in terms of self-efficacy. Taken together, in terms of training in child traumatic stress, those enrolled in an elementary school certification track perceived their teacher preparation program to be of lower quality, as well as had lower rates of perceived self-efficacy, than those in tracks for early childhood, high school, and K–12/all grades.

Qualitative Findings

The open-ended response items were designed to contextualize candidates' perceptions and experiences. Analysis also occurred on both universities' websites about their teacher preparation programs. Three major themes emerged: 1. Divergent depth and breadth of training in trauma, 2. Recognition of the innate value of trauma-informed practices, and 3. Misconceptions of trauma and of how identity intersects with trauma-informed teaching.

Divergent Depth and Breadth of Training in Trauma

Participants who discussed their training in trauma described traditional, yet inconsistent, teaching methods. For example, across universities, methods included lectures, discussion, videos, readings, and guest speakers. However, many shared how there was either no training at all or just a singular learning experience. At the private university, one junior shared how "some professors will embed the information into the curriculum so that every assignment touches on aspects of trauma," yet another stated, "I've only had one professor to incorporate this in a meaningful, humanizing way. They did so by having us read relevant texts, engage in open dialogue, and listen to great interviews with (non-White) experts, which was all very powerful." Furthermore, private university candidates stated how training was siloed into specific courses, such as school health, classroom management, or atypical childhood development.

At the public university, candidates' experiences greatly differed. The majority stated they received no training, while others shared about a limited experience. For example, one senior shared, "I have never had an instructor discuss trauma/childhood traumatic stress," and another senior echoed, "I do not feel learning of trauma was ever taught; the main focus [of the program] was teaching [in] Urban Schools and stereotypes." For those who did receive training, one senior described how "we had maybe one or two classes specifically about trauma, and we were told to keep students' trauma in mind throughout the course." A junior stated, "childhood traumatic stress has only been talked about in one class, and it was just explained to us what it is. We were not taught strategies on how to help support students with it." It is important to note that nearly all participants who claimed to have zero or little training were enrolled in elementary certification tracks regardless of university. In addition, document analysis of both universities' teacher preparation program websites revealed that trauma-informed teaching practices were not explicitly outlined in the goals of either program.

Recognition of the Innate Value of Trauma-Informed Practices

While teacher candidates' experiences varied, a theme of recognition emerged across universities on the critical value of trauma-informed training. When asked how their university could improve its instruction on trauma-informed practices, participants suggested these practices should be emphasized by embedding content or offering a class devoted to the topic. A private university junior argued that this should be "a continuing conversation" instead of "coming from one teacher one time." However, a more common response from participants at the public university was advocating to "actually teach it [trauma-informed practices]." Participants viewed these practices as crucial to being prepared for their role in the classroom. One private university participant argued that the program should "make sure teachers know this will be part of your job, no matter where you work," while others shared that they felt "unprepared" for their future role. One private university participant commented that their trauma-informed training was "not going to be enough once I enter the schools with my degree." Lastly, a public university senior shared that addressing trauma as "a real thing that both teachers and students experience" is essential. This statement was reiterated by participants who disclosed they had personally experienced trauma.

Misconceptions of Trauma and of How Identity Intersects With Trauma-Informed Teaching

Across both universities, participants often conflated trauma-informed practices with other content, such as special education, racial justice issues, or abnormal student behavior. When prompted about specific trauma-informed strategies learned, one private university junior responded, "we learned various ways to help those students in the classroom, especially when they are having a bad day." A private university sophomore stated that "we talked about EBD [emotional behavior disorder] and some tools to use when we are in the classroom, so don't touch them while having an episode. Let the professionals do that." Not only did some participants have a general misunderstanding of trauma, but many were also not able to connect racism and racial trauma to systems of oppression.

For example, one public university senior reported, "we had very little training on individuals with disabilities, or [students who have experienced] trauma. The whole four years was strictly minorities, BLM, and LGBTQ community. In my opinion, there are many other things future students should be taught." Despite learning about historically marginalized communities, participants did not learn about these communities' experiences through a trauma-informed lens. Another public university senior responded, "They haven't [discussed trauma]. We have only discussed racism." These participants did not identify how their program's discussion of race and racism might inform their understanding of racial trauma. Conversely, another public university participant discussed how a teacher's identity and experiences might impact students of color, noting that "outside of the pandemic responses, we have mostly addressed our responses to students experiencing the effects of trauma. Are we disproportionately sending Black, Indigenous Children of Color out of the classroom because of our lack of cultural understanding?" Document analysis reveals that a primary goal of the public university's program is "to adopt an anti-racist stance towards teaching," and the private university has a primary goal of "preparing students to meet the challenges of teaching diverse learners." Despite a focus on anti-racist teaching practices, racial trauma was not critically addressed among participants from the public university; racial trauma was not discussed at all from participants from the private university.

DISCUSSION

The culturally responsive, trauma-informed educator identity framework helps interpret the findings of this study, particularly by analyzing whether each component was present. First, our findings suggest that teacher candidates should acquire the knowledge and skills necessary to implement trauma-informed practices within their preparation programs to address their students' needs better. Consistent with Alisic et al. (2012) and Brown et al. (2020), participants want more training on the impacts of trauma and strategies to address them in the classroom. These impacts would include social, emotional, cognitive, and physical impacts as outlined in the culturally responsive, trauma-informed educator identity framework. Most participants believed that teachers should provide additional academic, behavioral, and emotional support to students experiencing child traumatic stress, yet 46.2% were dissatisfied with the level of training they received from their program.

When analyzing their responses on trauma-informed strategies, participants primarily described strategies to improve the classroom environment, engage in reactive responses to students, or foster the student-teacher relationship. These strategies included establishing daily routines, creating calming corners in the classroom, as well as building "relationships with your students so that they can feel safe being in your classroom and with their classmates." Although participants were aware of some specific strategies, there was no discussion of systems-wide thinking that would shape their use of culturally responsive practices. For example, participants did not discuss how systems of oppression influence school policies that negatively impact students who have experienced trauma (NCTSN, 2019; Thomas et al., 2019). While participants from the public university indicated that race and racism were addressed, it was evident that the program missed an opportunity to explore the connection between racism and trauma, given that systems of oppression can re-traumatize students.

As for differences between universities, the depth and breadth of trauma-informed practices content and curriculum varied between the private and public universities, though pedagogies were similar. Participants at the private university perceived their program to be of higher quality in trauma-informed practices training than those attending the public university. However, participants at both universities believe that teachers play a role in supporting students experiencing trauma (Sethi & Scales, 2020; Wiest-Stevenson & Lee, 2016). Participants also had similar rates of self-efficacy in implementing trauma-informed practices, and participants who rated their program as higher quality also rated themselves higher in self-efficacy. Moreover, participants enrolled in an elementary education program significantly rated themselves lower in self-efficacy and perceived their teacher preparation programs to be of lower quality. This finding may highlight elementary teacher candidates' beliefs about the value of trauma-informed environments or their awareness of existing research and resources on trauma. Additionally, consistent with Baweja et al.'s (2016) findings, many participants from the public university specifically stated how they did not receive any training in trauma-informed practices and described how they felt "unprepared" to address student needs.

Across both universities, none of the participants described how their identity, including their personal experiences (e.g., trauma) or demographic characteristics (e.g., race), might influence their ability to implement culturally responsive, trauma-informed strategies. Additionally, participants disclosing traumatic experiences noted their experiences might prepare them to be more empathetic and sensitive to student needs. This perception reveals that participants have a limited understanding of trauma-informed practices, as experiencing trauma does not equip participants with knowledge or skills to meet student needs. Additionally, participants did not contextualize their traumatic experiences within greater systems of oppression. Furthermore, while not directly asked, none of the participants mentioned engagement in self-care practices, adult SEL practices, or their own resilience, including those who disclosed prior traumatic experiences. This finding may indicate that teachers still need knowledge and skills to develop their resilience, adult SEL competencies, and self-care practices to support their well-being ((Thomas et al., 2019; Woolf, n.d.).

Participants did not reflect on how their cultural and racial identity may influence their interpretation of student behavior or their understanding of culturally responsive practices. Engaging in reflexivity on one's identity and worldview is critical in working with students exposed to historical and racial trauma (NCTSN, 2017). Many participants disclosed experiences of trauma and believed this equipped them to address student needs. This lack of reflexivity can be damaging, particularly for students of color, if teachers do not take an individualized, equitable approach to student needs (Iruka, 2020). In the school setting, trauma-related behaviors can lead to disciplinary actions that disproportionately impact students of color; students benefit when teachers recognize racial trauma and address their own biases that might influence their interpretation of student behavior and decision-making on appropriate disciplinary actions.

Document analysis revealed that for the public university, the teacher preparation program is not attending to all goals it has established. This program describes how teacher candidates will be able to "establish suitable classroom routines" and "communicate in ways that demonstrate a sensitivity to a broad range of diversity," in addition to one of its primary goals for candidates "to challenge barriers to educational opportunities, and to adopt an anti-racist stance towards teaching." Although participants from the public university described classroom-level strategies and the existence of marginalized communities, they did not articulate how they could work to dismantle racism, racial trauma, bias, or systems of oppression. For the private university, primary goals include "preparing students to meet the challenges of teaching diverse learners" with attention to the "dignity and unique development of individual learners." Despite not promoting trauma-informed practices in its promotional material, private university participants perceived that they were provided more training than those at the public university. Additionally, though participants did not describe engaging in reflexivity, particularly in terms of their identity, both universities promote reflective practice, with the public university's goal of having candidates "learn about learners and teaching through reflective practice," and the private university engaging candidates in a "continuous, lifelong professional development process based on authentic reflection." An opportunity exists for both programs to refine how they engage teacher candidates in reflexivity.

LIMITATIONS AND FUTURE DIRECTIONS

As this study was limited to two universities in urban cities the sample does not represent the entire teacher candidate population across universities in the United States. However, our sample reflects the demographics of the teaching force, considering the participants were primarily women who identified as White (National Center for Education Statistics, 2020). Additionally, the sample size between the universities was unbalanced. The public university had a much larger teacher preparation program and generated more responses despite a lower percent of their teacher candidates participating compared to the private university, which could impact results. Lastly, questionnaire responses reflect self-reported perceptions of participants' experiences in their teacher preparation programs, as this study captured the student perspective at their respective universities, not the perspective of university faculty or administrators.

Future research is required to attend to these limitations. To improve the diversity of the participant sample, it is recommended to gather participants from other types of teacher preparation programs, such as those housed in Historically Black Colleges and Universities or other minority serving institutions. Moreover, longitudinal studies that track teacher candidates' experiences upon entering their first years of teaching would be helpful in assessing the effectiveness of their training in trauma-informed practices. Finally, studies could investigate the university faculty and administrator experience in designing teacher preparation programs and their decision-making process on the content of trauma-informed training.

IMPLICATIONS FOR PRACTICE

This study contributes to the perspectives of trauma-informed practices from teacher candidates from both public and private universities. Findings indicate the participants attending the private university believed that their teacher preparation program provided better instruction in trauma-informed practices in terms of breadth and depth of training; however, many participants believed that their universities should provide more training, and both programs have opportunities to explicitly include content about racial trauma and the practice of reflexivity. Teacher candidates described classroom-level strategies that are trauma-informed, but they could not articulate initiatives or programs to address systemic issues that may re-traumatize students.

Moreover, the culturally responsive, trauma-informed educator identity framework informs us that the participants were not fluent in each component (see Figure 11.1). For example, it was evident that participants did not engage in reflexivity, as they could not articulate how their own identities might impact how students perceive their interactions, particularly from students experiencing trauma from differing cultural backgrounds.

Teacher candidates could utilize the framework as a tool to guide and measure their efforts in their future classrooms. For example, the framework could help teachers reflect on their pedagogy and relationships with students by reinforcing the need to understand how the impacts of trauma can manifest in different ways, the importance of being culturally responsive in their teaching methods and student interactions, and the role of promoting social-emotional learning for themselves and their students. Moreover, teacher preparation programs should include training in trauma-informed practices in a systematic manner. Specifically, programs can employ trauma-informed frameworks to help shape their training in trauma-informed practices. The culturally responsive, trauma-informed educator identity framework provides clear components that programs can teach and practice (see Figure 11.1) either through a foundational course in trauma or embedded throughout existing courses. Universities may need to start with curriculum mapping (Jacobs, 1997) to identify content and skills currently being taught in courses to help decide where to embed training in trauma-informed practices.

It is important to note that training in trauma-informed practices and developing educator identity cannot solely be embedded into teacher preparation programs. All personnel in schools, including principals, deans, bus drivers, cafeteria workers, and central office administrators (see Cole et al., 2013; Thomas et al., 2019), must be afforded this training. All staff trainings support a shared literacy and understanding of the impact of experiences of trauma on learning and behavior and help in promoting student and staff resilience. It is our hope that the culturally responsive, trauma-informed educator identity framework can be utilized to help guide educator preparation programs, districts, and individual schools.

REFERENCES

Alisic, E., Bus, M., Dulack, W., Pennings, L., & Splinter, J. (2012). Teachers' experiences supporting children after traumatic exposure. *Journal of Traumatic Stress, 25*(1), 98–101. http://dx.doi.org/10.1002/jts.20709

Anda, R. F., Felitti, V. J., Bremner, J. D., Walker, J. D., Whitfield, C., Perry, B. D., Dube, S. R., & Giles, W. H. (2006). The enduring effects of abuse and related adverse experiences in childhood: A convergence of evidence from neurobiology and epidemiology. *European Archives of Psychiatry and Clinical Neuroscience, 256*, 174–186. https://doi:10.1007/s00406-005- 0624-4

Bandura, A. (1977). Self-efficacy: Toward a unifying theory of behavioral change. *Psychological Review, 84*(2), 191–215. https://doi.org/10.1037/0033-295X.84.2.191

Baum, N. L., Rotter, B., Reidler, E., & Brom, D. (2009). Building resilience in schools in the wake of Hurricane Katrina. *Journal of Child and Adolescent Trauma, 2*(1), 62–70. https://doi.org/10.1080/19361520802694323

Baweja, S., Santiago, C. D., Vona, P., Pears, G., Langley, A., Kataoka, S. (2016). Improving implementation of a school-based program for traumatized students: identifying factors that promote teacher support and collaboration. *School Mental Health, 8*(1), 120–131. https://doi.org/10.1007/s12310-015-9170-z

Blaustein, M. E. & Kinniburgh, K. M. (2019). *Treating traumatic stress in children and adolescents: How to foster resilience through attachment, self-regulation, and competency* (2nd ed.). Guilford Press.

Brown, E. C., Freedle, A., Hurless, N. L., Miller, R. D., Martin, C., & Paul, Z. A. (2020). Preparing teacher candidates for trauma-informed practices. *Urban Education*, 1–24. https://doi.org/10.1177/0042085920974084

Carter, R. T. (2007). Racism and psychological and emotional injury: Recognizing and assessing race-based traumatic stress. *The Counseling Psychologist, 35*(1), 13–105. https://doi.org/10.1177/0011000006292033

Chafouleas, S. M., Johnson, A. H., Overstreet, S., & Santos, N. M. (2016). Toward a blueprint for trauma-informed service delivery in schools. *School Mental Health: A Multidisciplinary Research and Practice Journal, 8*(1), 144–162. https://doi.org/10.1007/s12310-015-9166-8

Cole, S. F., Eisner, A., Gregory, M., & Ristuccia, J. (2013). *Creating and advocating for trauma-sensitive schools.* Massachusetts Advocates for Children.

Cole, S. F., O'Brien, J. G., Gadd, M. G., Ristuccia, J., Wallace, D. L., & Gregory, M. (2005). *Helping Traumatized Children Learn.* Massachusetts Advocates for Children.

Collaborative for Academic, Social, and Emotional Learning. (2020). *Fundamentals of SEL.* https://casel.org/fundamentals-of-sel/

Copeland, W. E., Keeler, G., Angold, A., & Costello, E. J. (2007). Traumatic events and posttraumatic stress in childhood. *Archives of General Psychiatry, 64*(5), 577–584. https://doi.org/10.1001/archpsyc.64.5.577

Crenshaw, K. (1991). Mapping the margins: Intersectionality, identity politics, and violence against women of color. *Stanford Law Review, 43*(6), 1241–1299. https://doi.org/10.2307/1229039

Creswell, J. W., & Guetterman, T. C. (2019). *Educational research: Planning, conducting, and evaluating quantitative and qualitative research* (6th ed.). Pearson.

D'Cruz, H., Gillingham, P., & Melendez, S. (2007). Reflexivity, its meanings and relevance for social work: A critical review of the literature. *The British Journal of Social Work, 37*(1), 73–90. https://doi:10.1093/bjsw/bcl001

Farmer, E. M. Z., Burns, B. J., Phillips, S. D., Angold, A., & Costello, E. J. (2003). Pathways into and through mental health services for children and adolescents. *Psychiatric Services, 54*(1), 60–66. https://doi:10.1176/appi.ps.54.1.60

Felitti, V. J., Anda, R. F., Nordenberg, D., Willamson, D. F., Spitz, A. M., Edwards, V., Koss, M. P., & Marks, J. S. (1998). Relationship of childhood abuse and household dysfunction to many of the leading causes of death in adults: The Adverse Childhood Experiences (ACE) Study. *American Journal of Preventative Medicine, 14*(4), 245–258. https://doi.org/10.1016/S0749-3797(98)00017-8

Fowler, F. J. (2014). *Survey research methods* (5th ed.). SAGE.

Hydon, S., Wong, M., Langley, A. K., Stein, B. D., & Kataoka, S. H. (2015). Preventing secondary traumatic stress in educators. *Child and Adolescent Psychiatric Clinics of North America, 24*(2), 319–333. https://doi.org/10.1016/j.chc.2014.11.003

Iruka, I., Curenton, S., & Durden, T. (2020). *Don't look away: Embracing anti-bias classrooms*. Gryphon House.

Jacobs, H. H. (1997). *Mapping the big picture: Integrating curriculum and assessment K–12*. Alexandria, VA: Association for Supervision and Curriculum Development.

Krippendorff, K. (2018). Content analysis: An introduction to its methodology (4th ed.). SAGE.

Ladson-Billings, G. (2014). Culturally relevant pedagogy 2.0: a.k.a. the remix. *Harvard Educational Review, 84*(1), 74–84. https://doi.org/10.17763/haer.84.1.p2rj131485484751

Lawson, H. A., Caringi, J. C., Gottfried, R., Bride, B. E., & Hydon, S. P. (2019). Educators' secondary traumatic stress, children's trauma, and the need for trauma literacy. *Harvard Educational Review, 89*(3), 421–447. https://doi.org/10.17763/1943-5045-89.3.421

Metzler, M., Merrick, M. T., Klevens, J., Ports, K. A., & Ford, D. C. (2017). Adverse childhood experiences and life opportunities: shifting the narrative. *Children and Youth Services Review, 72*, 141–149. https://doi.org/10.1016/j.childyouth.2016.10.021

National Center for Education Statistics. (2020, May). *Characteristics of public school teachers*. https://nces.ed.gov/programs/coe/indicator_clr.asp

National Child Traumatic Stress Network. (2017). *Addressing race and trauma in the classroom: A resource for educators*. Justice Consortium, Schools Committee, and Culture Consortium.

National Child Traumatic Stress Network. (2019, Spring). Intercepting the school-to-prison pipeline. *IMPACT Newsletter*, pp. 6–7.

National Child Traumatic Stress Network. (2021). *Trauma-informed schools for children in K–12: A system framework*. https://www.nctsn.org/resources/trauma-informed-schools-children-k-12-system- framework

Newman, M., Gough, D. (2020). Systematic reviews in educational research: Methodology, perspectives and application. In O. Zawacki Richter, M. Kerres, S. Bedenlier, M. Bond, & K. Buntins, (Eds.), *Systematic reviews in educational research*. Springer. https://doi.org/10.1007/978-3-658-27602-7_1

Olsen, B. (2012). Identity theory, teacher education, and diversity. In J. Banks (Ed.), *Encyclopedia of diversity in education*. SAGE.

Raby, K. L., Roisman, G. I., Labella, M. H., Martin, J., Fraley, R. C., & Simpson, J. A. (2019). The legacy of early abuse and neglect for social and academic competence from childhood to adulthood. *Child Development, 90*(5), 1684–1701. https://doi.org/10.1111/cdev.13033

Reyes, M. R., Brackett, M. A., Rivers, S. E., Elbertson, N. A., & Salovey, P. (2012). The interaction effects of program training, dosage, and implementation quality on targeted student outcomes for the RULER approach to social and emotional learning. *School Psychology Review, 41*(1), 82–99. https://doi.org/10.1080/02796015.2012.12087377

Schonert-Reichl, K. A., Kitil, M. J., & Hanson-Peterson, J. (2017). *To reach the students, teach the teachers: A national scan of teacher preparation and social and emotional learning*. A report prepared for the Collaborative for Academic, Social, and Emotional Learning (CASEL). University of British Columbia.

Sethi, J., & Scales, P. C. (2020). Developmental relationships and school success: how teachers, parents, and friends affect educational outcomes and what actions students say matter most. *Contemporary Educational Psychology, 63*, 1–18. https://doi.org/10.1016/j.cedpsych.2020.101904

Substance Abuse and Mental Health Services Administration (SAMHSA). (2014). SAMHSA's concept of trauma and guidance for a trauma-informed approach (HHS Publication No. 14-4884). https://store.samhsa.gov/system/files/sma14-4884.pdf

Thomas, M. S., Crosby, S., & Vanderhaar, J. (2019). Trauma-informed practices in schools across two decades: An interdisciplinary review of research. *Review of Research in Education, 43*(1), 422–452. https://doi.org/10.3102/0091732X18821123

Wiest-Stevenson, C., & Lee, C. (2016). Trauma-informed schools. *Journal of Evidence-Informed Social Work, 13*(5), 498–503. https://doi.org/10.1080/2376 1407.2016.1166855

Williams, M. T., Metzger, I. W., Leins, C., & DeLapp, C. (2018). Assessing racial trauma within a DSM–5 framework: The UConn Racial/Ethnic Stress & Trauma Survey. *Practice Innovations, 3*(4), 242–260. http://dx.doi.org/10.1037/pri0000076

Woolf, N. (n.d.). *A comprehensive guide to adult SEL*. Panorama Education. https://www.panoramaed.com/blog/comprehensive-guide-adult-sel

ABOUT THE AUTHORS

EDITORS

 **Philip E. Bernhardt** is a professor of secondary education and associate director of the Honors Program at the Metropolitan State University of Denver. Dr. Bernhardt has spent over two decades working in public schools, including eight years as a secondary social studies teacher. He frequently presents on topics that include barriers to higher education; coteaching; academic tracking; teacher professional development; curriculum design and assessment; and teacher preparation, induction, and mentoring. Dr. Bernhardt has published numerous journal articles and book chapters, and he copublished *Digital Citizenship: Promoting Wellness for Thriving in a Connected World*, a textbook designed to support middle and high school students' understanding of their digital footprint and the unintended consequences associated with habitual use of the internet and social media. He also recently coedited a two-volume series on clinical practice in teacher preparation. Dr. Bernhardt earned his MAT in social studies education from Boston University, and he received his doctorate in curriculum and instruction from George Washington University.

Ofelia Castro Schepers, PhD, is an assistant professor of language and literacy at Purdue University and formerly an associate professor in elementary education and literacy at MSU Denver. Her recent work has examined the systematic implementation of trauma-informed practices for preservice educators in higher education. This work has provided a unique opportunity to consider how trauma-informed practices can center bilingual and multilingual children and communities. Ofelia teaches courses in multicultural education, differentiated learning, and culturally and linguistically diverse assessment. Her background in bilingual and multicultural education provides the necessary framework to ensure that preservice teachers who are not actively seeking out culturally and linguistically diverse education courses develop a critical lens and become advocates for all their students. She actively researches how race, class, gender, sexuality, and various identity factors are perceived by teachers in relation to their students in order to develop critical approaches to preservice education and professional development for in-service teachers.

Megan Brennan, PsyD, is a cofounder of Resilient Futures—a nonprofit that supports early childhood, K–12 educators and schools/school districts, university programs and youth serving agencies to implement and sustain trauma-informed practices that are equity centered. As a Licensed Clinical Psychologist with over a decade of experience working in the areas of children and adolescent mental health, Dr. Brennan practiced as a school-based therapist, with an expertise in providing trauma-specific therapies. She is an affiliate faculty at Metropolitan State University of Denver teaching in their Master of Education in Curriculum and Instruction, Trauma-Informed Practices concentration.

AUTHORS

Amee Adkins is Professor and Chair in Georgia Southern University's Department of Middle Grades and Secondary Education. She earned her PhD in Social Foundations of Education from the University of North Carolina-Chapel Hill. Dr. Adkins' teaching and research address power and identity in schooling; ethics; and qualitative research methods.

Dave Barry is an Assistant Professor of early childhood education at West Chester University. Prior to earning his PhD in Curriculum and Instruction from The University of Texas at Austin, he taught kindergarten in the Boston Public Schools for 10 years and was a Teaching Fellow at the Harvard Graduate School of Education for five years. His scholarly interests include preservice teacher education, teacher self-care and self-compassion, and supporting educators to develop trauma-informed practices.

Heather Bertrand has been working in the field of special education for over 17 years. Heather is a fourth-year faculty professor at Point Loma Nazarene University where she teaches pre-service special education teacher certification coursework. Her areas of expertise include UDL, MTSS, and language acquisition for students with disabilities and English Language Learners. She is a certified Trauma-Informed Practices trainer for educators and a certified assistive technology support provider. Heather is set to complete her doctoral dissertation in the summer of 2021 which focuses on trauma-informed training supports for novice special education teachers.

Erik Jon Byker is an associate professor in the Cato College of Education at the University of North Carolina at Charlotte. During 2019–20, he was the Resident Director of International Studies at Kingston University in London, England. He has a PhD degree from Michigan State University. He has conducted comparative and international research in Cuba, England, Germany, India, South Africa, South Korea, and across the United States.

Madeline Chimka is a project manager at HighScope Educational Research Foundation in Ypsilanti, Michigan. She earned her EdD in Educational Leadership and Policy from Vanderbilt University. Dr. Chimka previously taught middle school science in Metro Nashville Public Schools.

Merri Hemphill Davis received her PhD from George Mason University Carter School for Conflict Analysis and Resolution (2019). She serves as the Executive Director of the Center for Well-Being and Resilience. Her research interests include symbols as embodiments of collective trauma, historical memory and conflict, and influences of history and memory on gender constructions

Grace Fantaroni is a Professor of Special Education at Point Loma Nazarene University in San Diego, CA. A former special education teacher and district autism and behavior specialist, she loves using her experiences to teach preservice and graduate students with positive behavior supports, evidence-based practices and instructional techniques to empower all students. Part of the California Autism Professional Training and Information Network (CAPTAIN) and co-author of *Autism Is*, a social emotional curriculum for K–12 students to learn about peers with autism and other special needs, her research focuses on inclusive and evidence-based practices.

Ellie Haberl Foster is the Co-Director of education at the Kevin Love Fund where she is able to draw on her PhD research to build a free social emotional learning curriculum that takes an arts-based, social justice approach to emotional expression and storytelling. Her research focuses on critical affective approaches to welcoming and honoring teachers' and young people's challenging life experiences in school writing practices

Vanessa Gee is an educator in Indianapolis, Indiana. She is a second-year student in the Urban Education Studies doctoral program at Indiana University-Purdue University, Indianapolis. Most of Gee's teaching and research interest has focused on culturally relevant teacher practices and school-wide practices that ensure that all children succeed.

Lorna Hermosura is Assistant Professor of Instruction in the College of Education at The University of Texas at Austin. She teaches and researches Restorative Practices, Trauma-Informed Practices, Implementation, and the School-to-Prison Pipeline. Dr. Hermosura is the Principal Investigator and Project Director of *STEP UP Texas: Improving Juvenile Justice Outcomes through Trauma-Informed and Diversity, Equity, Inclusion Training*, a project funded by a U.S. Department of Justice grant.

Freda Hicks is the School Partnerships and Induction Counselor at North Carolina Central University and a former elementary principal. She earned a Bachelor in Elementary Education from Shaw University and a Master of Education in School Leadership from the University of North Carolina at Chapel Hill. Her research interests include teacher leadership and school induction.

Carly Laukai'ei'e Setsumi Ibara is a Secondary English Language Arts teacher. She currently teaches at Mid-Pacific Institute in Honolulu, Hawai'i as an 8th grade Language Arts teacher and National Junior Honor Society advisor. Mrs. Ibara is also a member of the Mid-Pacific Kupu Hou Academy and helps to facilitate professional development courses for teachers worldwide.

Vanessa Keener is the Director in the Department of Specialized Instruction at Savannah-Chatham County Public School System. She earned her EdD in Curriculum Studies from Georgia Southern University. After working as a special education teacher and Program Manager for Special Education Behavioral Services, Vanessa's interests have been related to critical disability studies, reducing disproportionate disciplinary practices in schools, social emotional learning, and a particular interest in the effects and resulting behavioral outcomes trauma has on students with disabilities.

Delores D. Liston, PhD, LCSW is Professor of Curriculum and Foundations at Georgia Southern University. She is author of *Joy as a Metaphor of Convergence: A Phenomenological and Aesthetic Investigation of Social and Educational Change, Learning to Teach: A Critical Approach to Field Experiences* (with Natalie Adams, Christine Shea, and Bryan Deever), as well as *Pervasive Vulnerabilities: Sexual Harassment in School* and *Promoting Social Justice Through the Scholarship of Teaching and Learning* (with Regina Rahimi). She is also LCSW licensed through the State of Georgia, practicing, and researching in social work for more than five years.

Cassandra Lo is Assistant Professor at St. Thomas Aquinas College in Sparkill, New York. She earned her EdD in Reading, Writing, and Literacy from the University of Pennsylvania. A former high school English teacher, Professor Lo now works with secondary preservice teachers in methods coursework and the student teaching seminar. Her research focuses on relational teaching practices, trauma-informed teaching, and supporting teachers of color.

Megan Lyons is an Assistant Professor at North Carolina Central University. In previous roles, she served as a high school special education teacher and Career Technology Intervention Specialist. She earned a Bachelor of Science in Communications Disorders and a Master of Education in Special Education from Auburn University. She later earned a Specialist in Educational Leadership from Columbus State University and holds a doctorate in Educational Leadership from Valdosta State University. Her research interests include social emotional learning and culturally responsive pedagogy.

Marisa Jucutan Mendoza-Maurer is a proud mother, educator, and proponent of the underdog. With a Master of Education in Teaching from the University of Hawaii at Manoa, her research aims to elevate the diverse voices of her students by utilizing metacognitive critical thinking strategies grounded within cultural frameworks. She is currently a Secondary English Language Arts teacher at Henry J. Kaiser High School in Honolulu, Hawai'i.

Lisa L. Minicozzi is a Clinical Associate Professor of Early Childhood Education and Program Director for Educational Leadership in the College of Education & Health Studies at Adelphi University. A former elementary school teacher and K–5 principal, Dr. Minicozzi values working with teacher and school leader candidates to prepare them for teaching in today's diverse and complex early childhood classrooms. She is a NYS Dignity for All Students Act (DASA) trainer, who coaches several teaching professionals on how to create positive learning environments for children.

Nigel P. Pierce is an Associate Professor in the School of Education at North Carolina Central University. Prior to his current position, he served as a Postdoctoral Research Associate with the Frank Porter Graham Child Development Institute at the University of North Carolina at Chapel Hill. Dr. Pierce's research interests include the effects of ethnicity, socioeconomic status, and linguistic differences on treatment and access to services for children diagnosed with autism spectrum disorder.

Regina Rahimi, EdD, is Professor of Middle and Secondary at Georgia Southern University and a former middle school teacher. She is author of *Pervasive Vulnerabilities: Sexual Harassment in School* and *Promoting Social Justice Through the Scholarship of Teaching and Learning* (with Delores Liston). She is currently researching trauma informed practice and residency models in teacher preparation.

Linda Reece is Associate Professor of Education at the University of North Georgia in Dahlonega, Georgia. A former middle school teacher and high school counselor, she teaches social studies methods courses as well as educational psychology and sociocultural diversity courses. Her recent research examines how mental health training impacts students' teacher confidence and willingness to reach out to students who may be experiencing mental health issues in the internship setting.

Ellen Spitler is Associate Professor of Adolescent Literacy in the Department of Secondary, K–12, and Educational Technology at Metropolitan State University of Denver. She earned her PhD from the University of Arizona. Her research examines preservice teacher literacy identity transformation, adolescent literacy instruction, multicultural education inclusive of culturally relevant and trauma informed pedagogy.

Devin Thornburg is Professor of Education at Adelphi University, teaching psychology, culture and learning within the frameworks of social justice and human rights. His latest work has focused on the experience of immigrant students in educational settings as well as those who educate them and a book on trust in learning across eight countries on 4 continents. He has collaborated on works on global perspectives on adolescence, international teacher education, and social media and social justice.

Molly Trinh Wiebe is Assistant Professor of Practice and Program Coordinator for Youth and Community Studies in the College of Education at The University of Texas at Austin. She teaches and researches Critical Pedagogy, Critical Literacy, Restorative Practices, and Social Entrepreneurship. Dr. Trinh Wiebe is also the coprincipal investigator of *The Education Innovation and Research Early-Phase Grant*, a project funded by the U.S. Department of Education.

Tommy Wells is an Assistant Professor at Bellarmine University in Louisville, Kentucky. He earned his EdD in Educational Leadership and Policy from Vanderbilt University. A former school counselor, Dr. Wells teaches graduate-level courses in trauma-informed practices and research methodology. His recent research examines education policy, trauma-informed practices, and school leadership development.

Printed in Great Britain
by Amazon

33696404R00132